Made in China

Made in China

Voices from the New Revolution

Robert Lawrence Kuhn

NEW YORK

Library of Congress Cataloging-in-Publication Data
available upon request from the publisher.

The publisher has made every effort to secure permission to reproduce copyrighted material and would like to apologize should there have been any errors or omissions.

TV Books, L.L.C.
1619 Broadway
New York, NY 10019
www.tvbooks.com

Interior design by Rachel Reiss
Manufactured in the United States of America

Contents

Preface

I first went to China at the invitation of the State Science and Technology Commission (now the Ministry of Science and Technology) in early 1989, as one of a group of American investment bankers to advise Chinese research institutes in their first, fledgling efforts to adapt to the incipient market economy. I was hooked from the moment I arrived. The Chinese had a fresh, if naïve, enthusiasm; they were eager to learn, and ready to improve their civic and material lives. "Entrepreneurship" was the new buzzword in China, and I knew then that the culture, history, and political and economic structure of the world's most populous country would matter a great deal to America. What I didn't know then was how much China would matter to me.

Since that initial visit, I have been occupied in various ways in China. I've worked with various enterprises and agencies of the government, including the Science and Technology Ministry, the State Economic and Trade Commission, the State Property Bureau, and the State Bureau of Radio, Film, and Television. I've conducted joint seminars with some of those agencies on the importance of mergers and acquisitions (M&A) as a key component of economic reform in China. I've argued throughout, to government officials and media reporters, that a strong M&A market in China would facilitate economic reform by accelerating the development of better enterprises, eliminating poorly managed companies, and encouraging foreign investment. I've also argued that a deep and free M&A market would, contrary to general opinion, protect the value of state-owned assets by preventing a few well-connected people from taking advantage of special relationships.

In today's China, business and finance are hot topics, and the art of the deal is a popular subject. Being an investment banker in China at this heady time has been a bit like being a minor rock star. In 1996, my book *Investment Banking Study* (*Touzi Yinhang Xue*: People's Beijing Normal University Press) was published in China—the first work on investment banking to be published there. It has been read widely by economists, government officials, and business leaders. In 1999, my book on deal-making (*Jiaoyi Ren*—literally, *Transaction People*: China Economic Science Press) met with equal success, this time with broader audiences.

Most directly relevant, I co-produced with China Central Television (CCTV) an eight-part documentary entitled "Capital Wave"—the first television series in China on mergers and acquisitions, which was broadcast nationwide in prime time on CCTV Channel 2 in April and May 1999. An English-language documentary, "In Search of China," giving fresh understanding of the New China, is being broadcast on PBS in the United States and syndicated internationally. It is the story of how the Chinese themselves, not only we westerners, are "in search of" the real China.

This book, *Made in China: Voices from the New Revolution*, accompanies the documentary and expands its themes, all of which are indeed "Made In China." It's not just the profusion of products—from red-white-and-blue fireworks used to celebrate the American Independence Day on July 4th to the multi-stage rockets used to launch American communications satellites—that are "Made In China." It's the uniqueness of China's history, science and civilization; it's how the Chinese people endured interminable foreign domination and humiliation and suffered incessant political upheavals and turmoil; it's the burgeoning of China's economy, the opening of China's society, and the diversity, complexity, vigor, and emergent personalities of China's people. This book is also the story of my own odyssey in China—a fascinated foreigner, one among many—which culminates in the production of the television documentaries and the writing of this book. All of this is "Made In China."

But I don't go to China just to give seminars, make documentaries, or sell books. I am drawn by the country's remarkable energy and optimism. Since Paramount Leader Deng Xiaoping began to institute his reforms, China has created what it calls a "socialist market economy." Part unbridled capitalism, part communist central planning, it is a hybrid system of personal and economic freedoms combined with rigid political controls. Some of it doesn't yet work—but much of it does. Here is the earth's largest population undergoing unprecedented transformation. How the Chinese people are adapting to these astonishing changes is nothing less than an historical epic. They and no one else will determine what shape China will take in the coming years. There is a new openness in today's China, and in their own words, this book is what the Chinese people have to say.

"Voices from the New Revolution": why voices? No description of China by foreign scholars or correspondents can express the emotion or the passions of the Chinese people as well as the Chinese themselves can with their own words, in their own voices. Voices are cacophonous; they do not tell a single story nor do they necessarily blend harmoniously like instrumental parts in a classical symphony. Cacophony is the defining sound of the New China. Iit is a healthy sign—indeed, it is the surest sign of an opening and maturing society.

Made in China is constructed with four interacting elements, each providing its own take of what's really happening in China today. The first is my own perspective, born of appreciation, experience, observation, idiosyncrasy, and hunch. The second presents my interviews with Chinese "movers and shakers," people who are making a difference, some of the leaders of China's New Revolution. The third offers excerpts from the working script of our PBS documentary, introducing a rich variety of real characters at all levels of Chinese society. The fourth is a series of short articles depicting diverse slices of contemporary Chinese culture, society, life, and opinion. The four elements, working together, portray a textured, nuanced, vibrant image of the most populous country on the planet.

Made in China is also a personal account of my doings and dealings in the People's Republic of China and of the friendships I formed there. I am not a Chinese scholar and not a professional "China hand," but I give my take on what I've seen and felt in this large land of escalating importance. All opinions expressed are my own, for which I take full responsibility.

It is a pleasure to recognize those who have been a part of this adventure—beginning with those who, in 1989, invited me on my first trip to China. I am most appreciative to Dr. Song Jian, who was then a State Councilor and Chairman of the State Science and Technology Commission and is now vice chairman of the Chinese People's Political Consultative Conference and president of the Chinese Academy of Engineering Sciences. Dr. Song has become a good friend whose wise counsel and advice I have come to rely upon. I express my continuing appreciation to my longtime mentor, Dr. George Kozmetsky, founder of the IC^2 Institute (for "Innovation, Creativity, and Capital"), an entrepreneurial think tank at the University of Texas at Austin, for arranging that first invitation. It was on this initial trip in 1989 that I met Adam Zhu, who was then working as a translator-cum-chaperon for the State Science and Technology Commission. Adam is now my partner in China; he deserves much of the credit for all that we do.

I appreciate the encouragement, cooperation, and assistance of my friends at the Information Office of the State Council of China, particularly Minister Zhao Qizheng, as well as Vice Minister Yang Zhengquan, Secretary General Zhao Shaohua, and Director General Gu Yaoming. Deputy Director General Yang Yang provided insight and support, as did Deputy Director Generals Li Xiangping and Ren Yinong. It was a pleasure to cosponsor with the Information Office, and co-chair with Minister Zhao, a three-day seminar in Beijing in January 2000 on "Media in the United States," which is described later in the book. And I appreciate the continuing support of Ambassador An Wenbin, Consul General in Los Angeles, and Liu Jikang, cultural consul.

I am most grateful and appreciative for the friendship, assistance and confidence of my many friends at the State Administration of Radio, Film, and Television and China Central Television (CCTV), including CCTV president Zhao Huayong; former Executive Vice Minister Xu Chonghua and Vice Minister Tong Xiangrong; former CCTV President Yang Weiguang; CCTV Vice President Zhang Changming; Director Generals Gao Jianmin, Li Peisheng and Zhao Yuhui; Deputy Director General Zhang Haichao; senior editor Professor Guan Runlin; Economics Department Director Wang Wenbin; and Li Qiang, our documentary director.

I am grateful for the advice and friendship of Yan Mingfu, the President of the China Charity Federation, who has provided historical perspective; and for the insights and assistance provided by Professor Bi Dachuan, Dr. Zeng Jinsong, Dr. Song Ning, and Zhou Nan. I am appreciative of the early support and continuing encouragement from Mr. Paul Blackburn, minister-counselor for press and cultural affairs at the United States Embassy in Beijing.

It is a pleasure to recognize the friendship, inspiration, advice, and counsel of Nina Kung Wang, chairwoman of Chinachem Group (and honorary chairwoman of K^2 Media Group, the company that produced the documentary). I am also appreciative of the ideas and assistance of Kevin (Shulin) Pu.

Since 1991, I have been president of The Geneva Companies, the leading M&A firm in the United States that represents private, middle-market companies (those with revenues from about $2 million to $200 million) in evaluating, growing, or, when appropriate, liquefying their equity in a merger, sale, or other financial transaction. I am grateful for my company's support—particularly that of my partner, David Troob, chairman of the Geneva Companies, and my assistant, Pamela McFadden.

I am pleased to acknowledge articles and photographs from *China Today* magazine, with thanks to its editor-in-chief Huang Zu'an, deputy editor-in-chief Ren Ying, Liu Hong, and Yu Xiangjun. Explicit recognition goes to the primary photographers, especially Zhang Wei (cameraman) and Li Qiang (director) from CCTV, Yu Xiangjun, and Adam Zhu; and in addition Huo Jianying, Liu Xiaoming, Lou Linwei, Wang Xu, Wang Yao, Wang Zijin, Xie Jun, Zhou Youma; and also to Adam Zhu and Aaron Kuhn who advised on photo selections.

I have benefited from ideas offered by Professor Lu Xiaobo of Columbia University, Dr. Wang Lihua of Northeastern University, Professor Yu Renqiu of the State University of New York at Purchase, and Professor Zheng Shiping of the University of Vermont.

I would like to thank Jeff Yang, founder and CEO of aMedia, for his help in shaping *Made in China* into its current form. Yang, who cowrote Jackie Chan's best-selling autobiography, *I Am Jackie Chan*, as well as the encyclopedia of Asian popular culture, *Eastern Standard Time*, provided invaluable editorial assistance late in the process of writing this book. aMedia publishes *aMagazine*, the nation's largest and most influential periodical for Asian Americans, and is the developer of aOnline.com, a dynamic website offering daily Asian-related news and content. I look forward to working with Jeff and aMedia in the future as *Made in China* evolves beyond this currrent book into more interactive forms.

I am appreciative of Sara Lippincott's always elegant editorial suggestions, Brian Knowles's assistance with the interviews, Professor Zheng's reading of the manuscript, and Adam Zhu's many insights.

I would also like to thank the key people who labored and agonized to produce the "In Search of China" television documentary: At CCTV: Professor Guan Runlin, Wang Wenbin, Li Qiang, and Zhang Wei; in the United States: Emma Morris, Aaron Kuhn, Rob Fruchtman, Niki Vettel, Dalton Delan, and Richard Thomas at WETA (the PBS affiliate in Washington), D.C., and once again, Adam Zhu, without whom this documentary and book would not exist.

I am proud to be considered an old friend *(lao pengyou)* of China, a high compliment indeed, achieved after over a decade of learning and teaching, and I am pleased to have been part of the team producing the CCTV and PBS broadcasts and this companion book. Today the Chinese people are torn between old communist ideals and burgeoning capitalist benefits, searching for individual identity while fearful of social instability. Presented here are the personal stories of China's newly rich and newly poor, the successes and pains of a nation in transition. Here are the ministers, the managers, the entrepreneurs, the workers—those who are flourishing and those who are floundering—as the energy, pride, and hopes of over a billion people are transforming a world power.

I look forward to enhanced communication between the Chinese and American people and improved relations between the governments of the People's Republic of China and the United States of America—especially since our two nations, in the twenty-first century, will shoulder much of the responsibility for world peace and prosperity. I therefore dedicate this book to those good people, particularly my friends and colleagues, whose commitment, foresight, persistence, and courage are helping to strengthen economic, social, and political reform in China and to help China understand the world and the world understand China.

Robert Lawrence Kuhn
Pasadena, California
New York, New York
Beijing, People's Republic of China
August, 2000

Pride and Stability

Chinese Pride

I arrived in China for the first time in March of 1989, one month before students began gathering in Tiananmen Square, but it would be years before I would begin to understand what was really going on. I've come to realize that you have to be aware of two overarching themes in order to understand China, and once you can recognize these themes in their countless variations, you know a lot about this country of 1.3 billion people. I want to open this personal account of my vision of China with a story that illustrates one of these themes.

In the early 1990s, not long after the Tiananmen crackdown, I became acquainted with a prominent academic—I'll call him Lu Xiaoning—who was cavalier in his criticism of the government and of communism in general. His comments were slyly comical, delivered with a mischievous glint of impolitic cynicism. Professor Lu was certainly not alone among the Chinese intelligentsia in criticizing the government—confiding to foreign friends in open spaces was the usual way it was done at that time—but I was nonplused when he offered these witticisms in much-too-public situations, such as when he was addressing a dozen of his professional colleagues. How could he get away with such an unbridled tongue, I wondered.

Since I couldn't recall Professor Lu ever having said anything complimentary about the communist political system, I felt secure, one fine day on the outskirts of Beijing, in applauding the action of the United States in preventing the 2000 Olympics from being held in Beijing. This censure was how the American government intended to punish the Chinese gov-

13

ernment for the repression in Tiananmen Square. Lu and I were alone, and I was fully expecting his hearty support of America's blackball.

"How stupid and insulting," he spat out, glaring at me as though I were the blackballer. "How stupid of your country, and how insulting to mine!" Never had he spoken to me like that, and I was quite unprepared for his attack.

It was my first lesson in what really counts in China. Don't let the criticisms fool you. Don't let the internal disputes cloud your vision. Don't assume that derogations of communism (or the government) indicate a diminished patriotism. The pride of the Chinese people—pride in their country, pride in their heritage, pride in their history, pride in their accomplishments, pride in their growing international importance—is a fundamental characteristic that one encounters over and over and over again.

Consider the long-standing internal debate at the highest levels of the Chinese government over whether to seek admission to the World Trade Organization. Although the contesting views pitted the economic benefits of foreign investment against the heightened competitive pressure from foreign companies, an underlying motivation, though it was rarely voiced, was that China belongs in the WTO because China is a great nation and should be counted as a world power.

"It involves the pride of the nation," is how Zhao Qizheng, minister of the Information Office of the State Council, characterizes recent Chinese advances in science and technology—and the explanatory power of his phrase is immense. That's the first theme—*Chinese pride*—and it energizes and influences a great deal of what is happening in China today.

Zhao Qizheng: "It Involves the Pride of the Nation"

The Honorable Zhao Qizheng is minister of the Information Office of the State Council of the People's Republic of China; a close associate of President Jiang Zemin, he exemplifies the new Chinese leadership. He was trained as a scientist in nuclear physics and worked in China's aerospace programs until he entered politics, becoming vice mayor of Shanghai under the then Shanghai Party Chief Jiang and Mayor Zhu Rongji. Zhao was responsible for building the spectacular Pudong New Area in Shanghai, the world's largest economic development zone and a remarkable success story. As minister of the Information Office, he is in charge of China's international media, including China's foreign language publications and broadcasts. At an informal dinner in Southern California, Minister Zhao mused that each time he has received a new job, what he would do with it has been underestimated. Whether as a scientist assigned a factory to manage in his early career, as the innovative and energetic vice mayor of Shanghai, or, most recently, as the high-profile minister of the Information Office, independent observers confirm that each time he has both exceeded expectations and been remarkably successful. A Dow Jones reporter recently remarked that Minister Zhao was "better known for his knowledge of markets than Marx." My interview with Minister Zhao, reported verbatim below, took place in the spacious formal conference room of the Information Office of the State Council in central Beijing.

ROBERT KUHN: Minister Zhao, what role has Chinese science and technology played in the reform and economic development of the country?

ZHAO QIZHENG: During the past twenty years, China has made remarkable progress both in technology and economics. I attribute this to the leadership of Deng Xiaoping. It was he who pushed for China's reform, who stirred up our nation's internal potential and moved us closer to the rest of the world. In the last two decades, we have made more progress than in the previous eight decades. We have progressed in science generally, and in specific applications, such as chemistry and electronic technology. We realize that scientific development contributes greatly to a powerful economy, and that China cannot become the strong and independent nation it seeks to become without aggressive development in science and technology.

KUHN: I sense that there is deeper meaning here to what a strong science and technology capability may imply, in addition to the economic benefits. Chinese people have a strong desire to learn and improve themselves.

ZHAO: The Chinese people have always held learning to be an important part of life, but for the past two hundred years we have been falling behind. Consequently, we are not where we should be in the use of technology. It involves the pride of the nation, and it will propel us to where we should be. We've come a long way, but we still have a long way to go.

KUHN: I've seen Chinese pride operating in many areas—for example, satellite and aerospace technology. In these fields, China has become a strong competitor in the world market. Why has China chosen aerospace as a prime industry?

ZHAO: We recognize the significance of the aerospace industry for the future. We've already successfully launched many satellites. Even though our scientists, engineers, and their institutions are less well funded than their colleagues in some other countries, our success rates are still competitive. By keeping our overhead low and emphasizing research and manufacturing methods, we're able to hold our own in the world market.

KUHN: I've also noted that China is emphasizing the development of communications technology—the use of personal computers, cellular phones, and the Internet. What will be their impact on Chinese society?

ZHAO: These technologies are changing the way we live and work. Because people are connecting, the level of work efficiency is improving. Though China is a huge country, people in one part of the nation are now able to communicate easily with people in other parts. We are also establishing communications links with the world outside China. This is vital if we are to participate in the global economy. Of course, China's telecommunications system is still in its infancy; compared with that of other countries, our per capita use is not yet significant. But the numbers are growing at an accelerating rate. China already has the largest number of cellular phone users in the world. Internet use, too, is increasing dramatically.

KUHN: Projections make China the second largest Internet market, after the United States. But—as in every other nation, including the U.S.—the Internet brings new challenges, such as the tensions between privacy and information, freedom and control. Tell us about this tension in China—in particular, between the need to empower individuals and the need to maintain government control.

ZHAO: Internet usage in this country is only a few years old, and our regulations are not yet mature. It will take time to work out the bugs. It is true that China has blocked some Internet sites—but only sites that are perceived to have a negative impact on our culture. We have been concerned about anti-China messages, pornography, hackers, and viruses. We don't yet have solid regulations or laws in place that will solve these problems, but we're working on them.

KUHN: How would you describe the personal freedoms of the average Chinese citizen, including students, as compared to twenty years ago?

ZHAO: There have been remarkable changes in China. When it comes to personal freedom, we reached a low point when the Gang of Four [i.e., political radicals led by Jiang Qing, Mao's wife] dominated the Cultural Revolution. All Chinese citizens were tormented in some way, many terribly. Scholars were forced to work on farms and students were denied the education they needed. The universities stopped accepting new students; many were closed. In some ways, this loss can never be made up. Today, that dark time is behind us. Things have changed. We all have much more freedom today.

KUHN: I can agree when it comes to economic freedom, but political freedom is still very limited. Doesn't that set up a coming conflict?

ZHAO: I think it's impossible for any country to have absolute economic and political freedom. There are always some restrictions, some degrees of freedom within law; that's true in any country. The Chinese people are becoming well-known for our economic development; we now have business partners all over the world. But businesspeople show little interest in learning about our political development; for the most part, they are ignorant of it. That's our fault, too, in a sense, because our own media have not stressed how much our political freedoms have evolved.

KUHN: Tell us what's been happening.

ZHAO: When it comes to democratic reforms—that is, elections—we've made great strides. We've also advanced in other areas, like human rights, minority issues, and family planning. One factor that limits the speed at which China can advance is our huge population. Not only that, but we still have many people who are illiterate. We don't want to make people's lives more difficult. Unwise government policies could cause yet more misery. The wrong solutions—or premature solutions—could create even greater problems.

KUHN: We have a saying for that: "The cure could be worse than the disease." You take great care—some would call it obsessive concern—not to inadvertently cause chaos. Why is stability so important for China?

ZHAO: In China, stability is actually more important than anything else. After a century of turmoil, the need for stability beats in every Chinese heart. Before 1949, the Chinese people lived with war and little else. During the Cultural Revolution, we again lived through chaos and disorder. The Chinese people have been through many trials. China cannot afford not to have internal stability, especially when its economy is not yet fully developed. If China were to become unstable, it would be a trial not just for the Chinese people but for the whole world. Can you imagine the impact on the rest of the world of *millions* of Chinese refugees? What country could, or would, receive them? Think of the refugees produced by the war in Vietnam, or in Kosovo. An unstable China would produce far more refugees than that.

KUHN: It seems that two of the axial political reforms that are now happening in China are the election of town officials and the average citizen's right to sue the government. Is this correct?

ZHAO: You're correct—both of these reforms are very important forward steps. Elections are in place in many villages throughout China, but not in all of them. In some villages, there are too many people still illiterate. They have to be educated first, so that they cannot be taken unfair advantage of. As education grows, so can democracy.

KUHN: What about the rule of law?

ZHAO: The law is the means by which the people can monitor their government. By giving people this right, the Chinese government hopes to improve the quality of government at the local level. The Chinese hierarchical system is huge. There are four levels: central, provincial, local, and city or town. Education levels and moral character vary from person to person. The bad apples need to be recognized and culled out. This can be done through citizens' lawsuits against the government.

KUHN: Let's look at the Chinese media, which is not free by western standards. As minister of the Information Office of the State Council, do you see changes in how the media functions?

ZHAO: We hope that the media can more accurately reflect Chinese reality and opinions. We encourage our journalists to report the truth to the Chinese people. We even encourage them to write criticism and to stir up discussion about real issues. This will foster—both in the media and in the people—a sense of responsibility for the welfare of our whole society. Of course, journalists should report on matters of common concern rather than simply using the press to grind personal axes.

KUHN: But if the media are to monitor the various levels of the government, don't they need to be truly independent? Does the current reform in China allow for truly independent media?

ZHAO: We don't use the term "independent media" in China, but for the most part the media are quite independent. The government manages the media, but it doesn't control them. Some regulations are necessary: for example, our newspapers aren't allowed to publish pornography or fake news. Beyond that, we have no intention of controlling the news media.

KUHN: Putting aside the issue of how news is determined to be real or fake, are people free to use the media to criticize government? Isn't there an increasing need for this right in fostering development in China?

ZHAO: China has more than two thousand newspapers. Most have at least a hundred thousand readers, who are free to express themselves on the many opinion pages. The government is also free to express its opinion in these pages.

KUHN: Would citizens get into trouble for criticizing the government in the media?

ZHAO: Chinese criticize the government often; of course, there are limits. As we've discussed, stability is of primary importance for China.

KUHN: Let's talk about China's economic reform. We've heard much about its benefits. Can we now talk about some of its problems? For example, many workers are being laid off as a result of economic reforms in state-owned enterprises. Would you address the negative impact of economic reform?

ZHAO: We're all familiar with the benefits of a market economy, and our reform is deepening. At the same time, some products have lost their markets. If the older, more traditional factories cannot compete by upgrading their designs and products, they lose out, and the result is layoffs. Dr. Kuhn, you are an investment banker, so you can help analyze this for me: China's economic situation is very strange right now—in fact, it is unique. No other nation has shared our precise situation. On one hand, we see some state-owned enterprises temporarily laying off workers—but we don't see a shortage of products in the marketplace.

The growth rate of China's GDP is still high, by international standards. So the economy isn't getting worse because of the layoffs.

KUHN: China's GDP growth rate has slowed—though you are right, it's
still very high [between 7 and 8 percent]. The problem arises because
some state-owned enterprises are so inefficient or so misaligned with
market demands that they cannot—indeed, should not—survive. Part
of the paradox, I think, is that these state-owned enterprises were per-
forming so poorly for so long that their downsizing or demise hardly
hurts the economy! The layoffs are only temporary, in the sense that
other employment may be found through new jobs generated by a
growing economy and by retraining of the workers for needed profes-
sions—but this is not guaranteed for all laid-off workers. What is the
government doing for these unemployed workers?

ZHAO: First, it's beginning to provide for their living expenses and offers
job training in special centers. It then introduces them to new job opportunities. In Shanghai's new Pudong district, where I worked, we established many foreign investment opportunities. The companies that
were formed absorbed many of the workers who had been laid off from
state-owned enterprises.

KUHN: Some believe that market reform has had a negative impact on traditional Chinese culture. For example, it has created competition, and
a more Western way of thinking. Do you have any sense of loss because
of this?

ZHAO: The essence of Chinese culture is in no danger because of market
reform. It is strong enough to absorb some of the great traditions of
Western culture—science, dance, music, and so on. We feel these
things are harmless to us; indeed, they reinvigorate us. We do need to
retain the essence of Chinese culture—this is very important to us—
and we need to reinvent some of our more traditional elements. We do
seek to prevent overtly negative entertainment, like excessively violent
films or pornography, from invading China. We are strict about such
things. But in recent years the more positive aspects of Western culture
have influenced our people. For example, China at one time refused to
build skyscrapers, because we saw them as symbolic of the American
way of life. Now we build skyscrapers here, too. Our clothing styles,
too, are now less traditional and more similar to Western styles. In
many of our cities, we have built concert halls that offer Mozart, Bach,

and Beethoven along with traditional Chinese music. In fact, I hope to have an opportunity to hear your wife perform in Shanghai soon.[1]

KUHN: Do you miss your scientific work?

ZHAO: Very much! Especially after having seen many of my classmates go on to become famous scientists. My feelings about that are complex. In my work today, as when I was doing scientific experiments, I have to be careful not to overstep myself.

KUHN: Do you keep up with the scientific literature?

ZHAO: Yes—but, to tell the truth, it's getting harder for me to understand those articles.

KUHN: Imagine us sitting here—with less hair—twenty years from today. What would we be saying about these times in China?

ZHAO: We'll remember today and praise it. The relationship between China and America will be better than it is now. We'll have fewer conflicts. I think China will be playing an important role on the center stage of the world. We'll have a friendly relationship with other countries. China and other nations will help each other. Your Chinese and my English will both be better than they are today.

Changes in China

Although economic improvement—a higher standard of living, financial success, luxuries of life—are goals in every country, there is extra energy to achieve these goals in China. The motivation goes beyond material benefits; the Chinese want to show the world that they are in every way a modern nation and in every sense a great power. If this demonstration requires material wealth, technological prowess, military strength, a world-class aerospace program, then these are what they must and will achieve.

It is hard for westerners to appreciate the momentous changes in China over the past twenty-five years—essentially, since the end of the Cultural

---

[1] Dora Serviarian-Kuhn, the author's wife, is a pianist who has appeared as soloist many times with symphony orchestras in China; she introduced the Khachaturian Piano Concerto in performances with the China National Symphony and China Broadcast Symphony.

Revolution in 1976 and Deng Xiaoping's initial reforms in 1978. The obvious improvement in the standard of living of most Chinese and the economic strength of the country is evidenced in virtually every city and town. The diversity in dress and entertainment, the new flexibility in sexual behaviors[2]—even the increase in divorce and legions of lawyers (see Appendix)—all speak to the uncontestable fact that China is no longer the drab, monolithic society so ingrained in Western consciousness.

But even more fundamental is the change in outlook and spirit. One need only speak with Chinese people in the major cities—educated Chinese and ordinary, person-in-the-street Chinese—to sense their newfound self-confidence and enthusiasm for life. They tell you plainly what they think—whether it's about how they are going to get a better job and make more money, or about their dislike of government bureaucracy, or about the omnipresent air pollution. They give you their opinions bluntly—you don't have to ask twice, and they don't look over their shoulder before they speak out. And what you discover is that for the Chinese—as for most people—what's most important are not the vagaries of national politics and international conflict but their own personal lives and their own personal futures, about which they are finally feeling confident.

They are also well informed—about China and (surprisingly) about the rest of the world. In our television documentary, you see an elderly, retired Chinese man, wearing his traditional clothes, walking his traditional paths, eating his traditional foods, and carrying a distinctly nontraditional portable radio, whereon he is listening constantly to market reports about Chinese companies and their stock prices ("Old Man Xiao," page 148). How current he is on international economics, like the financial crisis then brewing in Indonesia, as our camera crews follow him! And how clearly he understands the American way. "The U.S. would never send in its army like other coun-

---

[2] I have firsthand evidence of the changing sexual mores in China (but it's not what you may think). When my most recent book, *Closer To Truth: Challenging Current Belief* (an exploration of state-of-the-art ideas in science and their implications for the human condition), was being translated into Chinese I expected problems with the two chapters that dealt scientifically, but frankly, with sex. There were none. In fact, I detected a trace of condescending amusement that I would even think that serious sex talk would be a problem. (Oddly, the American public television series on which the book was based did have a problem, though the equivalent TV shows were intellectual, scientific, and all talk. In fact the entire twenty-eight episode "Closer To Truth" series had to be given a more mature rating, and those particular shows on sex had to be "flagged" so that stations could decide to preempt them.)

tries might," he confides to an old buddy, "their system would not permit it." He knows more about international economics than most Americans do.

Having lived much of their lives under a Maoist revolutionary regime with a central command economy, many Chinese are not used to thinking for themselves; they are just beginning to develop their own beliefs and sense of personal autonomy. When they are thrown into the market economy—an economy that demands, even for lower level jobs, a certain amount of personal initiative—many find themselves facing problems of adjustment and an unaccustomed struggle to survive.

The change in the economic lives of the Chinese people has been staggering: since 1978, China's per capita income has more than quadrupled. The Chinese economy is now the second largest in the world, and in thirty years it may well be the largest. Average salaries are low by Western standards—current annual per capita income is under $750 a year in urban areas and under $250 in rural income—but prices are also low, so that many people are living better than the income statistics indicate.[3] Almost a billion people have access to television; two decades ago only 10 million did. In 1978 there were 200 foreign companies doing business in China; today there are over 300,000. In fact, China absorbs more foreign investment than any country in the world except the United States. Chinese corporations are selling refrigerators and air conditioners and other such modern appliances around the world, and Chinese entrepreneurs are building private businesses on the Internet—yet 800 million of China's citizens are peasants[4] and over 100 million are still illiterate.

---

[3] Based on a calculation using Purchasing Power Parity (PPP), a system that normalizes for prices of goods and services relative to income or gross domestic product. The IMF, World Bank, and CIA use PPP in their analyses, but many others still use traditional monetary exchange rates, where approximately 8.3 *yuan* in Chinese currency equals $1.00 in American currency, so that China's relative position would be far lower. PPP explains how such significant improvements in Chinese standards of living are supported by such seemingly low per capita incomes.

[4] The common statistic has been that 80 percent of the Chinese people live in the countryside, but it is no longer true today. As many as 100 million rural residents are now part of the "floating population" in the cities. In addition, a rapid process of urbanization has turned many parts of the Chinese countryside into cities and towns. Finally, even if we may conclude that 65 percent of Chinese citizens still live in the countryside, not all of them are peasants (i.e., those who make a living by working in the fields) because many of them are engaged in rural commerce and town and village enterprises.

The old communist ideal of the glorious masses in common struggle is dead and buried, seemingly forever. It has been replaced by something new and dynamic, an economic engine fueled by personal dreams and national pride. Deng Xiaoping's reforms probably saved the Chinese Communist Party from extinction, but he has also unleashed forces that may radically change the system.

The Cultural Revolution

I spoke of pride as the first great motivational factor in the Chinese national psyche. I'll turn now to the second overarching theme—which I also learned from my friend Professor Lu. It had remained a mystery to me how, in those cautious days of recidivist repression after Tiananmen, he could remain so outspoken. One evening at dinner, I asked him (as I ask every Chinese citizen over forty) what happened to him during the Cultural Revolution, that horrendous decade (1966–76) of social turmoil and personal torment, when self-inflicted national mutilation turned the entire country inward against itself, pitting children against parents and friend against friend.

The Cultural Revolution was initiated by Mao Zedong in 1966 in the twilight of his mercurial career, in a sad and vainglorious attempt to re-revolutionize China and reaffirm his own potency and preeminence. Begun as an effort to ferret out elitist elements from society and expunge capitalists from the Communist party, it dissolved into colossal chaos and nearly destroyed the country. Universities were closed; intellectuals and professionals were exiled to farms; children were urged to denounce their parents; and young Red Guards, waving their little red books of Mao's quotations, stood in judgment over anyone they deemed counterrevolutionary.

Jolting quickly out of control and hijacked by radicals and self-aggrandizers, the Cultural Revolution was energized by a fundamentalist fervor; its adherents concocted a Mao-centered personality cult in order to assert their political dominance. Almost every institution of higher learning was shut down and virtually every educated person was conscripted to menial labor. As a nationwide frenzy of terror and anarchy paralyzed the country, an entire generation was lost. The human toll was horrific; torture was rampant; many millions died. Almost everyone of accomplishment in China suffered, and each of the survivors has a special story to tell.

Liu Shaoqi, the chief theoretician of the Communist Party and president of China, and Deng Xiaoping, then general secretary of the Party, were both purged. They were accused of advocating capitalism and op-posing Mao's major economic policies—the Great Leap Forward and Centralization. Their "crime" was that they supposedly gave individual farmers some freedom to own land. In truth, Mao feared that they, along with other high-level Party leaders, no longer followed his policies and he wanted an excuse to get rid of them. It is impossible to overstate the sear-ing memory of the Cultural Revolution—the accusations, denunciations, castigations, humiliations. I have not met a single educated person over forty years old who was not emotionally scarred by the experience.

Professor Lu said that he had been a graduate student when the Cul-tural Revolution began and, like all his colleagues, was forced to abandon his studies in an effort to achieve a true communist "purity."

"What did they do to you?" I asked, hunting for specifics.

"They put me into a room with other scholars and we were forced to criticize each other," he replied dryly.

"For how long?" I pressed.

"Sixteen hours a day."

"For how many days?"

"Seven years."

I went silent, stunned—so he continued. "My suffering wasn't special. There were millions like me. Many endured worse; many didn't survive. But I wouldn't let them take my soul. I continued with my study at night—I wouldn't let them thwart my development. So every night, all night, I would study. Of course, I would fall asleep during the endless self-criticism sessions during the day, and they, of course, would beat me up—with glee. But I was determined not to let them stop my learning. After all that they did to me then, what more can anyone do to me now?"

That's how I came to realize why Professor Lu was so nonchalant in his outspokenness. He had survived hell, and what hadn't killed him had made him stronger. And he was no renegade: later I would learn that he had made important contributions to national defense technology, and that his loyalty to China was unquestionable.

China's Stability

Professor Lu's experience during the Cultural Revolution reveals the sec-ond fundamental theme that, together with Chinese pride, underlies so much of what is happening in today's China. To understand it, we have to explore another paradox that I hadn't figured out earlier. (Frankly, it took me years to get it.) Despite all his clever criticisms of the Chinese government, Professor Lu was no proponent of Western-style democracy for China. What then to me seemed obvious (almost a tautology)—that if you reject communist-style central planning you must therefore espouse Western-style democracy—was not correct. Such simpleminded reasoning exposes the naïveté of Western perceptions. It seems one-dimensional and untextured to many Chinese, even to those who seek fundamental change in the political system. Professor Lu believed, quite in accord with government policy, that collective rights are more important than individual rights, and that improving the standard of living for all citizens is a superior good to allowing greater freedom of speech for some citizens.

The second great theme needed for understanding contemporary China is the Chinese desire for *stability*. Actually, it is more than desire; it is obsession—a deep-seated need for social order and an almost paranoid fear of turmoil and chaos. This is the legacy of the Cultural Revolution: the nightmare memories cannot be eradicated, and a recurrence in any form must be prevented at all costs. Stability is essential. This is what one continually hears in China; it is hard to overstate the importance of this concern. Professor Lu's personal experience during the Cultural Revolution is far from unique; among middle-aged people of some education or family stature or commercial position, it is almost universal. Moreover, much of what is happening in China today that is not good—such as the breakdown of traditional Chinese morals and ethics—can be traced back to the Cultural Revolution.

It may seem overly simplistic to reduce one's analysis of an entire nation—an entire people—to two basic themes. Nonetheless, if one characterizes contemporary China by the twin themes of pride and stability, one can explain a great deal. I ask you to keep them in mind—Pride and Stability—as you read through this book.

Civilization and History

Chinese Civilization

The word "China," in Chinese, is *Zhong Guo*, meaning the middle *(zhong)* country *(guo)*—the kingdom, as it were, at the center of the world. China has one of the oldest continuous civilizations in the world, and Chinese science and technology were well ahead of Europe's for the hundreds of years in which Europe endured the long, unenlightened period historians call the Middle Ages. Even as late as the fifteenth century, Chinese science and technology were supreme in the world. Gunpowder was not all that the Chinese invented; they were the originators of much that underlies modern civilization: paper (including paper money), the non-throttling horse collar, the wheelbarrow, cast iron, the helicopter rotor and the propeller, the decimal system, seismography, matches, an early form of printing, brandy and whiskey, the kite, elaborate astronomical clocks, the rocket, and the multistage missile.

No matter how embattled their circumstances, no matter how poor their condition, the Chinese have always considered their culture as being of the highest order. Foreigners have been characterized as barbarians—"long-nosed devils," to be specific. There is great pride in China about Chinese civilization and achievements, and great bitterness over the centuries of foreign subjugation.

The Legacy of Foreign Oppression

One cannot understand China today without appreciating this long history of foreign domination. The great pride that all Chinese citizens take in China's growing economic strength and increasing recognition as a world power has its roots in this history of humiliation. After centuries of domination and subjugation at the hands of foreign conquerors—Mongolian, English, Japanese—the Chinese are unified in their pleasure at taking their long overdue place at the center of power in international commerce and diplomacy.

It is difficult for non-Chinese to imagine the depth of the fury that Chinese people—no matter where they live—harbor toward their historic oppressors. In the thirteenth and fourteenth centuries, the Chinese were ruled by the Mongols. The British introduced opium into China in the late eighteenth century; there followed the so-called Opium Wars of the mid-nineteenth century, leading, among other things, to the forcible opening of Chinese ports to Western trade and the cession of Hong Kong to the British, a national humiliation only recently redressed. And then, in what seems to many Chinese like only yesterday, came the Japanese.

The Japanese occupation of China during World War II was brutal, sadistic, and deliberate; millions were murdered. The so-called Rape of Nanking alone consumed three hundred thousand Chinese, and the Japanese army, as a rule, treated the Chinese as little more than rodents. In what the Chinese still call the Anti-Japanese War—they do not refer to it as World War II, as does the rest of the world—the Chinese citizenry endured wanton slaughter, fiendish tortures such as grotesque medical experiments and bayonet practice on pregnant women, the gang raping of women of all ages, and the sexual enslavement of the "comfort women."

Only in recent years has the unspeakable abomination of comfort women come fully to light; as these women grew into old age, they became determined to surmount their decades-long shame. Here had been young girls abducted and forced to service Japanese soldiers—dozens of harsh sexual acts every day—and then they were tortured and killed when they could no longer perform that horrid task. All this is stamped indelibly on the collective Chinese consciousness.

A thirty-something Chinese-American entrepreneur was in my office in Southern California recently and noticed some mementos I had brought back from China. He ignored the beautiful watercolor paintings and the carvings of ancient warriors; all he could see, lying among a small collection of much older and more valuable Chinese swords, was one rusted Japanese sword. The young entrepreneurial glow faded from his expression. "I can still smell the Chinese blood on it," he muttered.

An op-ed article in *China Today*, one of China's largest English-language magazines, gives vent to the same smoldering resentment:

> What comes to the minds of Chinese people at the mention of Japan? I am sure that rancor would be one of the most common reactions. Certainly this deeply rooted animosity is reasonable. Japan is the country responsible for launching a series of aggressive wars against China during the past century that cost the lives of millions of Chinese.
>
> Unforgivably insulted and victimized, the Chinese people are still willing to step out of the shadows of the catastrophic past. Yet many Japanese, who often accuse China of dwelling on Japanese war crimes, are simply unwilling to admit the atrocities they have committed. Some Japanese must be ashamed of their ugly past. They consider themselves too civilized to have committed such hideous crimes. But it is clear that they will never escape their shame unless they face their actions squarely. However, many die-hard [Japanese] militants think differently. They revere the war criminals as national heroes and see the past as a precious legacy. Their only regret might be that their predecessors did not do their job well enough or there would be no evidence and witnesses left to trouble them now.
>
> Such an attitude toward whitewashing history, while alienating and angering the Chinese and other victimized peoples, does indeed have one benefit: it will constantly remind us that history remains part of the present. Never to forget our humiliating past, we shall keep a watchful eye over those who have never repented for their crimes.[5]

An extremely wealthy Chinese businessman in Hong Kong told me of his long-standing and continuing bitterness toward the British, who had recently returned the colony to China. No matter office or station, he said, any British had for decades and as a matter of course cut ahead of any Chinese standing in line, as if the Chinese person waiting patiently at the front of the queue at the bus stop or at the bank did not even exist—as if it were ordained that the British be the rulers and the Chinese the ruled. The fact that this Chinese tycoon now had more financial clout than virtually any Englishman left in Hong Kong had done little to dull his resentment.

---

[5] Xi Mi, *China Today*, January 20, 2000.

The Communist "Restoration"

Let no westerner think that because communism has failed China as an economic system, it has also failed to build a reservoir of goodwill among the Chinese people for restoring their national dignity and bringing international respect to their ancient civilization. Most Chinese look with pride on communism's nationalistic accomplishments. (However, the incessant political campaigns over the years, especially the Cultural Revolution, eroded much of this goodwill.)

Here is how a leading English-language Chinese publication characterizes China's modern diplomatic history. This account, intended (ham-handedly) to appeal to Western audiences, gives the (then) official view of China's relations with the United States (such "official views" are in constant flux). Note the reference to the American imposition, at the start of the Cold War, of an "all-around political, economic, and military blockade against China, attempting to arrest its development":

The hundred-odd years from 1840 to 1949 were a sad period, full of humiliations, in the history of Chinese diplomacy. Western powers launched aggressive wars against China, resulting in China being forced to sign treaties of national betrayal and humiliation. Since the Anglo-Chinese Nanjing Treaty signed in 1842, China was compelled to sign more than eleven hundred unequal treaties before 1949. It ceded territories, paid indemnities, and opened trading ports, being trampled by others at will, while Chinese representatives to the negotiations held in Paris could do nothing but sigh, "Weak countries cannot talk about diplomacy."

After 1949, New China entered the international arena as a sovereign state. On the eve of the founding of New China, Chairman Mao Zedong established the foreign policy of the new socialist China by first severing all links with the old foreign policy, or "setting up a separate kitchen," as he put it. The core of the foreign policy is independence and peace.

However, the United States had a hostile attitude toward the newly established People's Republic. It imposed an all-around political, economic, and military blockade against China, attempting to arrest its development. Only three days after New China was founded, the U.S. government declared its continued support of the Kuomintang regime.

On June 25, 1950, the Korean War broke out. The United States and other Western countries sent troops to Korea, extending the war flames to the bank of Yalu River, the border between Korea and China.

Meanwhile, the U.S. Seventh Fleet patrolled the Taiwan Straits, posing a severe threat to China's sovereignty and national security. Although under extreme difficulties, the Chinese leaders made a strategic decision to resist U.S. aggression and assist the Democratic People's Republic of Korea to safeguard their country. Chinese troops achieved a miracle in world military history by defeating a powerful opponent with a weak and underdeveloped force. The signing of the Korean Armistice Agreement ended the period wherein China always had to sacrifice national interests in diplomatic negotiations.[6]

For China, the Korean War (1950–53) marked a turning point in its relationship with the West. The stakes were far greater than the protection of neighboring North Korea: at issue was the reestablishment, after hundreds of years, of national pride. But Chinese self-determination and international respect is not limited to its relationship with the United States. The article continues:

> The issue of sovereignty tolerates no consultation. This is an outstanding characteristic of China's foreign policy of independence and peace. In 1958, leaders of the former Soviet Union proposed building a longwave transceiver station in China, commonly owned by the two countries, and establishing a joint fleet. Mao resolutely rejected the suggestion.

China's fractious relationship with the former Soviet Union—always combustible, in part because of a common and disputed border running for thousands of miles—exploded in the 1960s. One of the untold stories of this under-reported hot war was how Soviet tanks were unstoppable in their advance into Chinese territory until Israel, in highly secret arrangements and while China still refused to recognize the fledgling Jewish state, provided the Chinese with special weaponry to destroy those tanks. The

---

[6] "A History of Chinese Diplomacy," *Beijing Review*, January 10, 2000. The Kuomintang was the anti-communist Nationalist government, led by Chiang Kai-shek, Mao's mortal enemy, who fled to Taiwan in 1949 to set up the Republic of China in exile. Two other matters of note in the above article: the diplomatic priority established by the sentence "The core of the foreign policy is independence and peace"; and the fact that the cause of the Korean War—North Korean aggression, as established in recent years by declassified Russian documents—is not discussed at all, reflecting recent recognition among the Chinese elite of, if not outright North Korean culpability, at least a more nuanced and honest approach to the war's history.

long, clandestine military relationship between Israel and China, which continues to this day, has become critical, for different reasons, for the national security of both countries. I remember visiting a leading Chinese computer enterprise and asking about the rumored military relationship between Israel and China. My Chinese friend pointed out a factory for manufacturing defense electronics, built by the Israeli military in the early 1970s, when China was still denouncing Israel in its official public statements. The defense relationship between Israel and China is founded on the pragmatic fact that, for both countries, nationalism trumps ideology. The *Beijing Review* article again continues:

> In 1963, the United States, the Soviet Union, and Britain signed the Partial Test Ban Treaty, which was aimed at consolidating the nuclear monopoly of [the three] superpowers. While denouncing such an act, China broke the monopoly with its practical action. When a mushroom cloud rose to the sky from the desert in northwest China on October 16, 1964, the world marveled at the rapid progress of China's nuclear technology, as well as its determination to safeguard sovereignty and independence.

China's pride in its nuclear achievements, like its pride in its aerospace enterprises, bubbles over and cannot be contained, which makes the American accusations of Chinese nuclear spying all the more galling to the Chinese. The underlying affront is not the accusation of spying itself but the implication that China is incapable of developing advanced technology on its own. To the Chinese, an independent Chinese nuclear and aerospace capability makes the unmistakable statement that China will never again be humiliated by foreigners, that China will control its own destiny, and that if there is to be peace in the world, an independent China must be a major power to help guarantee it.

Mao and Deng

Mao Zedong, notwithstanding all his catastrophic mistakes and personal excesses, is unalterably held to be a great man in China: Mao is singularly revered as a thinker, a strategist, a statesman, and, most important, as the founder of the New China. He was the Great Helmsman who restored national pride. Mao's thought and personality is so deeply rooted in China, particularly with people over fifty, that his continuing impact on public affairs cannot be denied, and many Chinese compare his influence on contemporary Chinese culture to that of Confucius.

The differences between Mao Zedong and Deng Xiaoping are fascinating and complex. Lifelong Communists, Mao and Deng were both allies and adversaries, personally and ideologically. Most important, however, they shared the same fundamental goal—to make China into a strong country, with a high standard of living for its people and a high degree of respect among the nations. Mao was the first leader in modern Chinese history who envisioned China as a powerful, independent country. Deng wanted to develop the country, too, but he criticized Mao's theories of implementation and designed his own.

Deng was a pragmatist. He knew that change was necessary because the old system had failed. "It doesn't matter if the cat is black or white," Deng famously pronounced, "as long as it catches the mouse." It was his way of saying that if a market economy can produce the goods, that's what counts, and ideology could be set to one side.

But Deng's "socialist market economy," at its core, was a continuation of Mao's socialism. Superficial economics notwithstanding, the two approaches are not as distinct as they first appear. Mao wanted a socialist planned economy, while Deng wanted a mixed economy of free market business combined with government central planning. (Deng never used the term "capitalism" to characterize China's mixed economy.) Mao's era supplied Deng with a negative lesson in economics. The planned economy was demonstrably an outright failure; thus Mao gave Deng a good reason to reform.

Mao was an idealist, Deng a realist. Deng was a doer, not a theorist or a thinker. He didn't say much. He emphasized practice and learning lessons from mistakes. China's present reform follows Deng's advice: "Cross the river stone by stone." Reform progresses step by step, and it doesn't need ponderous theory to guide it. "The Cultural Revolution was a disaster," Deng said, "but we managed to turn it into our treasure."

Mao's political philosophy appears to have been—in the formulation of political economist Zheng Shiping, of the University of Vermont—"Political stability comes out of political chaos." He emphasized revolution and disruption. His back-to-back political movements and endless class struggles produced incalculable hardship and tragedy, as in the Great Leap Forward and the subsequent decade of catastrophic turmoil that was the Cultural Revolution. Mao is an important symbol not of stability but of Chinese pride—of the Chinese people standing together and for themselves.

Chinese feelings about Mao are emotional and conflicted. His reign produced terrible social chaos and economic losses. Nonetheless, the critical evaluation of Mao, authorized in 1981 by the Chinese Communist Party, stated that while Mao made "gross mistakes," his positive contributions outweighed his blunders in a ratio of 70:30; that is, Mao's historical accomplishments were 70 percent of what he did and his historical errors were 30 percent. (How does one cook up such specific numbers? It is amusing to imagine the tortuous debates and tense compromises among the Party leadership as they hurled competing percentages back and forth.) Do Chinese people accept this 70:30 evaluation ratio? Some say the reverse, of course—that his accomplishments were 30 percent and his mistakes were 70 percent, while others put it at 50:50.

The British journalist Philip Short concludes in his monumental *Mao: A Life* that the number of people who were killed by misguided policies under Mao's regime ranged from 23 million to 25 million, and that the Great Helmsman "brought about the deaths of more of his own people than any other leader" in history. Mao's delusions were revealed early, in a 1957 speech to Party leaders in Moscow, where he ruminated, "If war broke out, how many people would die? There are 2.7 billion people in the entire world, and one-third of them may be lost. If the worst came to the worst, perhaps one-half of them would die. But the world would still have one-half of its people left."

Mao's massive megalomania, along with his petty treachery, is symptomatic of a deep psychopathology. He could be a vengeful tyrant, manipulating all those around him and purging any whom he imagined as challenging his preeminence, even his closest colleagues. His above-the-law self-regard was cloaked in a brazen hypocrisy, and he flouted China's public policy in his personal behavior. While the government was proclaiming that extramarital sex was counterrevolutionary, Mao was populating his bed, as Short reports, "with as many young women as he wished"—often, it is said, with several of them at the same time. Yet Mao was also contemplative and literate, and while *Quotes of Chairman Mao* (excerpts from his speeches and writings) may be lampooned in the West, few westerners have actually read the words, which can express enduring truths of human hope and struggle.

Mao's portrait still dominates Tiananmen Square, and even though Mao's form of communism no longer exists, there is no sense that the portrait should be taken down. Mao embodies, quite literally in his image, deep symbolic meaning. It was he who changed China, who brought China self-esteem and international respect. What Mao symbolizes is Chinese unification, and the Chinese people will always remember him for that. He was the first person to unify China since the collapse of the Qing dynasty in 1911, and he set the trajectory for China to reestablish itself as a nation with international clout, as it had not been since the end of the Ming dynasty in the seventeenth century. This clout erupted suddenly in the Korean War, in which China suffered tremendous losses but showed that it was capable of standing up to the United States, the reigning superpower.

Hanging Mao's portrait in Tiananmen Square is similar to printing "In God We Trust" on America's currency—even though many Chinese may not actually venerate Mao, just as many Americans may not actually trust in God. Wang Lihua, a sociologist at Northeastern University in Boston, is on the mark when she compares China's reverence for Mao to America's reverence for God. In conversations for our documentary, she said:

> America and China are both multidimensional societies that require some identifying concept to maintain social unity. America is a melting pot where people have different origins, races, and beliefs, but there is only one God. I think the situation is similar in China. Class differences, regional differences, and sex differences have all emerged, and it is hard to find a single element to represent all of China. Thus Mao's image cannot be changed. Mao is like the first emperor; he represents unity rather than division, a spiritual cohesion. China needs such a symbol.
>
> After many years away, I went back to visit in 1991. It was the time of China's opening to the world. I had thought they didn't need Mao any more. But to my surprise, I saw many taxi drivers hanging Mao's portrait in their cars. When I asked why, they told me that Mao was God and could bring them luck. This made me realize that I had to rethink what I thought I knew about China. I had expected that reform would make the Chinese people admire a new leader. But they didn't need a new leader; they needed only Mao.

Maintaining the status quo and historical continuity are more important than the political winds of the present. When we asked the historian Yu Renqiu of the State University of New York at Purchase why the Chinese didn't take down Mao's portrait, he replied, "I don't think the Chinese can answer that question. They don't have a clear idea of what Mao represents. The image of Mao has had different meanings during different periods of time."

Economic History

Capitalism has in fact existed in China—particularly in and around Shanghai—since the early years of the twentieth century, but it was an immature form of capitalism. The Chinese economy was mainly agricultural. Over 80 percent of China's population resided in the villages. A few landowners controlled most of the land, and most Chinese people were very poor. Industry was controlled largely by the government. Such capitalism was bureaucratic, not free market, and companies, such as they were, could not freely compete with one another.

By 1949 when Mao's Red Army captured Beijing and the People's Republic was founded, the economy of China had been destroyed in the wars—the eight-year war of resistance against Japan and the subsequent civil war between the Communists and the Nationalists, which lasted nearly four years. The economies in large cities were on the brink of collapse, so when the Communists took over, their urgent task was to restore basic necessities. Mao announced: "The goal of the first five-year plan is to build an industrialized, highly modernized, culturally developed country."

Government power was the only choice, as were the extreme measures to control national resources, enterprises, and land. The new government established a planned economy out of necessity as well as Marxist-Leninist ideology. The state owned all the means of production and determined in advance how much each factory would produce. Mao had decided to adopt the Soviet Union's economic model.

Prof. Lu Xiaobo points out that after 1958, the economic development model in China was not the same as that of the Soviet Union. The Chinese economy was no longer entirely centralized and planned by the central government and some local enterprises began to emerge in many towns and counties along the coast. These small and medium-sized enterprises—which were collectively owned by the workers, not the state—would become the economic pillars of reform under Deng Xiaoping, and the predecessors of today's town and county enterprises, and would make great contributions to the economic development of China. Many of these enterprises were in existence even before Deng's reforms started, and they are a strong link between pre- and post-reform China.

China had been influenced by Marxism and Leninism since the 1920s, and it was widely believed that under a cooperative socialist system, all work and rewards would be shared and the country would grow rapidly. A planned economy, it was thought, was the only system that could raise productivity quickly so that China would be able to industrialize quickly. But the planned economy did not work in China, just as it did not work elsewhere—because of a profoundly erroneous assumption about human nature—and it made China extremely poor. The establishment of collective ownership was a fundamental mistake, arising out of a fundamental misreading of human behavior. Like it or not, most people work harder when they work for their own benefit.

The Great Leap Forward, which Mao concocted between 1958 and 1960, was an extreme economic experiment and an extremely spectacular failure. Mao wanted to enlist China's vast population, especially in large-scale rural communes, in a fanciful, harebrained attempt to attack China's industrial and agricultural problems in the shortest amount of time. The deeply flawed thought was that labor-intensive methods of industrialization, which stressed manpower rather than machines, would outstrip a slower and eminently more sensible process—that of industrialization through the gradual purchase of capital-intensive machinery. The Great Leap Forward was epitomized by small backyard steel furnaces in every village; these were supposed to eliminate the need to build large new factories.

Under the commune system, ideological purity was valued far more than technical expertise. The peasants were organized into brigade teams, military style, and communal kitchens were established so that women could be freed for work. All the while, the Great Leap was overseen and spurred on by fanatical cadres fighting a frantic war; the Chinese people were gathered and managed in a military style, and in such haste and with such lack of foresight that unmitigated disaster soon descended. The Great Leap Forward turned out to be a Huge Fall Backward. From 1959 to 1962, as a direct result of gross governmental mismanagement of agriculture, wildly unrealistic quotas, and forced labor, there was a national famine; at least 20 million people died of starvation.

Mao responded by calling for more revolution. His policies generated chaos in China. His so-called continuous revolution, back-to-back political movements, and class struggle, destroyed the economy, the social fabric and led to a huge loss of life. It had a devastating impact on the Chinese people.

To contemplate the passionate popular support for Mao's Great Leap Forward, which was expected to transform China into a superpower almost overnight, is to see the motivating energy of China's repressed pride. The Chinese masses, and not simply Mao alone, felt that China had suffered at the hands of imperialist powers because of its primitive economy.

They intended to right this wrong with a vengeance, a concerted will, and at an enormously impractical rate of speed. "Rushing Things Brings Disaster" is a favorite Chinese slogan, and the Great Leap Forward is a tragic example. Today all Chinese recognize that the Great Leap Forward was a huge mistake—a mistake whose enormity Mao never admitted.

In fact, Mao came to believe that the emergency measures taken to save the country from the disastrous consequences of the Great Leap Forward, such as decentralizing the communes, gravely betrayed his idealistic image of pure socialism. In 1966, yearning to reassert his misguided vision and restamp his megalomaniacal imprint, Mao launched the Cultural Revolution, which, as we've seen, visited even greater tribulation on his long-suffering countrymen, now decimating their spirits as well as their bodies.

3
Reform and Restructure

The Beginnings of Reform

For thirty years, people had no choice but to live and work where the government dictated. People were starving. As one farmer we interviewed said: "You had to sell every last egg the old hen produced."

In 1978, Vice Premier Deng Xiaoping, soon after Mao's death in 1976 and his own recrudescence, cautiously launched market reform. "If we do not start reform," Deng said, "then our goal to modernize socialism will be buried." Yan Mingfu, a former senior leader, remembers: "I had heard the word 'market' before, but it was always considered something negative. Deng Xiaoping was the first person to say that the market economy could exist under socialism. It made a deep impression on me."

Mao's hand-picked successor, Hua Guofeng,[7] then chairman of the Party and premier of the country, had resisted any change in policies. He was known for his "Two Whatevers"—(1) Whatever Chairman Mao said is Truth; and (2) Whatever Chairman Mao wanted us to do, we do. The newly re-emergent Deng Xiaoping challenged Hua's "Two Whatevers" by

---

[7] Hua Guofeng, who the Chinese consider decent but not terribly competent, had been Governor of Hunan, Mao's home province, before being anointed as Mao's successor. Hua's major contribution to China was perhaps twofold: he supported China's older leaders in removing and arresting the "Gang of Four" (the radical instigators of the Cultural Revolution, lead by Mao's wife, Jiang Qing), and he acquiesced in the reinstatement of senior leaders who had been jailed during the Cultural Revolution, including Deng Xiaoping.

saying, famously, "Seek truth from facts" and "Practice is the only standard to test truth." Deng's aphorisms were interpreted as a subtle challenge of Mao's godlike stature, not long after Mao had died.

The years between 1978 and 1980 are called the "Truth Debate" years,
when Mao's ideology was subject to secret discussions among the Chinese
leadership, and soon thereafter, when Deng finally prevailed, a nationwide campaign to redefine Truth was begun. The campaign was conducted
at every level of Chinese society, from grade schools to universities, from
the countryside to the cities, and featured official study documents from
Beijing (especially Deng's major speech on Truth) and open discussions
among the people.

It was a not-so-subtle effort to wean the Chinese people away from
blind obedience to the Great Helmsman, to reevaluate the infallibility of
Mao's utterances, and to commence a gradual but fundamental change in
sanctioning Chinese individuality. This debate changed Chinese history.
The Chinese people, perhaps for the first time ever, were encouraged to
think for themselves. Never again would any person's thoughts—whether
Mao, Marx, or even Deng himself—be accepted so blindly and uncondi-
tionally, and thus China was started on the long road to reform. Deng's
more pragmatic policy, amplified by his more dynamic personality, enabled him to win the power struggle: in 1980 Deng deposed Hua, and re-
defined Mao's role in Chinese history.

Simultaneously, deep in the countryside, a real-life change took place
that would soon have dramatic consequences. Socialism had failed, collective farming was not feeding China's people and an air of desperation hung
over the country. In 1978, eighteen households in Xiao Gang, a remote village of Anhui province in eastern China, were the first to experiment with
privatization (their motivation was pure survival; they could not have cared
less about economic theory). A severe drought had made many people, already very poor, into outright beggars. So these eighteen households held
a secret meeting and concluded that they could not survive under the collectivist system of mandated common ownership. They decided to split
the commune's cropland into individual plots, allocate them among the
member households, and adopt an individual responsibility system. They
decided to work independently, and pocket the fruits of their personal
labor. These few farmers would change the course of Chinese history.

They were so desperate that in October 1978 these Anhui peasants
signed a "blood" agreement to divide up the land. This was an extraordinarily risky initiative, because the political atmosphere at that time, so

soon after Mao's death, was still unclear. But these people were willing to take full responsibility. The pact said that if they were discovered and their leader arrested, the others would raise his son until he turned eighteen. So, sensing the grave danger but unaware of the historic import of what they were doing, they put their thumbprints on the formal document and divided the farm.

Within a few days, the secret pact was discovered by the county Party secretary, who thought that these villagers were promoting capitalism. But government officials had no options; what could they do? They realized the imminence of widespread starvation if they didn't start to allow a degree of autonomy. They therefore leased the commune's land to the farmers, household by household. The local Communist leader also thought that they had gone crazy from poverty, so what would be the harm in letting them try something new? Why not give them a few months? Let them try this experiment until after the harvest the following fall.

But after the harvest came the surprise: agricultural production had increased significantly. With this very small start, very large reform began in China. It wasn't really a market economy, of course, just a "responsibility system." But a fundamental change had occurred; a new incentive structure was at work on the Chinese mainland. After several months, this first, fledgling privatization began spreading to other provinces. Heated debates invaded the highest levels of the Party in 1979 and 1980. Should they change Mao's policy? Some thought the communist system was sacrosanct and must be maintained.

The Anhui farmers' success came to Deng Xiaoping's attention just as he was considering the possibility of economic reform. Deng said: "We need a brave plan to give the power to our people." The farmers' success spread throughout Anhui province and was soon approved by the central government. The essence of reform in the rural areas was the free access by farmers to the market, and letting farmers compete in the market. Because of that, China changed from a nation always short of agricultural products to a nation full of them.

Deng Xiaoping and other senior revolutionaries in the Party had been supportive of the division of farmland. As far back as December 1978, a couple of months after the Xiao Gang village farmers signed their contract, Deng had presented similar ideas to the Party in a report entitled (in the oracular tradition of such Party pronouncements) "Liberate Your Thoughts, Be Down-to-Earth, and Look Forward," in which he proposed to solve the problems in the countryside by giving autonomy to production-team and cooperative-union members. In 1980, Deng won the debate, and the central government sent out documents to officially promote dividing the farmlands. From 1980 to 1986, the government continually encouraged these so-called responsibility systems to expand and flourish.

Rural reform developed apace, and by 1984 longtime officials in the villages had finally recognized the dysfunction of the cooperative unions, which were no longer able to motivate Chinese farm workers, and these unions vanished. The responsibility system was so successful that by 1984 the agricultural output was experiencing annual double-digit percentage increases.

In our documentary we interviewed a typical farmer, named Guo Lanbao who lives in Northern China. Under collectivization he had no choice but to grow corn for his commune; with the move to the market economy he could make his own decisions. "In 1979 we got our first cow. By 1984 we had six or seven cows, and now we have more than twenty. In the beginning, only about two hundred families started doing this. Now the village has over a thousand. One year of income today is like ten years in the old days. My wife and I used to earn very little money from the commune and sometimes we had to go out and beg. Very often this corn is what we ate; we made fried rice with it. Even if it became gluey, we ate it. Our old house was built in 1962 when times were especially difficult—now it's used to store crops. We've built a new two-story house and our two sons have married. They eat all kinds of quality foods. Look at my grandson. He's only three years old and he looks so healthy. I could never have imagined life could be as it is today. The economic policy is open now and it's much better. You can work as hard as you want and even get rich."

It had been in the late 1970s when Deng first suggested that four small, poor coastal cities—Shenzhen, Zhuhai, Shantou, and Xiamen—be designated Special Economic Zones, as an experiment in urban reform. Shenzhen, adjacent to Hong Kong, was so designated in 1980. The rest, as they say, is history: the enormous successes of economic freedom in these cities set a pattern for the entire country. In November 1984, the State Council issued provisional regulations providing special tax benefits for foreign investments in these zones as the Chinese government launched its nationwide campaign of economic reform.

Reform was, from the beginning, very difficult. Every step was criticized by hard-liners as "creeping capitalism" and "turning backward." Several times Deng spoke up at the last minute to resolve disputes among different factions. Nineteen-eighty-four was the most glorious year for Deng since his return to power. Agricultural reform had been a great success, and for the first time in a generation there was optimism in the air. China had finally escaped the long shadow of the Cultural Revolution.

People's lives were getting better in so many ways that the thirty-fifth anniversary of the People's Republic that year, 1984, became a mass celebration of the new market approach. On that day in Tiananmen Square, students put up a banner with Deng's first name—"Hello, Xiaoping." Deng was popular among college students—he had restored the college entrance examination, which allowed them to enter universities. But his popularity was more general than that. The use of his first name expressed an intimacy between ordinary Chinese and their Paramount Leader; it would have been unthinkable when Mao reigned for anyone to say, much less parade, "Hi, Zedong."

As the chief architect of reform, Deng had achieved miracles. Most important, he had shifted the Communist Party's policy focus from class struggle to economic development. But making the change to economic self-determination was relatively quick and easy for individual farmers. It would be much harder and more complicated for industry, all of it owned by the state and all of it managed by government appointees.

Stages of Reform

We can consider three stages of economic reform in China. The first, beginning in 1978 and lasting until about 1985, focused on reform of the agricultural economy. The outcome was unmistakable—the living standards of peasants increased and the efficiency of agricultural production improved.

The second stage, lasting until about 1990, shifted reform to the cities and triggered some knotty problems. Urban reform was not as easy as expected, because it involved the emergence of a number of different markets (e.g., labor, securities, housing), the alteration of the system of pricing mechanisms, and the first reforms of state-owned enterprises. The impact came swiftly: first inflation, then corruption, then widespread corruption (where government officials and enterprise managers concocted unholy alliances to exchange undeserving preferences to businesses for illegal payments to individuals), which in turn led to the large-scale protests in Tiananmen Square in 1989.

By 1992, China's reform had entered its third stage, with a real commitment—notwithstanding the increasing problems—to deepen reform ("deepen" is a particularly Chinese adjective used to portray progression toward a market economy). Now state-owned enterprises became the center of attention. As Bernard College political scientist Lu Xiaobo puts it, reform's first two stages focused on increasing quantity whereas the third stage stressed increasing value. In its early stages, reform developed outside the existing system and did not touch the root of the old ways. Town and county enterprises emerged; private businesses were formed. The third stage tackled the most intractable problems of the economic system, increasing value in terms of profitability and efficiency. This third stage is by far the most difficult, but given the accumulation of experience over the past twenty years, the Chinese people—under the strong leadership of President Jiang Zemin, who became general secretary of the Chinese Communist Party in 1989 and president in 1993 (see page 249)—seem better able to deal with it than they were in the previous two stages. President Jiang seems determined to continue the commitment to reform made by Deng Xiaoping, and he has proved astute in navigating the uncharted waters where waves of economic uncertainty are amplified by torrents of political complexity.

In the initial stage of economic reform, no one—including Deng—had any idea of what the final goal was. Viewed from today's perspective, the goals of China's economic reform have been changing constantly. In fact, the goals set in 1978 have already been reached. At that time, the plan was to build China's economy so that people could live a comfortable life by the year 2000. That goal has been largely achieved. Although there are severe problems in China today, and although some people believe that as far as its ideology is concerned the old system had merit, there is no way for China to turn back. Too many people, too vividly, remember how much they suffered under the old system.

Problems of Reform

The biggest problem faced by the "New China" is a challenge to one of the two critical overarching themes discussed at the beginning of this book: instability. Since the purpose of economic reform is to improve efficiency and productivity, reform causes many people, at least initially, to lose their jobs. Government bureaus and state-owned enterprises have slimmed down, and this means that people who were once at least technically employed are now out of work. Further exacerbating the problem, peasants from the countryside are flooding the cities looking for jobs, just when many young people in those places are also entering the labor market. These three groups—laid-off workers, migrating peasants, and new workers—generate pressure on the job market.

The reform of state-owned companies is far from finished. Many are still losing money. Another problem area is finance—banking, tax, securities—where reform started more recently but needs to proceed more rapidly. Banks, for example, can no longer issue loans to prop up inefficient, market-dead, state-owned enterprises that constantly lose money. They must be commercially viable, responsible to market economics, not government dictates.

Then there's required reform in the rule of law, property rights, civil rights, and an independent judiciary. And ultimately, of course, there is the prospect of political reform. As China's economic reforms deepen, a middle class will grow more plentiful and powerful, and its members will want to express their political views. They will want freedom of assembly, freedom of speech, and other kinds of personal and collective freedoms. It is the government's hope that political freedom will never run too far ahead of broad economic development, as it did in Russia, to the great detriment of the Russian people.

Although virtually no one with any authority in China wants to go back to a wholly planned economy, there are some in leadership positions who would limit the market economy. Some of these conservatives are genuinely worried about unemployment, corruption, declining public ownership, penetration by foreign companies and, of course, the loss of control by the state over the economy and society, while others cleverly couch their reactionary ideology with expressions of concern for the person in the street and the peasant on the farm.

Yu Renqiu has pointed out that many ordinary Chinese citizens are truly frightened by the market economy. After living under the regulated Communist regime for their entire lives, they don't have the confidence or the independence of thought necessary to compete in such a world. Some Chinese, indeed, look back with longing at the Mao era. It's not that they are incapable of appreciating the new system; they are simply unused to it. Give them time, says Professor Yu, and they will come around.

A Matter of Attitudes

The death of Mao in 1976 was a turning point in the history of China, because after his death the new generation of leaders, the so-called second generation represented by Deng Xiaoping, took control of the political arena. In addition, the Chinese people were just plain tired of constant political movements, revolutionary upheavals, and class struggles, and they expected changes. But thinking was still ossified. After so many years of restriction and control, people had become afraid of thinking independently or differently. To them, Mao was God, a mythic hero, the decision-maker, the icon for everyone. The whole country worshiped him. All they had to do was to follow his instructions; Mao was not to be questioned or doubted. When Mao died, people didn't know which direction to go in. The tears at his funeral were as much an expression of great confusion as of genuine sadness. But deep in their hearts people wanted to see a big change of some kind. The death of Mao brought such a change, a turning point for reform in China.

The market economy has had a huge impact on people's perceptions and behavior. Citizens at all levels, from farmers to factory workers to enterprise owners, have begun to adjust. For example, before the market economy, salespeople in stores didn't bother to assist customers. You had to ask several times before anyone would show something to you. They couldn't care less whether you wanted to buy anything or not. It didn't matter to them: either way they were paid the same, there was no measure of success, and they couldn't lose their jobs. Their employment was guaranteed. Nowadays salespeople's sales directly affect their pay. If they sell more products, they get more money. Customers sometimes are scared away by salespeople who surround them, fighting to sell anything and everything in the store.

Change has been dazzling for the Chinese—not just in the construction of new buildings and modern cities but in the psychology and culture of the people. China was isolated from the world for decades, and while other countries were progressing, China stagnated. Because China began to modernize its thinking only about twenty-five years ago, a faster pace of change is needed if China is to catch up with the West.

The biggest psychological change has been the new conviction that change itself is possible. Before reform, no change was possible; after reform, no change seems impossible. Although no one has any idea where reform will end up, ordinary Chinese people are sure, with each step taken, that one way or another they will be better off.

Political economist Zheng Shiping likens the development of the Chinese market economy to what happened in Great Britain in the eighteenth and nineteenth centuries. At that time, capital was being accumulated in an impersonal, sometimes unethical, and frequently cruel process; as a system, capitalism was in a primitive stage. Now that other countries have supplied the experiences and the lessons, he says, China can do a better, more humane job in developing its market economy and avoid repeating the mistakes of history. That is, while developing market competition and market mechanisms, China should consider the social impact on people's lives and find ways to offset the negative effects that economic reforms inevitably bring.

Professor Zheng believes that although the market economy is competitive and impersonal, there is room to add some caring and personal elements to it. In his view, China should proceed not with an eighteenth-century model of mechanical and heartless capitalism, but rather toward the kind of economic development that includes social justice and social consciousness—a system that would include some form of social security, unemployment compensation, and other welfare measures. Europeans and Americans, he points out, did not establish these "safety net" provisions until they had endured painful times.

There is a new slogan in China today—"Enjoy Your Life!"—and the younger generation has accepted its directive wholeheartedly. This generation is markedly different from the one that grew up in the proletariat 1960s, when the central precept was to Forget Yourself and contribute to society. Today's young people put themselves first. Since self-interest is the behavioral core of capitalism, this new spirit augurs well for the economic development of China. But what happens to Chinese culture in the process?

Traditionally, China is a collectivist country, unlike America, which was founded on "rugged individualism." Collectivism in China didn't start with Mao; it has existed since the time of Confucius. When young people emphasize the self, they are flouting Chinese tradition, yet that tradition remains strong: people are still deeply attached to their families and friends. Although individualism is emerging in China, it is of a different character from that in America, where free choice has always been a key criterion of the good life. To many Chinese, free choice means anxiety. The Chinese people were used to the simple life, whereas the new consumer culture provides them with a panoply of choices and economic opportunities—for which certain sacrifices must be made. This conundrum has become an issue of import in China.

In my time there, I have seen evidence that the market economy is a major intruder into Chinese culture. Traditional Chinese culture emphasizes security and a peaceful life. The market economy shakes up such security and peace. These issues, as in other developed countries, are not of pressing concern to the young, but are important for older people. Back in.Mao's era, people's values were to create useful things for the collective society, but now people's values are to make money for their individual selves. But it is an oversimplification to conclude that everybody in today's China just wants to make money, and just because people want to make money doesn't mean that they are not doing good things for society.

The "Socialist Market Economy"

The semantics of China's post-Mao reform are interesting. In the mid-1980s, the government established a "planned commodity economy"—a hybrid phrase testing the waters. Officials didn't use the word "market" because it was still a suspect locution. Only after Deng's momentous visit to Southern China in 1992, when he revivified reform, and only after embarking on reform's third stage—the restructuring of the large state-owned enterprises—did the Chinese government finally begin using the unambiguous term "market economy." The system was then called "socialist market economy"—the adjective "socialist" being attached for historical continuity and political legitimacy. The phrase itself nicely allows for ambiguity: if you are more disposed to capitalism, then read "market economy"; if you tilt toward socialism, then read "socialist."

As for how much socialism is really involved, there is tacit understanding among the Chinese. Everyone knows that the country is moving from socialism to capitalism, at least a government-managed market economy not unlike those functioning in Japan, Taiwan, and South Korea. Everyone also knows that the government cannot blatantly say that it is now promoting capitalism. China is, after all, a socialist country (the tacit understanding goes), led by a Communist Party, which is the only ruling party. How then can it be promoting capitalism? While most formerly socialist countries have given up socialism, the Chinese are still weighing how much of traditional socialism they should retain and how much of Western-style capitalism they should adopt. This is as much a political problem as it is an economic issue.

The full new name for China's changing economy is a bit long, as you might expect, but when analyzed, is instructive: China enjoys a "Socialist Market Economy with Chinese Characteristics." Let's dwell on this pivotal, well-crafted phrase, which starts out sounding like doublespeak to our Western-tuned ears. There is actually more resonance with reality than one realizes.

The common assumption is that this mouthful is nothing but linguistic legerdemain to conceal China's embarrassingly overt embrace of capitalism and thus to confer some remaining economic legitimacy to the continued primacy of the Communist Party. The phrase "Socialist Market Economy" preserves Mao and Marxism and thus sustains the Party's continuing claim to leadership. Keep in mind why Chinese leaders believe that they need to maintain Communist one-party rule. This is the best way—perhaps the only way, in their opinion—to guarantee stability to their country and pride to their people. But how to justify communism when its foundational economic theory obviously never worked in China historically, is being repudiated in China currently, and has proved bankrupt everywhere it has been tried?[8]

The second adjectival idea is "Chinese Characteristics"; it actually modifies not only "Market Economy" but also the first modifier, "Socialist," and this is what gives policymakers the literary license to effectively bring the meaning back to a form of capitalism. (The common joke asks: What are these "Chinese Characteristics"? Answer: Capitalism.)

But all is not simply semantics. The "Socialist" appellation does in fact give a somewhat accurate description of China's current economic policy, if only to differentiate it from Western-style capitalism. The Chinese want to preserve a high degree of central control for reasons of stability and to temper the increasing disparity between rich and poor, which is an inevitable by-product of capitalism. So the government seeks to retain the primary elements of industrial production in its own hands, while the vast majority of state-owned enterprises are being privatized in one way or another. A recent strategic plan has decreed that about five hundred of the largest, most important state-owned enterprises will remain wholly government-owned, while the vast majority of the three hundred thousand state-owned enterprises in China are to be sold off or merged. Through the control of these five hundred or so giant enterprises, the government hopes to be able to direct the economy, thus giving some continued credence to the "socialist" label.

---

[8] It has proved bankrupt everywhere with the possible exception of the *kibbutzim* movement in Israel—the collective farms and villages that were created by socialist idealism and helped found Israel. Israeli *kibbutzim*, some say, are the only places that true communism was ever really practiced. However, though they worked for a while, these Israeli communes are now floundering in Israel's increasingly high-tech, entrepreneurial society.

The "Chinese characteristics" phrase adds both flexibility and mystery, enabling China to differentiate its form of self-defined communism from classic nineteenth century Marxist theory and from the twentieth century Bolshevik/Soviet catastrophe. China, it is said, has substantive differences between it and other countries, including its huge population, diverse (fifty-six) ethnic groups and geography, strong cultural and historical traditions, and entrepreneurial instincts of its people. These "Chinese characteristics" are what give the Chinese socialist economy a distinctive market flavor.

Li Yining: "All Three Criticisms Were Proved Wrong"

Li Yining, a professor of economics and dean of the Guanghua School of Business and Management at Beijing University, is one of China's most famous and influential proponents of the market economy. Dr. Li is vice director of the Financial Committee and a standing committee member of the PRC National People's Congress. I interviewed Professor Li in his spacious office at Beijing University, just before he was to teach an evening class. He apologized for not having a great deal of time for our discussion, but, he explained, he needed to have a small dinner prior to class so that he could be at his best. I was quite moved by the interview, experiencing through Professor Li the protracted intellectual conflicts and political tensions hidden within China's historic transformation to a market economy.

ROBERT KUHN: As an economist noted for liberal thinking, you've observed that China is going through a "dual transition." What does that mean?

LI YINING: China is transitioning, at the same time, both from a planned economy to a market economy and from a traditional agricultural society to a modern industrial society. Few countries had to undergo these two transitions at the same time, but China is doing so now.

KUHN: Give us some sense of the history of the market economy in China.

LI: If you want to know the market economy in China, you have to start with the planned economy. Why did the planned economy last so long in China? Because people had two wrong concepts about it: first, they thought a planned economy facilitates productive forces; second, they thought that only in a planned economy could the government guarantee that Chinese citizens would get equal salaries and equal rights—in other words, fairness. But they were proved wrong on both counts.

KUHN: What are the underlying reasons that the planned economy was proved wrong?

LI: After several decades under the planned economy, the facts tell us that enterprises and people are not motivated. Since they are not motivated, productive forces cannot be developed. Under the planned economy, there is no competition, there are no equal opportunities, and people are not allowed to relocate. Fairness cannot be realized under those conditions. After the Cultural Revolution, China's economy was on the brink of destruction. At that point, the Chinese people had no choice: they had to choose a new system. And they chose the market economy.

KUHN: The transition was neither fast nor simple.

LI: Right, the planned economy was too stubborn to retreat from the stage. So China's economic reform started in rural areas. Then some "special economic zones" were permitted and built. All the reform started on the periphery in China, away from the major centers. The initial success of the market economy was completed between 1979 and 1984, but the planned economy was still too stubborn to withdraw. Starting in 1984, the reform took aim at the core of the Chinese economy—that is, the state-owned enterprises. These enterprises were inefficient and unproductive and had to be reformed. It was decided that each should be in charge of its own production, not continue to be dependent on abstract planners in some far-off ministries.

KUHN: What was your role at this point?

LI: Some economists, including me, proposed that state-owned enterprises should take the form of the stock system, where tradable shares would be issued to their owners. We had discussed the stock system at length and had concluded that it was the best system for China.

KUHN: When did you first have the intellectual realization that the market economy was the best system for China?

LI: If you ask me when I first felt this internally, it started in the 1960s. I had many opportunities to see how labor operated in the countryside, and I saw that the peasants were very poor. I thought that in order to structure and motivate them to abolish poverty, the planned economy should be abandoned and the market economy should replace it. But I didn't dare to speak of it. It was only in the late 1970s that we dared to speak out.

KUHN: So for about fifteen years, you knew that the market economy was best for China, but you didn't publish any of your ideas?

LI: I could talk only to my friends; I couldn't publish or lecture about it at all. Otherwise I would have been labeled an antirevolutionary.

KUHN: Did your friends agree with you?

LI: Yes, they agreed. If not, they would have turned me over to the authorities. There were two Beijing Universities then. One was in our minds, and in our candid, confidential exchanges between friends. That was the real Beijing University. The other was the Beijing University where the Cultural Revolution was going on and all ideas were stifled. Only by appreciating these two universities—the real one and the superficial one—can you really understand modern China's scholars and scholarship.

KUHN: It's fascinating to witness through your eyes this protracted forty-year sweep and struggle through recent Chinese intellectual history.

LI: I think the young generation is very lucky. They haven't gone through what we have had to go through. So they are quick at accepting whatever is new, whatever makes scholarly or practical sense. But we are different. We had to endure terrible hardships, physical and mental. We were also heavily influenced by Russian scholars who promoted the planned economy. All the scholarly papers I wrote in college were on the planned economy. My intellectual conversion occurred, as I mentioned, during the 1960s, especially during the Cultural Revolution. I began wondering why we Chinese were so poor while other countries were so developed. I figured that our problems could only be blamed on our system. That was when I surreptitiously started to desert the planned economy and get on to the market economy.

KUHN: What was your status in the Cultural Revolution?

LI: Although I was only thirty-five then, I suffered a great deal, experiencing and enduring everything, like doing forced labor, my house being searched, and my head being shaved. I was compelled to work at menial labor on the farms for ten years. But you can't imagine how good a manual laborer I was! I am proud to tell you that when I was working in the countryside, I was very good at planting seedlings—one of the best.

KUHN: After you returned to Beijing University, how did you start promulgating your then-radical theories on the market economy?

LI: At that time, the general atmosphere here was to propose the market economy and a stock system for enterprises. Many economists shared this view; it wasn't any individual's special contribution. The only difference was that some economists wanted to move to a market economy faster and some wanted to move slower. I wanted to move faster.

KUHN: There must have been controversy in those early years, politically if not intellectually.

LI: Sure, there was controversy. We say that the stock system experienced three ups and three downs in China. Sometimes our ideas were not so much appreciated. But if you feel that your opinion is right, you should insist on your opinion. In the Chinese economic reform, there was a trap of putting more emphasis on theory and less on practice. But actually, in the real world, the leaders of various enterprises did a great deal of the work—proving in practice that the market economy was the best system. They had begun to issue shares, and they accomplished a great deal.

KUHN: How were your early theories promoting the market economy criticized?

LI: There were three criticisms of our ideas. The first was that if we developed a market economy and implemented a stock system, it would mean that China was going over to the capitalist side. The second criticism was that the Chinese economy needed to be well regulated, and that if we developed a market economy, the Chinese economy would devolve into a mess. And the third criticism was that since at that time the prices for various commodities were stable, if we allowed prices to fluctuate according to market conditions, prices would become chaotic. But all three criticisms were proved wrong.

KUHN: At that time, in the heat of intellectual and political battle, how did you answer each criticism?

LI: I answered the first criticism in this way: the market economy and stock system could be used both in a capitalist society and a socialist one. If it is helpful for the development of the economy, then it could be used.

And since all those countries that have a planned economy are poor, maintaining the old system would push the Chinese people to a dead end. Just because ideas are used in capitalist society doesn't mean we can't incorporate them into our socialist society. I answered the second criticism by explaining that the market economy is quite helpful in keeping society stable and also for increasing people's standard of living. I turned the second criticism around and argued that if a market economy isn't used and some crisis arises, then society will really be in a mess. To the third criticism I responded that although on the face of it you could say that in a planned economy prices are stable, in fact people can't buy the commodities they want, because those commodities aren't available! Furthermore, when the government artificially controls prices, it is actually a kind of inflation. If those price controls are released, the prices immediately go up. It's like pushing a ball into water: if you release your hand the ball will immediately pop back up. It's not good to keep prices stable by controlling them; this practice, too, has been proved wrong.

KUHN: You stated that a market economy with a share system can be socialist as well as capitalist. What is a socialist market economy, and how does it differ from capitalism?

LI: In my personal opinion, there is no real difference. The only apparent difference is that the environments are different. One is capitalist and the other socialist. In the market economy, all the problems that can be solved by the market should be solved by the market. If there are some kinds of problems that can't be solved by the market, they should be solved by the government. So the market is the first way to regulate, and government policies are the second way to regulate. It is important to remember that there are significant historical modifications in how the market economy has operated in the United States over time. In the nineteenth century, the market economy was completely free—not controlled by the government at all. But problems and crises arose [such as rapacious monopolies, robber barons, and the Great Depression], so that in the twentieth century the government had to step in and regulate some aspects of the market. The real differences are between the traditional market economy and the modern market economy.

KUHN: So, in essence, the American market economy started with no regulation by government, but when problems arose the government had to intervene and introduce some regulations. In comparison, the Chinese market economy started with total regulation by government—the planned economy—but when that proved to be flawed, many freedoms were introduced. Are you saying that both American and Chinese economic systems are merging into a middle ground—into some optimal mix of free markets and government intervention working together?

LI: The market economy and the planned economy cannot coexist and cannot be merged. There can be only one major factor [governing an economy]. In the market economy, the market is the major factor; and in the planned economy, government control is the major factor. But regulatory methods can coexist. The two systems cannot coexist, but the two methods can. But I should be clear here: China is not merging the two systems. China is deleting the planned economy and enabling the market economy to develop itself.

KUHN: Does regulation of the market in China differ from regulation of the market in the United States?

LI: There is no major difference in the matters regulated by the government. The only difference is the political system. The United States is a capitalist society, which uses the capitalist system, and China is a socialist society, which uses the socialist system. But the government regulates the economy by playing the same kind of role in each, using financial policies, tax policies, monetary policies, and the like.

KUHN: How does the market system currently developing in China differ from the market system practiced in the United States?

LI: There are some differences. In China, there are many state-owned enterprises, and the shares of the most important enterprises in the most important industries are controlled mainly by the government. But I have my own feeling about this: I agree that the government should control the major industries and enterprises, but I think the ratio of their ownership should be decreased a little. Let me tell you a story; it comes from Japan. Once there were some fishermen, and all the fish they caught were dead. But there was one fisherman whose fish were all alive, and no one could figure out why. Before this fisherman died, he told his son his secret: "You should always fish in places where there are two kinds of fish, because they will fight each other and thus develop the ability to survive." This is similar to conditions in China. If there is only one system, such as only state-owned enterprises, the economy will die, but if there are many kinds of enterprises—private, foreign, and community enterprises—then the system will thrive.

KUHN: I still don't understand why it is better long-term for the government to own shares of any industrial companies. If all companies were owned by private shareholders, there would still be strong competition.

LI: In the initial period of a socialist market economy, the state-owned enterprises should continue to be a major factor, but the system should also include the other kinds of enterprises.

KUHN: Let's project forward twenty years. How will the Chinese economy differ from today?

LI: Economists cannot predict the future, but we can analyze the present conditions to make some predictions. I think that in twenty years state-owned enterprises will account for one third of the Chinese economy, cooperative enterprises will account for another third, and private enterprises will account for the final third.

KUHN: Almost every senior executive of every state-owned enterprise with whom I've spoken has said that he or she hopes that more of the company's shares can be owned by private citizens—managers, employees, or members of the public. Almost everyone has told me this.

LI: My idea about the division of the system into thirds applies to all aspects [of industrial structure and enterprise organization]. But maybe in the future the state-owned enterprises will be multifaceted—not purely state-owned but also invested in and owned by managers, employees, and outside investors.

KUHN: As you sit here today in Beijing University, the intellectual heart of China, do you have any concerns about the future—about a potential reversal of reform?

LI: I'm not concerned about reversals, because it has been thoroughly demonstrated that the market economy is the best way to develop China. It's common knowledge, so I'm quite optimistic about the future.

KUHN: If you felt that the state should not own any part of China's industrial companies—which is contrary to government policy—would you feel free today to publish and speak about your dissenting opinion?

LI: As you know, I don't feel that the state shouldn't own any of the industrial companies, but if I did, I would speak it publicly and publish it frequently, so that scholars and officials could comment on my opinion. Actually, any kind of opinion has to be put into practice; the only accurate proving ground is the real world. But to reiterate my opinion, I firmly believe that—at least for now—my idea of a three-way split in ownership is an optimum one for China. As for the far future, my research shouldn't be used. That research has to be done by the younger generation.

Reform and Restructure

China is still a portrait of contrasts: the recently rich and the permanently poor, prosperous provinces on the coast and backward provinces inland, high technology start-ups and hopelessly outmoded factories, modern dress and ancient traditions. The standard of living of millions of Chinese has risen dramatically. But so has the disparity in wealth, a catalyst for social combustion. Migrant workers flood the cities in search of jobs, and the government creates huge construction projects to employ them. China is restructuring its inefficient, state-owned enterprises, laying off tens of millions of workers. It is estimated, unreliably, that 12 to 20 million urban workers are unemployed (including those laid off) out of a total workforce of about 140 million, in addition to about 130 million unemployed rural residents (who have never been employed by the state).

The need for reform is unquestioned; how to reform is the tricky question. Under Mao Zedong, China followed the Soviet model of the 1950s, developing huge enterprises in heavy industries—steel, petrochemicals, machinery. These giant factory complexes do not make consumer goods, and most are ill suited to the new market economy. China has no model to guide it out of this vexing quandary. No other country can offer its experience; only China is exploring such a massive transition. Chinese leaders must make decisions of enormous consequence with no guidelines and no precedents. They have thrown away Mao's extravagant use of ideological theory and are crossing the river, in Deng's aphorism, stone by stone. In China today, everything, it seems, is being "restructured"—another buzzword of economic reform. Enterprises are being cut loose from their government bosses and can now make what their customers want, not what out-of-touch bureaucrats decide.

The impact of the Tiananmen movement on reform can be viewed both politically and economically. Political reform was set back, because the government became more cautious and tightened its controls. But economic reform was accelerated, a historical fact not appreciated by westerners. The protests and crackdown in Tiananmen Square influenced China's economy in two ways. First, directly: from 1989 to 1991, China's economic development lost ground. The hardline conservatives in the Party used the student movement, which they called counterrevolutionary, as an excuse to assert that economic reform in the direction of capitalism was not in the best interests of China. But then, in 1992, Deng called for continuing—indeed, for reinvigorating—economic reforms. Since Deng's clarion call, such reforms have deepened and accelerated; in fact, reform has been more successful in the past decade than it was in its first decade.

Second, and equally important, was the indirect impact of Tiananmen on reform. The tragedy made many Chinese realize that political reform cannot happen with revolution; it must happen gradually, with evolution. Economic reform must come first; stability must be maintained and assured, before moving on to political reform. Paradoxically, the June 4 event seemed to teach Deng the lesson that Tiananmen-style solutions to problems were archaic and counterproductive, that further reform in China could not be conducted in an authoritarian way, that a hardline approach could only be temporary, and that reactionary policies were not in the interest of the Communist Party. In the long term, the stability of China and the survival of the Communist Party would depend on developing the Chinese economy, which in turn would depend on reform. This real world, empirically-based process exemplifies Deng's application of his own cross-the-river-stone-by-stone theory. If one way doesn't work, recognize the mistake and try another.

The student movement had made it plain to the government that the government's existence was relatively fragile. If the leadership didn't do well for the people, it could be toppled by the people. Such a realization was something new to modern Chinese leaders, especially in the wake of the almost sudden collapse of the communist regimes in Eastern Europe and the Soviet Union, and so the government decided—for reasons of self-preservation if not ideological conviction—that the best way to consolidate its position was to continue reform and develop the economy so that people could live better lives and protests would never arise. My own opinion is that a surprisingly large number of China's senior leaders genuinely desire real reform, and I suspect that the self-preservation argument may have been the pragmatic way to influence their more conservative colleagues.

Along the crowded shopping streets of Beijing, the market economy is in full swing. There is action and availability, expressed in the brisk pedestrian pace, the current fashions, the cellular phones ringing everywhere. Eleven years ago, when I first started coming to China, nearly all businesses were owned by the state. Today private enterprise is the engine of growth, from the corner shop owner to the Internet entrepreneur, signaling a sea change from the China that existed under Mao.

But the price of economic restructuring is clear—millions of angry, unemployed workers and the resentment of power-deprived bureaucrats. But the biggest change that economic reform has brought to the private lives of the Chinese is the shift to individualism. People are learning how to pursue their personal goals and satisfy their personal values. This was impossible before reform; in fact, it was an attitude criticized as capitalistic—sometimes it was even criminal. The entrepreneurial spirit—long a characteristic of Chinese culture—was eradicated, almost by design, in the planned economy. With the advent of a market economy, that spirit has emerged again, as if from a long sleep.

For three decades, China's economy was classic communism: the state owned all the means of production and dictated production quotas for each farm and factory. People had to live and work where they were assigned. They had no civil rights and even the expression of personal beliefs was controlled. Today, in a market economy regulated by supply and demand, many people can live where they want and work where they want. They can own private property and they can start private businesses. People can think what they want, too—even criticize the government if they like, provided that they do not threaten the singular leadership of the Communist Party. That's the deal.

The Reform of State-Owned Enterprises

In 1998, at the Ninth National People's Congress, Zhu Rongji was elected the premier of the State Council, and he pledged to turn the state-owned enterprises around in three years. It was a startling goal, and although unattainable in fact, Zhu's vision set a new economic agenda. Realistic and rough, Zhu is apparently unconcerned with personal tenure and permanent power (see page 252). He really thinks he knows what to do and he is prepared to sacrifice anything, including himself, in order to get it done. Zhu, who had been dean of the business school at Qinghua University, enumerated a number of bold initiatives for his new administration: "Guarantees" (growth, inflation, devaluation), "Repositionings" (reform of state-owned enterprises, reform of financial and banking systems, streamlining the government), and "Reforms" (food and supplies, investments, housing, medical care, and taxes). Certainly on slimming the bureaucracy, Zhu delivered, reducing the number of ministries, notwithstanding the hoots and howls of high-level, newly unemployed bureaucrats. Making state-owned enterprises profitable would be a matter more messy.

The state's share of China's industrial output had already fallen markedly—from 80 percent in 1978 to around 35 percent in 1997. Today there are approximately three hundred thousand state-owned enterprises in China, employing over 70 million people. They still dominate the urban labor markets, employing two-thirds of the workers in the cities. Non-state-owned enterprises—private businesses, rural township and village enterprises, joint ventures, and foreign-owned companies—have experienced a concomitant rapid growth.

Westerners can be confused when they hear the terms "state-owned," "public," and "private" as applied to Chinese companies. In the United States, a public company is one that has issued shares to the general public, is listed on a stock exchange, and is subjected to specific regulations, such as disclosure requirements; a private company does not issue shares to the public and is not subject to such regulations; and there are virtually no companies "owned" by the state (other than, say, the post office).

In China, these definitions are different. A "private" company is one that is not owned by the state, whereas a company that issues shares to the public and is listed on a stock exchange is usually owned or at least controlled by the state. In 1998, for the first time under the Constitution of the People's Republic of China, private enterprises received an official approval and were legalized. Although they had been allowed and indeed encouraged for years, private businesses were made legitimate by this formal legalization, and the change was significant. For example, Chinese banks are now encouraged to give loans to good private companies and joint ventures, and the stock exchanges are beginning to allow them to be listed so that they can raise public capital. All this is in recognition of the enormous importance of private businesses in furthering the country's economic reform and development.

In fact, much of the growth of China's economy comes from the burgeoning private sector, which can be divided into several classes. First, there are those private companies that are owned solely by one or more Chinese citizens and have not been financed by the government. Second are the foreign or joint ventures. Third, and most pervasive, are the collectively owned enterprises. If we add up the outputs from all these non-state-owned enterprises, the total comes to between 55 and 60 percent of China's gross domestic product.

Chief executives and managers of state-owned enterprises are not allowed to own stock in their own companies. They are also prohibited from taking advantage of their position to boost their salaries or gain other monetary rewards. The idea is that such stringent limitations on executive compensation prevent corruption (when in fact the reverse may be more true). These restrictions also preclude any large salary disparity between executives at state-owned companies and their putative bosses in the government. State-owned enterprises are restricted in other ways. They are not completely free to run their operations: to get bank loans, for example, approval is needed from the Chinese government, the Bank of China, or other government-owned banks. And managers cannot freely fire people, because this will worsen unemployment.

When an enterprise is said to be owned by the state, what does this really mean? Which part of the state is the owner? And how does the state exercise its ownership? Classically, the massive ministries in Beijing were the owners of the large, national enterprises, while medium-sized and small enterprises were under the control of provincial or municipal governments. Each government owner would work under a centrally administered plan that determined in advance what each of its factories was to produce.

You can imagine the "fun" when, under a new policy instituted in 1997 encouraging mergers and acquisitions, an enterprise owned by one province purchases and downsizes an enterprise owned by another province. By "fun," I mean lawsuits—brought against one province by another—quite a novel experience in China. And what happens when multiple agencies of government share ownership in a single enterprise? Then add the compounding complexity of privatization—such as stock ownership by the public, and various management and employee options—and one can begin to appreciate the confusion of ownership in China today.

Sometimes such confusion works for the benefit of the company and its management. One successful young Chinese manager who is chief executive of a growing state-owned company with business interests in trading and technology put it this way: "Who is the owner of my company?" he asked rhetorically. "Who is 'the state'?" In his case, "the state" happened to be a number of entities, including a subsidiary of a company owned by a municipality, an offshoot of a central ministry, and a quasi-independent scientific association. So who really owned his company? There was a board of directors made up of representatives of these entities, but this young executive, in effect, was the unconstrained boss, reporting effectively to no one. And the results have been outstanding; his company has grown rapidly and profitably, opportunistically going into diverse businesses unencumbered by bureaucratic decision-making and thus offering increased employment and technological advancement to the country.

The central state-owned enterprises, as noted, were originally established and owned by the central government in Beijing, and thus their ownership has been well defined. But the situation with regard to ownership of the local state-owned enterprises is fuzzy, and the reasons are historical. In the late 1950s, local governments implemented the so-called "Walk with Two Legs" policy established by Mao: one leg represented the central government and the other the local governments. Both were to be actively involved in owning enterprises, and as a result local governments made investments in developing their local economies. But these investments were generally small, so that local enterprises operated on small scales, usually with poor financial results.

Later there emerged collectively owned, neighborhood enterprises, which are even more confusing. The assets of collectively owned enterprises—the public assets of communities or neighborhoods—belong to individuals; nevertheless, the local government also "owns" them, sort of, by dint of heavy presence and influence. So collectively owned enterprises are difficult to categorize—even more so today, since some entrepreneurs have borrowed the name of collectively owned enterprises and then run them as private enterprises. So should collectively owned or neighborhood enterprises, along with centrally and locally state-owned enterprises, be classified as part of the system of state-owned enterprises in China? Most analysts say no. Who really owns the assets of the collectively owned enterprises? The private individuals who may have built them? Or the neighborhoods in whose name they have operated? More clarity is needed here, since vague ownership of enterprises creates confused lines of authority and conflicting interests, thus retarding efficiency of operations.

There are several models for reforming state-owned enterprises. One is the corporation, in which shares of ownership are held by the employees, the company managers, often some other companies, and one or another government bureau or quasi-governmental association such as the Chinese Academy of Science's ownership in Legend Holdings, China's largest computer company. (State-affiliated organizations usually own the majority of shares, though this rule is being broken with increasing frequency.) As shareholders, the workers are now newly motivated to improve the company and increase its productivity, and although individuals own a minority of these shares, they usually have a say in company management and operations. Moreover, when new companies or enterprises are founded, the initial funds often come from the government or quasi-governmental organizations. As such, high salaries are not possible, but substantial benefits and other compensation can be given. The company can assign cars to its executives (and they can be the best models) along with other conveniences, like drivers and expense accounts.

An early goal of economic reform was to create a new management class; managers were to be free to run their businesses with optimum efficiency. In most management-related matters, this is being accomplished, but in matters of personnel it often is not. The Communist Party is still a player in state-owned companies, where it runs, in essence, a parallel organization; frequently the local Party secretary is more powerful than the president of the company, and sometimes the secretary *is* the president. In appointments and promotions, especially at high levels, the Party has more say than anyone else, and company managers are still not authorized to make personnel decisions freely.

The deregulation of medium-sized and small state-owned enterprises means that these local businesses must sink or swim on their own (many collectively owned enterprises are included in this category). These enterprises are now allowed to go bankrupt, merge, or be acquired by private investors. Many economists believe that a key to reform is lowering the state ownership of virtually all state-owned enterprises to less than 51 percent of the company; several senior advisors propose one-third as the proper level of state ownership (see my interview with Li Yining, page 50).

Critically important is enabling state-owned enterprises to streamline operations by eliminating unnecessary personnel; this will be possible only if the government sets up a social security system to protect laid-off workers. A legacy of the planned economy, state-owned enterprises have traditionally provided for all the needs of employees and their families: housing, food, education, and even cemetery plots, as well as pensions and health care. How to provide these services when state-owned enterprises are downsized or closed is a central problem of China's transition to a market economy.

Yi Li Ice Cream Company: "Army Of The New Economy"

China's largest ice cream factory is located in Inner Mongolia, an underdeveloped province stretching out across north central China. The Mongolian people are one of China's fifty-five minorities, and the Mongolian language, with its distinctive letters, is often displayed bilingually underneath Chinese characters. The majority of the people are farmers and herdsmen, but Huhehaote, the capital, is a polluted industrial city. Even in this out-of-the-way province, however, the "socialist market economy" mantra of reform, efficiency, and profit has been heard loud and clear. Yi Li was once one of those communist-style state-owned companies, unburdened by the need to compete. With the move to the market, the government found it could no longer afford to prop up nonessential industries like ice cream manufacturing. Yi Li's management led a complete restructuring and reform of the company's operations and business practices—and transformed a lagging, bankruptcy-bound business into a market leader. We examined the Yi Li story for our PBS documentary. Our CCTV camera crews spent a great deal of time in Inner Mongolia, including a frightening trek during winter when a stalled vehicle would have meant a frozen death. A transcript of the Yi Li segment of our documentary follows.

DR. ZHENG SHIPING (POLITICAL SCIENTIST AT THE UNIVERSITY OF VERMONT): It was no big deal if there was one less ice cream factory in China. The government wouldn't interfere if Yi Li went bankrupt. This said to Yi Li that they had to survive by their own means, they had to succeed in the market.

NARRATOR: Yi Li churned out its allotted quota of ice cream, irrespective of demand. Its ice cream didn't taste very good either. But Yi Li has since restructured, selling some of its government shares to the public. Its leaders have modernized the company and turned it into China's most popular brand. [Note: Today, Yi Li's ice cream tastes very good, less sweet than Americans are used to; speaking personally, I had three popsicles when touring the factory, more than I've had in years.]

MR. ZHENG (PRESIDENT OF YI LI): We made the decision to model Yi Li ice cream after the Chinese military.

MR. NIU GENSHENG (VICE PRESIDENT OF YI LI): I've seen the movie *Patton* many times, and I've studied the ancient Chinese generals, because a disciplined army is the most powerful force.

YI LI SQUAD LEADER: There's no laughing in the military.

NARRATOR: Employees at Yi Li take two weeks of compulsory basic training, as if they were army inductees before starting their jobs. It's enough to make American workers go screaming to their unions. But there is a reason for Yi Li's practices: they are remedial, not punitive. In a planned economy, Chinese workers never had to worry about efficiency. In a market economy, only the efficient survive. So the penalties at Yi Li teach workers that resources cannot be wasted, that profits are important.

PRESIDENT ZHENG: In the beginning, the workers said, "We want to work, not join the army."

MALE WORKER #1: At first I wasn't used to it; all of this seemed meaningless.

FEMALE WORKER #2: I thought the bosses wanted to punish us.

FEMALE WORKER #3: I'm ashamed to go out into the street. The girls in city are so much prettier, and since the training I'm so tan.

MALE WORKER #4: Before the training, I was very undisciplined. But now I've come to think of myself as a soldier.

VICE PRESIDENT NIU: The only thing in our hearts is the field of battle and the marketplace. Our minds are consumed by the fire of competition and the smell of the battle is very strong.

DR. LU XIAOBO (POLITICAL SCIENTIST AT COLUMBIA UNIVERSITY): In China it was easier for economic development to occur along the southeast coast. In the remote regions like Inner Mongolia it was much harder to develop the market economy, because historically, westernized companies never existed there. So there was very little understanding of the market, and there were no MBAs. So what do they do? Some look to their own personal experiences and local culture, then mix them together and apply it to management.

Dr. Zheng: Why does Yi Li's management wear military uniforms at meetings? It seems funny, but reflects the fact that companies like Yi Li need to utilize all kinds of strategies in order to survive. The CEO is using the military model to develop their business and strengthen the employees' discipline and sense of responsibility. During the Cultural Revolution, every factory and school in China was managed by the military. Chinese are familiar with the military model because China used to be like one huge military camp. Everyone was learning from the People's Liberation Army (PLA), which used to be the model for everything.

Huge Chinese Slogan At Yi Li: The Chinese are not inferior to the West. We can do it ourselves.

Vice President Niu: All these workers were farmers, so our greatest task was to make them feel the pressure and anxiety of being replaced.

Narrator: Many companies in the province are laying off workers. Yi Li is paying $75 a month, the highest in the area. There's no shortage of applicants.

Vice President Niu: The workers are constantly reminded of the crowd waiting outside ready to take over their spots. And the managers are constantly aware of those who have more knowledge and better skill and who are lusting for their positions.

Yi Li Leader A: How many times do I have to tell you? You've broken company rules several times. This one is Sheng Hongxia.

Female Worker #5: But I didn't know.

Leader A: Who is Zheng Weihui?

Man: Me. Don't write me down.

Leader A: Be careful next time.

Interviewer: Why did they take your ID card?

Female Worker #6: Because I didn't walk in line.

Interviewer: What's going to be your punishment?

Female Worker #6: Well, I'll definitely be fined.

WOMAN IN FATIGUES: One time, I forgot to push my chair in at the end of the day. If you break this rule, you get fined ten *yuan.*

MAN IN YI LI CAFETERIA: If you don't finish all your food, you get fined five *yuan.*

INTERVIEWER: What happens if the child can't finish?

WOMAN WITH SON: Then the adult must finish it for him.

HUGE CHINESE SLOGAN AT YI LI: If you don't work hard at your job today, you'll have to look hard for a job tomorrow.

PRESIDENT ZHENG: *(in Yi Li War Room, with all executives clad in battle fatigues)* Currently, Yi Li has a market share of less than three percent. This expansion project is very important as Yi Li pursues the goal of being the global "King of Ice Cream." This is a life and death struggle for Yi Li. And we must connect our hearts to accomplish our goal. Are we confident?

WHOLE STAFF: Yes!

PRESIDENT ZHENG: Dismissed.

PRESIDENT ZHENG: *(distorting himself in front of a mirror)* Every factory entrance in Yi Li has a fun house mirror. It's there to remind us that we're all very small. We're constantly motivating employees to grow. You see me directing and managing so many workers, but I still feel very small.

PRESIDENT ZHENG: *(in executive meeting)* The head of our manufacturing department officially sent in his resignation two days ago. This seems to be a trend nowadays. Two days ago, Li Luo's vice president came by, supposedly to check out a possible purchase of our product. But the truth is that he was here to hire away our workers.

YI LI MANAGER: After a half year, Li Luo will come out with similar milk products to compete with us and there will be a mess in the market.

PRESIDENT ZHENG: We need to fix our policies so that the employees think that tomorrow they could be vice manager, then maybe the managing director the next day, and maybe even the CEO after that. Whether it's for honor or whether it's for money. If we don't have this ambitious culture, the problems will continue to occur. Our company is going to change from labor intensive to machine automated. When that happens, we can use other methods to replace this militarized management method. We won't need all these thousands of workers. Maybe we'll just pick the top ones and we'll have to come up with a new management method to replace the old one.

Mergers and Acquisitions (M&A)

In 1997, at the Fifteenth Congress of the Communist Party of China, President Jiang Zemin put forward further initiatives, including mergers and acquisitions, to reform the state-owned enterprises—its guiding motto was "Control the large ones, and free the small ones," and let the market decide their fates. It was a historic pronouncement and it would change dramatically how business and industry would henceforth be structured in China.

Although mergers and acquisitions in the United States have been maligned as examples of unbridled capitalism—and the excess financial leverage (i.e., debt) and financial frenzy of the 1980s gives some justification to the charge—the primary economic driver of such takeovers is often an underlying inefficient structure and complacent management. Whenever the value of the parts, or divisions, of an enterprise is greater than the value of the entire enterprise itself, that enterprise is probably not optimally structured, and its management is either not acting in the best interests of the shareholders or is just incompetent. In the U.S., the bloated, overgrown conglomerates fashioned in the 1960s and taken over in the 1980s are prime examples. The existence of a free and fluid M&A market enabled those inefficient enterprises to be acquired and divided into optimal parts, with financial profit for the acquirers and ultimate economic health for the resulting new and smaller companies. Though workers are often laid off and dislocated in the painful downsizing, the ultimate result is that the companies are better able to function in an increasingly competitive global economy. In developed market economies, the private M&A market has emerged as the mechanism to restructure and refinance those companies that cannot or should not go public, that seek to grow faster than internal growth can permit, that are structured inefficiently to compete in the market, and/or are troubled and need to be restructured.

Everyone in China knows that the profitability of state-owned enterprises is generally low or negative, and only a few of these companies are competitive in the market economy. In the old planned economy, the government decided the input and output of factories and continually revised their management policies—a system that resulted in overstaffing and other inefficient use of assets, little concern for customers, and low productivity. In 1998 about a third of the state-owned enterprises were losing money—some estimates give a less generous one-half.

Since 1997, the major goal of economic reform has been to focus on the large state-owned enterprises—those that play a strategic role in the national economy or defense—and deregulate the mid-sized and smaller ones, allowing them to seek alternative ownership structures. Every effort is being made to prevent the large state-owned enterprises from going bankrupt, including attempts to improve their efficiency and competitiveness by merging and restructuring them.

I have been speaking and writing about instituting a mergers-and-acquisitions market in China for over a decade,[9] including guest lectures at Beijing and Qinghua universities. Initially I was told that although my ideas were interesting, they did not apply to China, but I felt that although the Chinese economy had substantial structural, historical, and cultural differences from the American economy, there were still fundamental market principles that require an effective M&A market as an integral part of any efficient economy. I was given much support by friends and associates in China who saw the benefits of M&A for China and who educated me in the differences and special nature of the Chinese economy.

I also argued that a deep and free M&A market would protect the value of state-owned assets by preventing a few well-connected people from taking advantage of special relationships. The protection and proper valuation of state-owned assets is an important consideration in China's economic reform. Why is valuation such an issue? In the early stages of reform, when privatization was beginning, many of the initial divestitures of government property were sold at fire sale (or sweetheart—pick your

---

[9] My thesis was that M&A would bring numerous critical benefits to China's emerging market economy: (1) M&A aligns owners and managers for optimum productivity (i.e., the right shareholders can make a huge difference in economic performance); (2) M&A replaces inefficient management by economic forces; (3) M&A resizes enterprises for optimum effectiveness (there are natural economic laws that determine best sizes for enterprises and these ideal sizes differ by industry — e.g., certain consumer goods should be produced by smaller enterprises that can react more quickly to market changes, whereas certain telecommunications equipment needs sufficient corporate mass to handle complex projects); (4) M&A provides a source of liquidity for investors (i.e., converting stock ownership into cash), which is critically important for companies that cannot go public, thus encouraging the initial investment.

metaphor) prices, far below what they were really worth. Often the buyers were overseas Chinese—usually from Hong Kong or Taiwan—who were generally in some underhanded partnership with local officials on the take. The Chinese people, who had built those assets by working for the state, have every right to be concerned at this kind of corruption.

What I said during those early years of cautious privatization, in lectures and in the press, was that the underlying cause of this looting of state-owned property was not too much M&A, but too little. My prescription ran counter to the prevailing opinion at the time. Most felt that since state-owned property was being given away by what appeared to be an M&A mechanism, then M&A itself, that pinnacle of rapacious capitalism, must be the problem. I said the reverse. Hole-and-corner deals are where corruption flourishes, while the creation of a broad and open M&A market in China would establish a climate for the competent and standardized valuation of state-owned assets, by establishing a market basis for sales and transfers. The greater the number of M&A transactions, the more buyers and sellers in the market, and the more efficient the M&A market becomes for all participants.

In fact, there is no better, more efficient way to assure the proper valuation and transaction value of state-owned assets than by establishing a vibrant M&A market. Moreover, by enabling the best Chinese enterprises to utilize a domestic M&A market, more Chinese businesses would be bought by other Chinese companies rather than by foreign investors, thus strengthening the best Chinese companies and diminishing the advantages of foreign acquirers.

The now rapid development of the M&A market in China appears as a fast forward recapitulation of the progressive development of the M&A market in the U.S. China is experiencing in a few years the same stages, complete with the same problems, that occurred over roughly a hundred-year period in America—and whereas in America these phases occurred sequentially, in China they are all happening at once, in parallel.[10]

---

[10] M&A in the United States is said to have passed through six phases: (1) Consolidation within similar industries (ca. 1893–1904); (2) So-called horizontal mergers (1915–1929), resulting in oligarchies—that is, a few dominant firms in each major industry; (3) The friendly M&A of small private companies (the 1940s) due to burdensome estate taxes forcing sales; (4) The conglomerate era (ca. 1955–1969), which was until recently the largest M&A wave and was based on the theory of diversification—M&A was thought to lessen risk of economic cycles and make for the efficient allocation of capital; these transactions used accounting techniques and

As economic reform deepened in China, and as soon as national policy permitted, M&A was accepted with a sudden intensity and a naïve enthusiasm. It was as if a dam had burst. Chinese entrepreneurial spirit was set free, but because the Chinese had had no M&A experience and were now exercising little restraint in its pursuit, problems surfaced quickly. Almost overnight, M&A had emerged as a panacea for all the country's economic ills, and many companies propelled themselves headlong into the M&A market.

So just as suddenly, I found myself on the opposite side of the M&A barricades, now urging great care and caution in its use. I likened M&A to a "great amplifier" or "great accelerator," so that if a company's strategic direction was poor or misguided, and if that company acquires another company, then the result would amplify or accelerate that initial poor strategy, making the combined companies much worse much faster. Only if a company's strategy was good and its management sound would its participation in the M&A market prove useful. I illustrated my fears with examples of American takeovers that had produced sub-optimal results, including numerous failures and some outright disasters. I found myself lecturing more on the problems of M&A than on its benefits, cautioning against shoddy financial analysis, overeager decision-making, over-optimistic financial forecasts, a lack of planning for post-acquisition integration of the acquired organizations, the difficulty of achieving operational synergy, the fool's gold of diversification in excess of corporate competence, the debilitating clash of different corporate cultures, the potential for conflict among senior managers, the underestimation of how much time and money it takes to make a merger or acquisition really work, and similar problems. It wasn't that I was against M&A, of course, I was just against its misuse.

Another potential misuse of M&A in China is coercing successful enterprises to absorb unsuccessful ones on the theory that a forced merger is better than bankruptcy, in that jobs are preserved and good management can oversee underutilized assets. The danger is that those jobs may be a

---

Wall Street stock accretion to generate artificial increases in value, which later led to the takeovers of the following phase; (5) The deconglomeration of large diversified corporations (mid-1970s to mid-1980s)—mostly hostile takeovers (using high debt and junk bonds) of large public companies that were inefficiently managed with respect to operations and financial return, and the divestiture of their sideline or unprofitable divisions; (6) Strategic and synergistic acquisitions across multiple industries (mid-1990s to the present), often driven by pressures of globalization and rapid technological change, engineered both by public companies and financial groups building companies and then going public with them.

burden, those assets a liability, and management focus will be diverted. Prospering in a competitive market economy now global in nature is hard enough without extraneous burden, liability, and distracted managers.

China's debt-ridden trust and investment enterprises may be one sector where mergers and acquisitions are a solution; at least, it's hard to imagine a better one for such a severe situation. These diversified holding companies, often under provincial or municipal aegis and frequently a locus of personal privilege reflect China's early efforts at adapting to a market economy. The 1998 bankruptcy of Guangdong International Trust & Investment Corporation (Gitic), once an international financial darling and then loaded with $4.7 billion in debt, shocked foreign lenders. Gitic was China's second largest trust, yet it was not bailed out, as everyone had expected, either by the prosperous southern province of Guangdong or the central government in Beijing, which was worried about triggering a crisis of confidence. It is estimated that 150 of China's 240 trust companies must be merged or closed, and that the total amount of bad debt exceeds $25 billion—a mess more dangerous than the savings and loan debacle in the United States, because in China the financial sector is more interdependent and much more fragile. China's aggressive approach to this problem by putting many of these trusts out of business suggests the kind of resoluteness and toughness that will be necessary across the economy.

Wang Hai: Double Star's "Sole Survivor"

While some managers struggle with productivity and suffer the pressure of market forces, others revel in their newfound freedom to maneuver. These are the people who are revolutionizing China, like Double Star president Wang Hai, who once fought Americans in Vietnam and now fights Chinese bureaucrats in the government. He is a born salesman who can finally use his talents. And since Wang Hai enjoys speaking his mind, irrespective of whom he might offend, you can understand why we asked our CCTV camera crews to virtually live with him in preparing this story for our PBS documentary. Our editor later remarked that Wang Hai was one of the best characters he had ever seen in any documentary.

HOST: *(at celebration)* The president of Double Star Shoes, China's most successful shoe company, Mr. Wang Hai.

WANG HAI: A reporter once asked me if I wore my own shoes. I quickly reacted and took off my shoe. I know of course that to take off your shoes in public is very impolite, but I really wanted to prove to him that the shoes I wear are always Double Star. I'm the president of the company. If I don't wear my own shoes, I'm not qualified to be a shoemaker.

NARRATOR: Double Star is a state-owned enterprise that sells more shoes in China than Nike, Reebok, and Adidas combined; it has 13 percent of the shoe market in China and exports its shoes all over the world.

WANG HAI: If you go by population and market share, I am the world's most famous brand. What's funny is that our own government is giving us trouble. They said to me, "Who approved your claim that you're the world's most famous brand?" I said to them, "That's crap. Do the world's most famous brands get approved?" I said, "Who gave the approval to Nike? Did they vote for Pierre Cardin in the United Nations?" We give respect to artists, politicians, scientists; we should also give respect to entrepreneurs. We've got to be taken seriously, and I think the government is having trouble understanding who we are.

NARRATOR: Double Star, one of the oldest footwear companies in China, was nationalized in 1952. When Wang Hai was appointed president, it was outmoded and losing money.

WANG HAI: In the early 1980s, Double Star was making shoes that nobody wanted. However, no one knew it was due to market problems. I had no idea what the market was.

NARRATOR: At that time in China, manufacturers had no say in how their products were sold. A state agency handled that.

WANG HAI: I said, "If I can make shoes, why can't I sell them?" So I decided to break new ground. I carried shoes on my back to the department stores, trying to get sales. I was probably the first factory director in the country to sell shoes to the stores. Nobody could believe it. I was treated with contempt. Even my employees said I was not doing the job I was supposed to do. They said, "Why is a factory chief peddling shoes?!" What they didn't know is that I was trying to understand how the market works.

NARRATOR: Wang Hai had to reinvent the wheel, and then learn to sell it, rediscovering techniques that socialism had discarded.

WANG HAI: *(in shoe store)* You don't have many shoes here.

SALESGIRL: Basically, I have every style displayed.

WANG HAI: *(picking up a shoe)* This style is pretty good.

SALESGIRL: Actually those aren't selling well now.

WANG HAI: You can't just leave it here. You have to claim it's some type of warm shoe. Just name them yourself. Something like "The Newly Arrived Warm Boots." "A One-Week Only Special." In fact, it's still the same price, right? But when people see that, they'll come running for it.

WANG HAI: What kinds of methods can we use to educate the employees? The old method of saying "We all own the country" just doesn't work.

WANG HAI: *(to salesgirl)* You are going to make a fortune. How old are you?

SALESGIRL: I'm twenty-two.

WANG HAI: Twenty-two. At thirty-two you'll be a capitalist.

DR. ZHENG SHIPING (UNIVERSITY OF VERMONT): Why were Wang Hai's employees ashamed of his salesmanship? After the market economy was introduced, many companies had to struggle to survive. The success of Wang Hai's company had to do with the managerial strategies he implemented. Wang Hai viewed a CEO's job as selling shoes just like a salesperson. This was very novel to Chinese people. They had the impression that senior management was always high above, commanding the lower-level employees. Wang Hai is a very unusual CEO.

NARRATOR: For Wang Hai, being a good salesman and being Chinese go together. He's built his own Chinese shoe city, in the shadow of the Double Star towers in downtown Qingdao, a beautiful city on the sea in northern China, better known for its beer than its shoes.

HUGE TALKING BUDDHA STATUE: Good wishes to you.

WANG HAI: *(laughing)* It's very unusual that a Buddha can talk. And the Double Star Buddha is the only one that can talk.

TALKING BUDDHA: May you get rich and have an easy life.

WANG HAI: I found that some of our Chinese culture can be borrowed and made use of for the purposes of management. However, what I use from Chinese culture is not superstition. Superstition is simply that I do nothing but pray all day long, recite the scriptures and be a vegetarian, and while you pray all day, the shoes just come out of Buddha's ass. Being good at your work is like doing charity or being a good Buddhist, and nobody wants to be bad. Look at the [giant] Santa Claus in the corner. It emphasizes that our Buddha is better. This is to encourage us. Historically, westerners treated the Chinese badly. This is to remind us of that history, and also to punish them. That's what Santa in the corner means.

INTERVIEWER: And is it also practical?

WANG HAI: *(laughing)* Yeah. Very practical. Because it's a bathroom.

SIGN NEAR SANTA CLAUS STATUE: Two cents to use the bathroom.

WANG HAI: *(reflecting privately at home)* On the surface of the earth, only the Chinese have defeated the Americans. The first time was in Korea and the second was in Vietnam. I missed Korea; however I did not miss Vietnam. I was in Vietnam from 1965 to '66. It was the time when the Cultural Revolution was going on in China. I was about twenty-five or twenty-six years old. We were the first group to enter Vietnam. We even had to wear Vietnamese clothing. I have experience in both the battlefield of the market and the battlefield heavy with the smoke of gunpowder. People who want to be successful on both these battlefields first need to have the will to defeat their enemies. I could have been a goddamn general in the Communist army, and I'm absolutely confident that I would have commanded very well in war. However, I ended up being a shoemaker. Shoemaker is the tougher profession.

WANG HAI: *(agitated and annoyed, redressing a Double Star executive)* What the hell is this? How can you do things like this? You'll ruin the stores! If you give them whatever they want, there'll be a huge financial hole. How can you ask me for four million at once? Do you think that I can just print money?

DOUBLE STAR EXECUTIVE: I'll return the money in March.

WANG HAI: *(screaming)* This is an international joke! Take it away. Is this the way you do things? You have no sense of money!

INTERVIEWER: Has Wang Hai ever criticized you like this before?

DOUBLE STAR EXECUTIVE: I've seen worse.

WANG HAI: To yell at the employees is the best way to release the pressure for me; that's why I'm always so healthy. When I'm angry I release my tension right away.

WANG HAI: *(in giant, multi-tiered Double Star shoe museum)* Look at these, shoes from the Qing Dynasty.

NARRATOR: While the government wants managers like Wang Hai to make companies profitable, it has yet to provide them with personal incentives. Afraid of corruption and conflict of interest, it forbids company presidents from raising their own salaries or profiting from their success.

WANG HAI: All of this, the entire company, is my creation, and even though our stock is traded publicly, I don't own any of it.

INTERVIEWER: Is this fair?

WANG HAI: No, it's not fair, but there isn't absolute fairness in this world.

NARRATOR: Wang Hai is in Pingdu to celebrate his company's purchase of a knitting factory that supplies its fabrics.

PINGDU OFFICIAL: I would like to take this opportunity, on behalf of the Pingdu Communist Party committee, to extend warm congratulations to the establishment of the Double Star knitting factory.

NARRATOR: Seventy percent of workers in state-owned companies are in so-called "nonessential" industries like this one. Beijing realizes that if they fail, serious unemployment would follow. So the government is pressing successful state companies like Double Star to take over money losers and turn them around.

WANG HAI: In my opinion, state-owned enterprises are hopeless. If there were no entrepreneurs to make them ready for the market, they would never survive.

INTERVIEWER: Do you think you have sufficient freedom to run the company the way you wish?

WANG HAI: I don't. It will take a long time for this to come true. Why do I say this? Because the company was born in a planned economy. It's still a state-owned enterprise and thus not truly free.

DR. ZHENG SHIPING: State-owned enterprises aren't completely free because China doesn't have a genuine market economy. Wang Hai can't freely fire people because this will affect unemployment. What's more, he needs approval from the government to get loans. Wang Hai was appointed by the government, so he has to respond to them.

CHINESE PREMIER ZHU RONGJI: Within three years, we want to make most mid-sized and large state-owned companies completely change their poor performance, and in that way build a modern enterprise system.

HE QINGLIAN (ECONOMIST AND JOURNALIST): Reform must involve changes in our politics, our economics, and our ideology. So far we have only changed our economics, and nothing has changed in our politics or the way we think.

WANG HAI: The way they think will never change. What they're running is still a planned economy. This is impossible to work out. It's bullshit. The officials send somebody down to the factory. You know his opinion is no good. And if you don't do what he says, that's no good either. Saying it's a market economy is a joke. They say they want to reform into a market economy in three years. The government is full of hot air.

Breaking the Iron Rice Bowl

The catchphrase "iron rice bowl" refers to an entire life that was guaranteed under the socialist system: people not only had stable jobs but also stable living. A bowl made of iron will never break, unlike one made of glass or ceramic. The iron was iron in more ways than one. If you were a college graduate, a high school graduate, or a graduate of a professional school, your subsequent job would not be the result of your own job search but instead would be assigned to you by the government. And regardless of whether you enjoyed your job or not, you had to stay in it for a very long time, usually a lifetime. Under socialism, theoretically, every worker, whether manager or laborer, had permanent job security.

Since the late 1980s, China has been reforming the labor market. Workers find their own jobs instead of being assigned to jobs by the government. So now when they are hired, they can be fired; jobs are no longer secure. Often, a prospective employee must sign an employment contract with his or her employer. Upon the expiration of the contract—in two years, say, or five years—the employer may decide not to renew. There is reciprocity here: the employee can quit at any time and accept a better job elsewhere.

Most Chinese young people—people who are new to the workforce or just entering it—like this kind of freedom; they are at liberty to decide what enterprise they want to work for and how long they want to work there. If the work is unpleasing, they can leave whenever they want. But older people who have worked in a company for a long time are not used to such uncertainty. If they are fired, it's hard for them to find new employment—for all the same reasons why it is hard for people past their prime to be hired in capitalist countries. And there is the added psychological trauma of having been abandoned by a company that was supposed to have been one's guardian for life.

Moreover, these middle-aged people had been the ones sent down to the countryside during the Cultural Revolution, thus losing the opportunity to become educated; they do not possess the practical skills to survive in today's technological economy. And so they are the first to be laid off when state-owned companies are downsized. The breaking of the iron rice bowl is hardest on long-tenured employees.

Although the government can no longer afford to pour money into bottomless pits, many of these failing enterprises, bleeding red ink, live on, dependent on continual transfusions of loans unhappily supplied by government-owned banks. For the time being, many enterprises that should go bankrupt cannot, because bankruptcies make unemployment even worse. There are already too many laid-off workers, and rising unemployment feeds social instability—an anathema in China.

In China, laid-off workers can be differentiated from the general unemployed. They are not technically unemployed, because they are still attached to the factory they worked in, and this provides them with a small amount of living expenses, perhaps 200 to 300 yuan per month (about $24–$36, between 10 and 15 percent of their regular pay)—extremely low wages by any standards. If it is not destitute, the factory can cooperate with the local government to set up a reeducation center to help these laid-off people find jobs in new enterprises or open a small shop or business for themselves.

Bankruptcy is still alien to the post-1949 Chinese economic system, and it is shocking to employees when their factory is declared bankrupt. Until the beginning of economic reform, Chinese workers assumed that once they had been hired, they would be employees of that company until their retirement or their death. And in fact, many companies provided company graveyards as well as nurseries for literal cradle-to-grave care. The social contract operating under the communist system held that a person worked for an enterprise for his or her entire life, and that this enterprise would in turn take good or at least reasonable care of its employees for life. But bankruptcy in effect says to the worker, "Your company will not take care of you any longer. You're on your own!" It is a psychological blow from which most workers have difficulty recovering.

Under the state-owned system, everyone was guaranteed not only a job but also food, clothing, a place to live, medical insurance, workmen's compensation, and retirement pensions. These obligations have continued to burden state-owned companies and put them at a disadvantage when competing with foreign companies and the newly formed private companies now operating in China, who do not have such historical burdens of worker responsibility. Even if the state-owned companies match the operational performance of these enterprises, the foreign and private companies will enjoy greater profits, which can then be invested back into the company to make it more competitive, thus leaving state-owned enterprises further behind. Such disparity is not appreciated by westerners, who decry various regulations giving state-owned enterprises some compensating advantages, such as easier access to bank loans. When Chinese executives in failing enterprises want to reduce expenses, an easy way is to cut down on welfare: China is therefore now considering public pension plans supported, directly or indirectly, by the government.

To assure the successful reform of state-owned enterprises, many Western observers, myself included, believe that China must establish a nationwide social security and pension system—a Chinese governmental safety net—and indeed, departments of labor and social security have recently been established. All employers would be required to set aside money in a social security fund, to be used for the living and medical expenses of fired employees.

But when these westerners ask why China does not already have a governmental safety net such as unemployment insurance, they betray a misunderstanding of socialism. According to historian Yu Renqiu, formal socialism was basically that—a social security system. The government had control of all industries and took care of all citizens for life. Political economist Zheng Shiping reports that when Chinese friends of his visited the United States and observed our national Social Security and local unemployment welfare systems, they wryly commented that America was the socialist country and China the capitalist country. China was once *in loco parentis* for its people. Clearly, it is the government's responsibility now to ease people's pain so that they can survive the transition and make it to the new system. Minimum security for China's citizens is essential during this reform period.

Shao Ning: "Competition Creates Losers"

> *Shao Ning is director general of the Department of Enterprise*
> *Reform of the State Economic and Trade Commission, which is*
> *responsible for industrial structure in China. As such, he coor-*
> *dinates the central government's decisions determining which*
> *failing enterprises will be allowed to go bankrupt. It is difficult*
> *work. I interviewed him in his office in Beijing.*

ROBERT KUHN: Bankruptcy is an aspect of the market economy that is
much misunderstood, even in the United States. Please discuss the
role of bankruptcy in China.

SHAO NING: There has been a fundamental change in the way Chinese
people understand bankruptcy. In a planned economy, it isn't supposed
to exist. When the market economy was introduced, so was the principle of competition. Competition creates losers. The way we extricate
losers is through bankruptcy proceedings.

KUHN: How do you feel about your job?

SHAO: I have several feelings. The first is that it's very significant work. If
the reform of state-owned businesses is successful, then China's economic development has a bright future. My second feeling is that this
job is quite a challenge, because we have no experience in reforming
state-owned enterprises. Third is that this will be a very difficult undertaking. After all, there are about three hundred thousand state-
owned enterprises, employing over 70 million workers. That means
reform must involve the general participation of society as a whole.

KUHN: What are the primary benefits of economic reform?

SHAO: The biggest change is that China as a whole has been transformed
from a very poor nation to a generally wealthier one. Twenty years ago,
those who had the chance to go abroad were shocked at the relative
prosperity in other countries. They found supermarkets whose shelves
were full. You could buy anything. In contrast, the shelves in our stores
were sparsely stocked. Now our supermarket shelves look much like
they do in other countries. For the ordinary citizen, this is probably the
most noticeable change.

KUHN: As China develops a market-based economy, a natural phenomenon is occurring—the growing gap between rich and poor. What will be its impact on Chinese culture?

SHAO: From the inception of the market economy, the wealth gap has been growing. As you say, this is natural. I think the divergence between rich and poor can actually be helpful in improving economic efficiency. However, if the gap becomes too great, it will become an issue of fairness, and that could affect stability. The government should actively redistribute some of this new wealth by levying higher taxes on the rich. So the issue of the gap between rich and poor becomes one of reasonableness. As the mechanisms of the market economy are perfected, the gap will become more reasonable. In traditional Chinese culture, egalitarianism did not play a significant role. It came to prominence with the idea of "equal distribution," which was an idealistic and influential tenet of the planned economy. A reasonable gap in wealth is normal, and it shouldn't have a negative effect on traditional Chinese culture. If the government actively makes the appropriate adjustments, the culture will easily absorb the impact.

KUHN: What kinds of inefficiencies does China face in moving to a market economy?

SHAO: Near the beginning of economic reform, we found that those who were not supposed to become rich became rich, and those who were not supposed to become poor became poor! This was because the developing market economy had loopholes in it. Over the years, this situation has gradually changed. We are now seeing that people with good educations can more readily get rich—merely being willing to take risks isn't enough anymore. Those who are capable of becoming richer will do so.

KUHN: You might like to come to America to lecture some of our politicians on these matters. But back to China. Even though the wealth disparity is normal in a market economy, it's alien to communist thinking.

SHAO: I believe in communism. Ideally, communism is supposed to be built upon a very wealthy society—one that has been created by hard work and to which everyone contributes. Given the mindset of our society and the current level of development, I'm not sure that egalitarianism is realistic. We think, based on the current level of economic development and morality that exists in China, that stressing greater distribution efficiency and creating a fairer society are the best ways to go.

KUHN: You have articulated the current government position. But some people who live and work in China disagree.

SHAO: I was speaking for myself when I said that. You are only interviewing me, and that is my feeling. However, I think that as the economy continues to grow and a real market economy emerges, most people will accept the new realities. In today's China, the flavor of egalitarianism is less and less appreciated. People who make a greater contribution should have a greater income. This is the point of view of successful labor. The government, of course, is concerned about fairness and has to find ways to help those who are disadvantaged.

KUHN: All governments say the same thing. Let's talk about the Acheng Sugar Factory in Harbin, China's first large bankruptcy (see page 84). Why did the process take two years?

SHAO: I assume that during that time the factory management worked hard to change the way employees thought about bankruptcy. After all, workers have always been conditioned to believe that bankruptcy shouldn't, or couldn't, happen to a state-owned enterprise. The decision to file for bankruptcy was passed through a committee of employee representatives. I'm sure they looked for other ways to solve the problem, but they discovered that there was no other way to bail out the enterprise, so they agreed on bankruptcy. The fact that they did indicates a change in the mindset of employees.

KUHN: Clearly a market economy has many advantages, but could you talk about its disadvantages?

SHAO: You're an American, and Americans know more about the negatives of a market economy than we do. So I'll leave that to you. What I can talk about are the negatives of a planned economy—something with which I'm more familiar.

KUHN: OK—let's do it.

SHAO: The primary negative of a planned economy is its decision-making apparatus. When the central government makes a plan, it affects the whole nation. Such plans cannot possibly predict changes in demand across the whole country, because so many variables affect demand.

Therefore, many of these plans fail. A second negative is the lack of motivation on the part of people at all levels to implement these plans. Just telling people that things are supposed to be done according to the plan is not in itself a motivation. Because in a centrally planned economy, nobody's interests are [directly] served by carrying it out. Consequently, most people down the line are "passive implementers." In earlier times, a successful implementation might have meant a political reward. Today, there's no political or material reward, so it's very difficult to motivate people. For these reasons, efficiency in a planned economy is something less than optimal.

KUHN: An excellent explanation! You're right, that was the question I should have asked you. Looking forward, how will state-owned enterprises develop?

SHAO: First of all, it's very hard to predict anything. Twenty years from now, I think, we'll have solved the problems and obstacles faced by state-owned industries. State-owned enterprises are supposed to be the major force in market competition. "State-owned" simply means that the state holds the majority of shares. In the market economy approach, state-held shares can be sold, transferred, restructured, or retained for reinvestment. In the future, I think human resources will be more market-oriented as well. With a good welfare system in place, people will be free to move around the country to pursue the jobs that they are best qualified for. This is achievable.

KUHN: What's the general feeling about political reform over the next ten or twenty years? Does the government see it as necessary to continuing economic reform?

SHAO: This is another big subject. Our major job is to reform state-owned enterprises. This sometimes leads to the need to address political issues. It may simply be the harmony between personnel management and administration. At this level, we can see clear needs for reform. We would like to reform the management mechanism in state-owned enterprises. For example, if a given department is responsible for protecting the value of public property, and yet it does not have the power to make decisions about the personnel involved, how can it do its job? There's no way! Of course this principle has a much larger implication, but we can't seem to address that. We are limited to the immediate sphere of our activities. But someone should deal with it on the larger scale.

KUHN: In restructuring state-owned enterprises, is corruption a significant obstacle to success?

SHAO: It's not so much an obstacle as a very serious problem that must be solved. The government is currently sending auditors to evaluate and supervise the performance of management in state-owned enterprises. We have found the area of purchasing to be a serious problem. The auditors classify it as "Managing the Comparison of Purchase Prices." The problem involves commissions.

KUHN: I've saved the most important question for last. After you've been successful in reforming state-owned enterprises, and you've put yourself out of a job, what work would you like to do in the new market economy?

SHAO: I haven't thought about that one! The reform of state-owned enterprises is very challenging, so it's hard to think beyond that. If the government continues to trust my ability, I may be doing this job for another thirteen years, then retiring. I can't envision the job being finished at that point.

The Acheng Bankruptcy: "A Losing Proposition"

As Shao Ning says, competition creates losers. Capitalist societies have had to find ways to counter the human costs of the free market: the downsizings, bankruptcies and unemployment that are the flip side of growth and innovation. Now China has to face these problems too. Before 1949, Manchuria was a relatively wealthy region, with rich natural resources, a diverse culture, and the most industrialization in China. But then the communist government, supported by the Soviet Union, decided to make Manchuria the base of China's heavy industry—and what worked in a planned economy was ill-suited for a market economy. Massive state-owned enterprises were proved to be inefficient and not competitive, and a large number of workers have lost their jobs. Acheng was China's first and largest sugar factory, built a hundred years ago by a Polish businessman, during the last days of the Qing Dynasty, in Harbin, Manchuria. After the revolution, Acheng became a pillar of the planned economy, the most automated and largest sugar plant in China, producing over three thousand tons of beet sugar a day. Now it's old, deep in debt and too expensive to modernize. Eventually even social-ist economies must measure costs against income. For thirty years, China put off the reckoning; by the time we were filming our documentary, they no longer could. As the chief executive of Hu Qing Yu Tang, a pharmaceutical company, told us: "The market is merciless. If you don't adapt you'll be eliminated." Fol-lowing is the transcript from our television documentary. I have to point out how our CCTV camera crews, led by Director Li Qiang, spent many months in Harbin, following this crucial story. Braving nonstop freezing temperatures and poor living con-ditions, they captured the heartbreaking story of China's first major bankruptcy and the resulting human tragedies.

MUNICIPAL JUDGE: *(in formal court session)* The ruling of the Intermediate Court of Harbin City is the following: The applicant, the Acheng Sugar Factory, and Zhang Xiaoqian, its president, applied to us for bankruptcy. Due to poor management and other reasons, the debts increased every year. The decision is: the Acheng Sugar Factory, with all its branches, is granted a bankruptcy. This ruling becomes effective immediately.

NARRATOR: For forty years, there was no major bankruptcy in China. No matter how inefficient or overstaffed or incompetently run, big compa-nies just weren't allowed to die. Acheng is the first. Unable to compete with more efficient producers, Acheng went bankrupt in 1998, with over $80 million in debt. This put 4,500 employees out of work. Restructur-ing companies may be necessary, but the consequences can be wrenching.

ACHENG PRESIDENT ZHANG: *(in his office)* This is the work of the market economy: the winners stay, the losers are gone. According to the natu-ral law, the first to be born is the first to die. Bankruptcy is a new thing for our country, like our big bankruptcy, but in the market economy bankruptcy is a normal thing.

SHAO NING (DIRECTOR-GENERAL OF THE STATE ECONOMIC AND TRADE COM-MISSION): The bankruptcy of the Acheng Sugar Factory is due to two fac-tors. The first is that the price of sugar beets had gone up. And the second is that a factory like this has a lot of unnecessary workers and retired workers, so it carried a heavy financial burden that increased the operat-ing costs. The factory could simply no longer compete in the market.

PRESIDENT ZHANG: My next step will be how to settle with the workers. If the workers are not properly taken care of, history will view me as a sinner. Let me be straight about this: the factory is bankrupt; the company doesn't exist anymore.

LAID-OFF WORKER #2: I haven't been paid for twenty-five months.

LAID-OFF WORKER #3: How come it's bankrupt now?

PRESIDENT ZHANG: *(in his office, with the three laid-off workers)* We're all in the same situation. We're all unemployed. This is part of the process.

LAID-OFF WORKER #1: Process? The process wasn't reasonable. You must face the people.

LAID-OFF WORKER #2: Let's kill ourselves on a train track. When you have nothing to eat, death is the only solution.

LAID-OFF WORKER #3: I've lost my job, got nothing to eat. We've worked like donkeys our whole lives and now they want to kill the donkeys.

ZHENG GUOZHONG: My grandfather, my father, myself, even my children have all worked here. Now our whole livelihood is gone.

NARRATOR: Allowing bankruptcies is a risk for China's leaders—tens of millions of unemployed workers could trigger social turmoil—but it is a risk they must take to secure long-term economic stability. Bankruptcies are necessary in a market economy to eliminate inefficient enterprises. The personal tragedy of Acheng is great, but its bankruptcy signals the maturity of a government willing to take short-term social risks to create a long-term stable society. Historically, in the Chinese planned economy, all a worker's benefits came from the "Danwei"— the work unit within the state-owned enterprise. If your enterprise goes bankrupt, it means the end of your "iron rice bowl."

DR. WANG LIHUA (SOCIOLOGIST, NORTHEASTERN AND HARVARD UNIVERSITIES): The iron rice bowl had several meanings. For workers, they were permanently employed and never afraid of being fired. Their food and salaries and other welfare were guaranteed.

LAID-OFF WORKER #1: You're just bullshit! Bullshit! Nobody's telling the truth. All of them are bullshit! I'm the only one who's telling the truth. I was raised by communism. I'm not afraid of being punished by the Communists. Do Jiang Zemin's and Zhu Rongji's words mean anything? What are the local officials doing? Why is there nobody to execute? A seventy-year old man like me, I have today but maybe not tomorrow. I have the morning, but perhaps not the afternoon.

SHAO NING: When the strong enterprises push the weak enterprises out of the market, we don't have measures to deal with the consequences.

DR. ZHENG SHIPENG (POLITICAL SCIENTIST AT THE UNIVERSITY OF VERMONT): The reform in China is a very painful, stern and cruel process. The nation as a whole has benefited, however many individuals have lost out. The Chinese government does not yet have a good idea of how to deal with either the unemployed or laid-off workers. The only solution is to build up a social security system and unemployment benefits system, the sooner the better.

LAID-OFF WORKER #2: We'd rather not listen to the radio. They're not reporting the truth. They only report the positive news. That's why people don't want to listen. Don't worry, the lies won't last too long.

NARRATOR: Harbin is not a pleasant place to lose one's job. It is very cold: for six months a year the temperature doesn't climb above zero, and minus forty is not uncommon.

KANG SON: There's nowhere to go and nothing to do. All forty-five hundred of us workers are now without jobs, so how can you find a job?

NARRATOR: The Kang family lives not far from the sugar factory, where mother, father, and sons, all once worked. Now all have been laid off—permanently.

MRS. KANG: *(in decrepit housing)* Don't you think we're pitiful? The factory president lives in his nice apartment and we live here. We have to buy coal; we have to pay for the wagon. Who can we talk to? If you go see the president, he'll scold you like you're a kid. Why did they mess up the factory? I feel like I could die.

DR. YU RENQIU (HISTORIAN AT PURCHASE COLLEGE, STATE UNIVERSITY OF NEW YORK): The workers are not prepared for the new situation they are facing. This is a very difficult problem. Because of the Cultural Revolution, lots of people didn't have the chance to go to school and therefore do not possess the practical skills to survive in today's economy.

MRS. KANG: We need to rest. I'm so tired; I can't bear it.

NARRATOR: The Kangs have lost more than a paycheck: they feel the loss of a future.

KANG SON: If the factory had not closed, I would've been married by now, because the factory gave you a nice, secure living.

MRS. KANG: It's very simple. First you've got to be a government official. You've got to be rich and have a house. These are the requirements to get married. Can we qualify? If not, there's no marriage.

DR. WANG: I think the market economy is very disruptive to traditional Chinese culture, which emphasizes security and a peaceful life. The market economy has shaken this up so the traditional values of good and bad are shattered.

MRS. KANG: Maybe there is still hope if the leaders do right. Otherwise, the factory may be closed forever.

KANG SON: But you still don't understand. Bankruptcy means that the sugar factory is gone for good.

MRS. KANG: Oh, my God.

INTERVIEWER: The Acheng sugar factory is no more.

MRS. KANG: Then what is there to do? What will all the workers do? How will they make a living? If by any chance the factory is open again, I'm going to work. They have to have me back. We are getting poorer and poorer. There is nothing to say. Eat.

PRESIDENT ZHANG: You think being a factory chief is easy? These three years have been like thirty years for me. I didn't get paid a penny either. What kept me going? My loyalty to the Communist Party.

MRS. KANG: We raise these goats so that by selling the wool and drinking the milk, we try to stay healthy. That's how life is now. Whenever I step through the factory gate I get sad. I think of the good old days when we used to take care of one another.

KANG SON: We've spent all day trying to work, and the money we'll make won't even be enough to buy food.

MRS. KANG: My only wish now is for all of my sons to get good jobs and for them to settle down with their own families and be happy. Then I can stop worrying and close my eyes for good.

PRESIDENT ZHANG: I hope you won't forget me. This is the biggest bankruptcy in China, and when people think of me, they'll see me as the sinner. This might be the chance for them to have me arrested. Don't come only when I've been arrested and not when I've made a comeback. Whether or not we can be reborn, we have to make the effort.

Foreign Enterprises

Foreign businesses have been a major driver of China's economic development and foreign investment is a major motivation encouraging China to make concessions in order to join the World Trade Organization (WTO). A wholly-owned foreign enterprise (whimsically known as a WOFE) in China is 100-percent owned by a foreign company. The foreign firm retains complete control and directs the operation without Chinese partners. But establishing a WOFE can involve many difficulties, since the foreign firm may have little experience in operating in China and no knowledge of the local area. WOFEs are generally set up as manufacturing or assembly plants whose products are intended for export. Technically, in certain industries, they are not allowed to sell their products in China's domestic market, but most use creative export-import methods to do so (which increases costs and prices). Most of the WOFEs are located in China's Special Economic Zones, where they can take advantage of favorable tax rates, improved infrastructure, and a variety of local suppliers and services that support foreign companies operating in the zones.

Joint ventures (JVs) are, as the term suggests, businesses in which a foreign firm invests with a Chinese partner, and are the original and still preferred structure. The ownership ratio varies, but it is often 51:49, with the foreign firm taking the controlling share. Foreign companies enter into JVs for various reasons, the most common being to gain access to China's enormous domestic market. Without a local partner, it is difficult for foreign firms to gain market access. The Chinese partner has, as any Chinese citizen has, the right by law to sell domestically without incurring tariffs or other charges. If the business is profitable and sales in China are essential, JVs are the best choice. They allow access not just to markets but to the knowledge and expertise of the local partner in doing business in China and the local area. This is especially true for first ventures, where it is critical to get government approvals, line up local services and suppliers, and secure domestic distribution channels. The structure of a JV is typically one where the foreign partner contributes technology, equipment, and most or all of the financial capital, and the local partner contributes land, labor, and various essential intangibles.

President
Jiang Zemin
initiating new
waves of
reform.

President Jiang Zemin
meeting with Ameri-
can executives prior
to a concert of the
China National Tradi-
tional Orchestra in
Lincoln Center in
New York as part of
the cultural exhibi-
tion, "A Close Look
at China" (September
8, 2000).
From the left:
Zhao Qizheng, minister, the State Council Information Office; Jiang Zemin, president, People's Republic of China; Sun Jiazheng, minister, Ministry of Culture;
Michael Johnson, president, Walt Disney International; Nina Kung Wang, chairlady, Chinachem Group; Robert Lawrence Kuhn; Gary Benanav, chairman, New
York Life International. [This photo, taken by the Xinhua News Agency, appeared
on the front pages of all national newspapers in China, including *People's Daily*.]

Premier Zhu Rongji announcing policies for his new administration in 1998.

Fiftieth anniversary parade in 1999.

Zhao Qizheng, minister, the State Council Information Office.

Exploring cooperation and opportunities with public television in the U.S. Right to left: Liu Jikang, Cultural Consul (far right); Mel Rogers, PBS board member and KOCE-TV President (third from right); An Wenbin, Consul General (back to camera); Minister Zhao Qizheng (second from left); Yang Yang, Deputy Director General (far left).

The Pudong New Area of Shanghai, developed by then vice mayor Zhao Qizheng.

The Pudong New Area of Shanghai with "Oriental Pearl Tower" in the fore-ground.

美国总统克林顿先生戴的是
TINO COSMA 领带

Chinese luxury goods store.

No time to waste
in China's new
market economy.

Mao Zedong announcing the founding of the People's Republic of China in 1949.

Mao overlooking
fireworks in
Tianamen Square

The Great Leap Forward: zealous, idealistic young leader.

The Great Leap Forward: women making backyard steel furnaces.

The Great Leap
Forward:
brigades of
workers
contructing a
reservoir.

The Great Leap
Forward:
communal eating.

The Cultural Revolution: Red Guards hurling propaganda.

The Cultural Revolution: President Liu Shaoqi denounced and humilated

Chairman Mao lying in state.

Mourning the death of Mao Zedong.

Deng Xiaoping in 1965.

Deng Xiaoping
begins reform
in 1978.

中美两国是伟大的国家

Deng Xiaoping with President Carter in Washington, D.C.

Deng Xiaoping: a "cowboy" in America.

Anhui villagers: pioneers of reform.

Anhui villagers: the contract in blood.

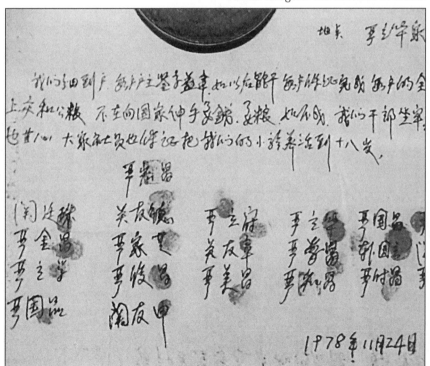

Reform brings
riches: farmer
Guo Lanbao with
his grandson.

Reform brings
happiness.

Student banner, "Hi Xiaoping!" in the thirty-fifth anniversary parade in 1984.

1984年10月1日

Deng Xiaoping's portrait in the fiftieth anniversary parade in 1999.

Toward the new millenium: President Jiang Zemin at the fiftieth anniversary parade in 1999.

Senior leaders at fiftieth anniversary parade.

Professor Li Yining, Dean, Guanghua School of Business and Management, Beijing University.

Lecture on mergers and acquisitions at the Guanghua School of Business and Management, Beijing University.

New social problem: beggar woman.

New rich ethnic groups: Mongolians.

Yi Li Ice Cream Company in Inner Mongolia.

Yi Li Executive Committee.

Flamboyant
entrepreneur:
Double Star
president
Wang Hai.

President Wang Hai teaching how to sell.

Talking giant Buddha at Double Star Headquarters.

Santa in the corner: "Twenty cents to use the bathroom."

Wang Hai's morning exercises on the beach in Qingdao.

Shao Ning, Director General, State Economic and Trade Commission.

Harbin Courthouse bankruptcy proceedings for Acheng Sugar Factory.

Zheng Guozhong,
pensionless retired
worker at Acheng.

Laid-off:
Mrs. Kang
herding goats.

Kang Son:
"Labor for
Hire."

Changing Mao's portrait in Tiananmen Square.

4
Society and Its Problems

The New Social Contract

The Chinese people now dress as they like (and do so with great diversity and style), choose from a diverse array of entertainment options (foreign movies, local rock stars, and a multiplicity of broadcast and cable television channels that are competing for their attention), and they can discuss whatever they like, even criticizing any level of government (as long as they do so privately). They may even sue the government before a judiciary that is slowly but seriously becoming independent. All this with the one proviso (and to the West this is still a touchstone for infringement of human rights) that they do not challenge the primacy of the Communist Party or form organizations that could become sources of alternative, independent political power.

This is the social contract that the Chinese people—particularly the educated urban elite—have struck with their government. (The point has been well made by Thomas L. Freedman of *The New York Times*, and I agree with him.) The contrast between the early 1990s and today in the attitude of the Chinese intelligentsia toward their government is startling (and to traditional Western liberals, disheartening). Then there was smoldering resentment; today there is genuine agreement. While they still expect progressively greater degrees of freedom consistent with social stability, and look to a future when full democratic principles and individual rights will prevail, the Chinese elite—the country's intellectual and professional leaders—accept this social contract and give the government credit for having delivered on its part of the bargain. This tacit deal between the government and the people has unleashed an enormous reservoir of energy and entrepreneurial spirit among Chinese of all classes and regions.

Sure, there is censorship; many foreign newspapers and magazines are not available to ordinary Chinese and the websites of annoying organizations, like CNN and *The New York Times*, are awkwardly blocked. But it is amazing how well informed the Chinese people are; they have learned how to take what foreign news they do get, and sense the spin on the local news, to tease out a close approximation of truth. What I enjoy is speaking with censors; the ones I've met (and perhaps I've self-selected or have been fed the good ones) are literate and reflective, believing that they are maintaining the standards of a civil society, yet embarrassed with their roles and titles and honestly hoping for a continuing opening of the media. "Please don't tell people in the West my real position," pleaded one censor with a rather bland English title; "They wouldn't understand."

Human Rights

It is surely true that despite a degree of relaxation in China's economic and political life, serious problems of human rights remain. Even today, more than ten years after the student uprising in Tiananmen, individuals who try to organize opposition to the Communist Party are restricted, detained, or jailed. Trials are perfunctory, severe, and sometimes held at mass rallies; they are designed to intimidate others from repeating the transgression. Criminals may be peremptorily tried and publicly executed. The persecution of Falun Gong, a harmless, hapless, health-oriented sect, is a salient case in point. The PRC government has banned the movement and imprisoned its leaders, leveling extreme charges against it via every public vehicle. Virtually unknown before 1999, when it quietly organized ten thousand followers to gather in a street near the Zhongnanhai Compound (where China's senior leaders live) in Beijing, Falun Gong suddenly became evil incarnate in China, and its peaceful protest reached the front pages of newspapers around the world.

Falun Gong's great sin was not its medical superstitions and advocacy of strange spiritual rituals—practices that seem archaic and mind-numbing at best and dangerous and delusional at worst—but its ability to bring together an intimidatingly large group of people. If its members had practiced their beliefs alone or in small groups, Falun Gong would never have been bothered—and most westerners would never had heard of them.

That they persuade their naïve followers to avoid proper medical care is a social evil, certainly, but given the greater social ills in China it would not have been cause for official alarm. That they could gather in the heart of Beijing was infinitely more threatening to the Chinese leadership. Chinese internal policy has drawn a sharp, bright line between individual beliefs and collective action—with surprising freedom for the former and unrelenting restriction for the latter. People can now believe virtually anything they want and even discuss their opinions with friends. What they cannot do is what Falun Gong did: organize.[11]

There is a new sense of individual freedom in China that Western media generally don't get, because they miss the distinction—obvious to Chinese, subtle to us—between voicing private opinions and organizing public demonstrations. Organizing in furtherance of a nonpolitical matter, as Falun Gong did, is deemed a far greater threat than private, individual expression of antigovernment opinions.

The readiness of westerners to criticize the Chinese for human rights violations frustrates or infuriates most Chinese, even those of sophistication and liberal leanings. It is instructive to understand the foundations of this typical Western criticism and this typical Chinese frustration. Rarely a week goes by without major Western media reporting some new Chinese

---

[11] So severely has Falun Gong affected Chinese public thinking, that just because the Falun Gong claims to use "parapsychology and ESP" (in the most ludicrous and perhaps deceptive fashion), even serious scientific study of parapsychology and ESP—diametrically opposed to the superstitious nonsense of this sect—has become sensitive territory. As a result, it was recommended that the two chapters on parapsychology and ESP be omitted from the Chinese translation of my newest book, *Closer To Truth* (which brings leading scientists and scholars together to debate how fundamental issues in the sciences affect human meaning and purpose). It didn't matter that my coverage of these topics was analytical and critical as well as descriptive and exploratory, and that I featured only leading skeptics and serious researchers. Although Falun Gong obviously misappropriates parapsychology and ESP and uses pretense and illusion to delude its naïve followers (as do so many sects, groups, gurus, books, movies, and TV shows in the West), the Chinese government is so sensitive to Falun Gong's organizing power that the government-controlled media has literally polluted the connotations of the simple words themselves. I need to point out that this personal episode was not classic censorship, since I could have easily decided to include those mischievous chapters—my Chinese (government-owned) publisher told me it was entirely my decision. However, I concluded that these two chapters on parapsychology and ESP at this time in China would overwhelm the other twenty-six chapters and distort perceptions of the book and its themes.

violation, such as the detention of a Chinese-American librarian who had visited China in order to collect old newspapers from the Cultural Revolution, or the case of a Chinese national who was jailed for exchanging lists of e-mail addresses, or the Chinese reporter who was followed and harassed by State Security agents whenever he talked to foreigners. Westerners extrapolate from the particular rights of individuals to the well-being of all Chinese society and thus tend to equate life in China today, on the basis of these isolated, albeit deplorable, events, to life under the authoritarian regimes with which they are familiar, such as the police-state communism of the Soviet Empire or Mao's rigidly closed society.

But most educated Chinese are proud to be building their country, for the first time in centuries, into a respectable and respected nation, and they are dumbfounded when what they have accomplished—indeed, the freedoms they have won—remains unappreciated and often unknown. Some fall prey to conspiracy theory, imagining that America's primary motive is to keep China on the defensive and that the keen American media interest in human rights, which the Chinese consider biased and badgering, is simply a pretext. It is true, as westerners claim, that China will not become a great nation until it has the maturity and self-confidence to grant all its citizens substantial freedoms of expression, and it is also true, as Chinese claim, that China has already made enormous progress in human rights and fears that too-rapid change will threaten its vaunted stability.

I was embarrassed for the Chinese leadership when they detained that librarian, jailed that e-mailer, and harassed that reporter. I also regret—but I am less offended—when they deal crudely with those whom they deem dissident, such as Wei Jingsheng, a long-time, oft-imprisoned advocate of political reform, since Chinese leaders see immediate linkage between disruptive individuals and social chaos.

When the Chinese government thwarted an attempt by a U.S.-based human rights organization to donate $25,000 to families of students killed in Tiananmen Square, some apologists claimed that the much-publicized donation was more a calculated plot to provoke the government than a sincere effort to help the needy. Be that as it may, the harassment by state security agents of Ding Zilin, a retired professor of philosophy who formed a network of grieving families after her own son died in the 1989 crackdown, is considered an outrage by many observers in the West. Ding's house in Beijing is often surrounded by agents who monitor her conversations and sift through her garbage, presumably looking for evidence of subversion. Professor Ding, a formerly grieving, now fiercely galvanized, elderly woman, personifies the unhappy conundrum that China's leaders face. To allow legitimacy to Professor Ding and her organization would signal to the symbol-sensitive Chinese an incipient reversal of the historical assessment of the Tiananmen movement, and though Chinese leaders may believe such to be the ultimate assessment, this instant legitimacy could, in their opinion, loose the uncontrollable genie of social volatility, now well confined. It's this kind of judgment call that China's leaders must make nearly every day.

Ironically, while Western media and politicians make much of human rights issues in China, the Chinese people overall are much freer today than they have been at virtually any time in their long, illustrious history. In addition to being able to live where they want and work at whatever job or profession they choose, their beliefs are more than ever their own.

Although religion in general is not encouraged in China, the government is not concerned with whether or not you believe in God; its only concern is whether religious cultists will rebel and cause turmoil. The government is focused on the economy and the standard of living of its citizens, not spiritual ideology and the ultimate destiny of its people—and they are smart enough to realize that, anyway, they cannot control the perfusion of foreign influence streaming into China, not if they want China to become a great nation.

Back in the 1950s, everyone read Mao's little red book—in some sense it was the Chinese Bible. Now Mao's thoughts alone are no longer sufficient, and actual Bibles can be found everywhere in China. The Chinese people, like people everywhere, find comfort in the Bible; they form support groups, just as people do in America, to share their problems and try to cope with them. The underground church in China, the pick-up religious groups not officially sanctioned by the state, is flourishing. But unless these worshippers sit themselves down in the town square, the government doesn't much mind.

What Chinese Leaders May Believe

Most westerners assume that the primary interest of the senior Chinese leadership is to maintain power for the sake of the power itself. After all, such is the way, to some degree, of all political institutions or personalities, whether in democratic or authoritarian states. But I see more in this picture. I think the current Chinese leadership is different, not just in degree but in kind, from past generations. Here is how I imagine the secret internal plan of the Chinese government. But first a disclaimer: what I am about to say I have not heard expressed by anyone in China, certainly no one in senior position, and I assume that when Chinese officials read it they will repudiate it. I have no idea whether senior leaders have discussed this plan among themselves, although I am virtually certain that this is what most of them think when they are alone. For I believe that this generation of Chinese leaders, by and large, are honorable men whose primary interest lies in the well-being of their citizens and the development of their country.

I believe that China's senior leaders know that a kind of democracy close to what we have in the West will eventually come to China, and that the full economic energies of the Chinese people will not be realized until such political freedoms, including freedom of the press, are realized. Such freedoms are necessary, as I think they believe in their heart of hearts, for China to reach its rightful position in the world as a leading power and as a proud people. This is the Chinese-pride factor, and it is a prime motivating force.

However, in order to maintain stability, the other prime motivating force, Western-style freedoms cannot be allowed until China's senior leaders are sure that social stability will be maintained. If Western-style democracy were to come too soon, they think, the country might well be torn apart by political infighting. (Recent Russian history confirmed their concerns.) The key is to continue to raise the standard of living for all Chinese, so that once the majority of the population, including its 800 million peasants, are enjoying a reasonably good life, there will be every incentive for the citizenry to maintain the status quo, and the forces of chaos and fragmentation will have no grounds to foment trouble.

I believe further that China's leaders are intent on creating a civil society, a society where the role of government is to create an environment in which its citizens enjoy comfortable lives, solving their own problems without the government imposing on their daily lives—a society managed by civilians. China in fact has begun to allow citizens to run important social organizations whose power balances the government.

A present-day example is the China Charity Federation (CCF), which is a nongovernmental organization that carries out focused social objectives in accord with government policy, though not under government control, which is more, I believe, than a difference in semantics (see my interview with CCF founder and president, Yan Mingfu, on page 123). If, over time, these nongovernmental organizations fulfill their stated purposes, they will gradually replace government agencies, with the vital added benefit of having enhanced the confidence of the public in self-government and having begun to redistribute social and political power. Under socialism, the government was mainly responsible for such humanitarian tasks, the theory being that private charities symbolized a bourgeois class suppressing and controlling a proletariat class. But now the government is withdrawing from these activities, which it can neither afford nor manage, and allowing private charities to become an independent social sector.[12]

Political reform in China is not entirely a matter of what the senior leaders intend to do but rather of the natural result of advancing economic reform. Economic development is increasingly dependent on the free flow of information, the same nutrient that feeds political reform. I do not think that many senior leaders of China doubt the coming of political reform. The only issues are its kind and speed.

It has been said that a market economy teaches people how to choose—that individual ideas and independent decision-making are crucial for commercial success, and that these attitudes of mind are essential in promoting democracy. Before reform, there were virtually no alternatives from which to choose: you lived and worked where you were assigned, there were hardly any choices in consumer goods, clothing looked alike, the little entertainment available was all the same, and when a leader said something, you agreed and obeyed. With economic reform, more and more products arrive with increasing variety in multiple markets. All of a sudden, ordinary people begin to experience what it means to assess, determine, decide, choose, and critique. When people grow accustomed to selecting from among a great variety of detergents, say, or fashions, or magazines, or sports programs on television, they will reach a point where they will think it natural to exercise this same kind of discretion in the selection of their political leaders. The behavioral implications of a market economy are far-reaching and will be a driving force in the development of democracy in China.

Thus, there may be a direct relationship, if we project into the future, between the economic standard of living of the people and the degree of political democratization of the government. This is a simple equation

---

[12] The Chinese government keeps close watch on these new charities. They all have to register with the Ministry of Civil Affairs, and they must disclose the source of their funds, since they are not allowed to accept donations from foreign political groups. In addition, some successful Chinese enterprises are beginning to recognize their responsibilities to fund activities beyond their businesses, such as the arts, education, and sports.

that many in the West do not understand. I anticipate that the voices of China will become progressively more free, in synchrony with economic growth and enhanced lifestyles. The more people have to lose, the more they will seek to protect what they have. When the most populous country on earth is undergoing history's fastest transformation, when a country has been so beset by subjugation and oppression for so many generations, such long-term political strategy may actually make sense.

The bargain may sound Faustian to us in the West; we may think of it as a sellout—because we think we would not compromise individual rights and freedoms for the sake of national pride, national stability, and individual economic gain. We have been brought up to believe that individual rights are the highest good and that if individual rights are protected, the greatest number of people enjoy the greatest amount of good. Feelings are generally different in China—not just among the leaders of the Communist Party but among many other educated Chinese as well. They view the rights of the collective as more valuable than those of the individual, and they believe that the rights of the collective are best protected by the maintenance of social stability. Hence, the object is to maintain the preeminence of the Communist Party for as long as is practical.

There is also, not so incidentally, a continuing belief in the idealistic elements of ideological communism, and although this belief is far less pervasive than in years past, it is a mistake to assume that it has disappeared. Let's understand what this means. Notwithstanding widespread disregard (and even contempt) for the Party's past economic orthodoxy, Chinese citizens respect the Party's avowed responsibility for the welfare of the people. If the Party can no longer credibly claim to practice communism as an economic ideology, it can still practice communism as the framework of China's social conscience and the expression of China's nationalism.

Corruption

Unfortunately, to understand China, one must understand corruption. It is a ubiquitous and poisonous problem, pervading all levels of commerce and government, threatening both economic development and political stability. It even could undermine the legitimacy of the state. The problem of corruption has spread dramatically as China has implemented reforms and moved toward a market economy. But corruption is not a new issue in China, nor are efforts to root it out. What is new is that the government of

President Jiang Zemin and Premier Zhu Rongji is serious, perhaps for the first time in modern Chinese history, in really doing something about it.

At the Ninth Session of the National People's Congress in early 2000, Minister of Supervision He Yong pledged that China will continue to intensify its anticorruption campaign and resolutely punish those found guilty of corruption. He said that thorough investigations will be launched into major corruption cases, regardless of the department or person they may involve, and that no lenience will be shown in dealing with those involved. Minister He stressed that the punishment of corrupt officials like Hu Changqing, a former vice governor of east China's Jiangxi Province, is a remarkable achievement of the nationwide anticorruption struggle. Hu Changqing, convicted on charges of bribery and possession of huge amounts of property, was sentenced to death on February 15, 2000, and executed the next day.

Corruption loads a heavy burden onto a state and its citizens. It not only illegally transfers resources from society to individuals, effectively stealing from everyone, it also leeches efficiency out of the economy by enabling suboptimal transactions or risky ventures to go forward. Corruption has been called "crony capitalism," and it was largely blamed for the Asian Crisis of 1997. Corruption in China is said to pervade virtually every segment of the economy, but it is remarkable how much the economy has grown despite it.

Though corruption is overtly repugnant, there are behavioral forces that can explain its pandemic presence, especially during times of economic transformation. First, fortunes are made with astonishing speed when huge portions of state resources are privatized, and it can be tempting, to some officials, to reach up and take some of the low-hanging fruit. Not only do they see others making a great deal of money very rapidly, they also see their own positions of power eroding over time. Furthermore, everyone seems to be doing it and getting away with it, including those much more senior in authority. So motivated by a combustible mixture of envy, jealousy, greed, and anxiety, they fall victim to base instincts.

Some say that the fundamental cause of current corruption is the long-term corrosive impact of the Cultural Revolution, which destroyed traditional Chinese culture and mutual respect, so that there remains little natural immunity to the disease of avarice and personal aggrandizement. The market economy surely gives opportunity for corruption, but it was the Cultural Revolution that truly destabilized Chinese society.

Exemplifying China's desperate determination to fight corruption, the *People's Daily*, long the Only-Good-News-Thank-You mouthpiece of the

Chinese Communist Party, quoted Li Jinhua, auditor-general of the National Audit Office (NAO), that as much as 125 billion *yuan* (about $15 billion) in funds for poverty relief, resettlement, or water projects in China had been misused or embezzled in 1999. This outright looting of state property included the embezzlement of $600 million from the Three Gorges Dam project, China's controversial effort to build the world's largest hydroelectric generating facility. The revelation that around 12 percent of the entire Three Gorges budget to relocate 1.13 million people was embezzled in a single year indicated the scale of the corruption swirling around the vast project. The stolen money was used to construct buildings, set up companies, and buy shares on the stock market. Li Jinhua also reported that an audit of a poverty relief fund revealed that from 1997 to mid-1999, 4.3 billion *yuan* had been spent for illegal expenditures, such as constructing government and private buildings, and buying cars for official and personal use.

In another article, the *People's Daily* reported that Wei Jianxing, secretary of the Central Commission for Discipline Inspection of the Communist Party of China (CPC), China's top anticorruption body, said that in 1999 Party discipline inspection and supervision departments completed investigations into 130,414 cases and punished 132,447 corrupt officials. Among those punished, 17 were minister-level officials, and more than 4,400 had responsibilities for bureaus, prefectures, departments, division offices, or counties. In addition, a total of 19,458 companies run by the People's Liberation Army, the armed police, the police, and legal departments were shut down, and 6,494 were put in the hands of local governments. Wei pointed out that despite this success, rampant corruption has not been effectively curbed and the situation remains severe.

To step up the anticorruption campaign, Wei said that family members of high-ranking officials are to be restrained from running businesses or assuming certain positions within the administrative scope of their parents or spouses, and are forbidden to receive gifts and money by taking advantage of the influence of their parents or spouses. Officials are not allowed to take part in tourist activities arranged by their subordinates at the expense of public funds, or use public money for private computers or Internet access. Wei urged governments at all levels to adopt a strict fiscal system that will prevent corruption, and to inform the public about their administrative activities.

The President of China's Supreme People's Court, Xiao Yang, said more than 15,700 people were sentenced in 1999 for corruption-related crimes. These included graft, bribery, and misappropriation of public funds. Mr. Xiao was interrupted by applause eight times during his speech to the National People's Congress. Mr. Xiao said the Supreme People's Court will punish severely and without mercy anyone who commits economic crimes. China's top prosecutor, Procurator-General Han Zhubin, told the Congress that the anticorruption campaign will intensify. He said it will focus on cases involving high-level officials and large sums of money. Whoever is involved in bribe-taking and smuggling, Mr. Han said, will be brought to justice, with no exceptions.

Capital punishment in the West is largely limited to premeditated murder, and administering the death penalty for any crime, no matter how heinous, remains controversial. Not so in China. Executing people for economic crimes may seem harsh and cruel, grating against our Western sensitivities, but this extreme punishment is widely supported in China. The reasons reside in our twin themes of Pride and Stability. In China, the good of the collective is more important than the rights of the individual, and when the pride and stability of the country are undermined, the individual must be eliminated. Corruption emasculates pride by impeding China's economy and ruining China's image; it threatens stability by delegitimizing the government.

One of the biggest corruption cases has not been discussed openly. It allegedly involves billions of dollars in fuel oil and other products smuggled through the southeastern port of Xiamen, just across the strait from Taiwan. Hundreds of corruption busters were said to have descended onto Xiamen, where, it was rumored, virtually the entire leadership of the city was involved in these massive crimes. The case may involve figures close to some of China's top leaders. But all reports came from outside China, since the Chinese media remained ominously silent.

In his 1997 paper, "Daring to Fight Tigers: Anticorruption Work in China," Peter Nimerius of Stockholm University states that "the Chinese proverb *zhi da cang ying, bu da lao hu* (to kill only mosquitoes and flies, but not fight tigers) traditionally described the Chinese approach to corruption, but times have changed and "tigers" are now being hunted.

First introduced in the "Three-antis" and the "Five-antis" anticorruption campaigns in 1951–52, this proverb implies that only the unimportant low-level corrupt bureaucrats, the "mosquitoes and flies," are punished, while the real culprits, the "tigers," remain free. The expression "tigers" in this case may either point to high-level leaders or to the system itself. In the

1950s it definitely aimed at all those who indulged in "bureaucratism," i.e., in putting their personal position and career before serving the public. The proverb was again used by the students in the Tiananmen Square demonstrations in 1989, but this time it was aimed at the Party and government leadership, which was accused of shielding its corrupt members from investigation and punishment.

After the dramatic events in June 1989, the Communist Party of China (CPC) acted rapidly to elevate the ardent anticorruption champion from Shanghai, Jiang Zemin, to a high position in the Party. During his time as mayor and Party secretary in Shanghai, he had established himself on an anticrime and anticorruption political platform. In the 1990s, anticorruption work has taken on new forms, and the CPC has openly proclaimed that it is going for the "tigers" as well as the "mosquitoes and flies." A number of mid and high-level political officials have been tried and sentenced for political corruption. Anticorruption work reached unprecedented heights in spring 1995, when a number of high-level officials were caught in the web, among them Chen Xitong, Party secretary in Beijing and member of the CPC Politburo. The question remains whether the law and anticorruption work can function satisfactorily in a country still entirely dominated by the rule of the Communist Party.

At the Eighth International Anticorruption Conference (Peru, 1997), China's deputy minister of supervision, Feng Tiyun, stated that only the rule of law can assure the integrity of government, and that corruption can only be cured by a comprehensive mechanism that combines investigation, education and prevention, as energized by resoluteness and perseverance. He stressed that China would focus on those leading administrative organs, judicial bodies, law enforcement departments, and economic managing agencies that are vulnerable to corruption. Fighting corruption, he said, has three fronts: first, the promotion of integrity and self-discipline among leading officials; second, the investigation of cases involving high-ranking officials; and third, the establishment of professional ethics and the correction of wrongdoings in public service.

Corruption flourishes in the dark crevices that are shielded by the shadow of authoritarian protectionism. Only the bright light of a truly free press operating without restriction or fear and the enforcement power of a truly independent judiciary, operating under a rule of law, can root out and stamp out corruption. This is why the Chinese government is encouraging (intermittently) investigative reports in the media —like it or not, only a free press has the resources and the motivation to expose corruption. (But a new media enjoying new freedoms may become a new media hard to control, and therein lies a subtle contradiction for the Chinese leadership. See page 192.)

Social critic and economic journalist He Qinglian has made the fight against corruption the core of her withering criticisms. In speaking with the bluntly outspoken Ms. He, and in reading about her merciless pounding of the current politico-social fabric, I wondered how, in this freedom-restricted country, can she get away with it? I suspected (though I had no way of knowing) that the answer lies in the fact that eliminating corruption is so central to the Chinese leadership, and that Ms. He, without political position to protect or sensitivities to respect, is able to say what many leaders themselves would like to say. Perhaps she's a trial balloon; perhaps her extreme pronouncements make the positions of others seem more reasonable by comparison.

As this book was going to press in July 2000, two seemingly contradictory (though hardly coincidental) events took place that highlighted the unambiguous fact that corruption had become China's most noisome and sensitive problem. On the one hand, corruption investigations were expanded dramatically to include Shantou, a busy port on China's eastern coast, and Shenzhen, the vibrant cradle of reform adjacent to Hong Kong, even as they continued intensely in Xiamen. On the other hand, corruption critic He Qinglian was demoted from her job as journalist and editor in Shenzhen, and censors banned state media from publishing her sensational though scholarly works. (Reports claim that her salary was cut as well, although this seems generally inconsistent with past practices in such situations.)

That the war against corruption had escalated, a reality that is not pleasant for the government to admit publicly, was made manifest shockingly when a suspicious fire at a Shantou hotel killed four members of a high-level anticorruption team from Beijing, who were in Shantou investigating a huge smuggling case. It was a temporary setback for the Central Commission for Discipline Inspection, which in the past two years has launched vigorous inquiries into official malfeasance and administrative graft.

But what seems oddly contradictory to Westerners—i.e., intensifying investigations of corruption while silencing corruption's most prominent critic—is calmly consistent to Chinese. Once again, stability is the key; it is the overriding good for China's society. Since the investigations of corruption have now been kicked seriously into high gear, Ms. He's public goading is no longer needed to break through the bureaucratic morass. And since the investigations would no doubt confirm the widespread existence of corruption, much of it at embarrassingly high levels, her incessant public reporting would become irritating, grating and debilitating to society, and thus delegitimizing to the Communist Party and destabilizing to the country.

This is why central government policy about investigative reporting in the media seems so capricious and erratic. Too little allows covert corruption, especially in distant provinces and municipalities, to scurry, hide and flourish. Too much erodes social confidence and undermines both government and Party.

Following is my complete, uncensored interview with He Qinglian, recorded by China Central Television (CCTV) crews in September 1998. Personally, I found the fetching Ms. He (whose persona betrays a bit much intoxication with celebrity status) to be, on the one hand, incisive, rigorous, relentless, and fearless, and on the other, dogmatic, mordant, unnuanced, and supercilious. I enjoyed the interview.

He Qinglian: "In China, Power Went to the Market"

He Qinglian, an economist trained at Fudan University in Shanghai and a journalist at the Shenzhen Legal News, is the author of China's Pitfall *(Zhongguo de Xianjing, Hong Kong: Mingjing Chubanshe), characterized in a long review in the* New York Review of Books *(October 8, 1998) as "the first systematic study of the social consequences of China's economic boom, [which] vindicates the skeptics so resoundingly as to force us to reconceive what 'reform' has meant." I interviewed Ms. He, one of China's sharpest social critics, in a tranquil park in the west of Beijing where she had come to attend a confidential conference. Her comment on the cause of moral degradation is particularly penetrating.*

ROBERT KUHN: China has experienced remarkable economic development in recent years. What are the main problems in making the transition to a market economy?

HE QINGLIAN: The process is still incomplete. National resources are still controlled by the state, and this creates problems. For example, about

40 percent of national investment funds have been stolen by corrupt officials. Even when investment money does find its way into projects, the quality [of those projects] is often low. We've had a few "tofu crumb" projects at the Three Gorges dam site [on the Yangtze River in central China, it will be the largest hydroelectric dam in the world]; a bridge that was being built in Sichuan collapsed; and a school that was being constructed for the Hope Project [for dropouts] fell apart. Part of the problem is that the government is not properly positioned for efficient economic reform. It does too much of what it should not do, and it doesn't do well what it should do.

KUHN: You assert that China's economy is not yet a real market economy.

HE: That's correct. Readers of your book would be mistaken if they thought I was living a pastoral life.

KUHN: How do you deepen economic reform without endangering China's stability?

HE: It's possible to change while remaining stable. China's stability can be attained through reform. Many of China's economic problems are caused not by the economy itself but by other factors. People find it easy to blame the economy, though, because it's a visible target.

KUHN: What political changes are being brought about by economic reform?

HE: Political changes are unavoidable. The longer we refuse to face that fact, the deeper our problems will become.

KUHN: Specifically, what kind of political changes do you view as necessary?

HE: The media should have the right to monitor the government, and freedom of speech should be ensured. Interest groups should have means of free expression. Currently, workers, peasants, and intellectuals have no such forums. The 1999 amendments to the constitution established some rights for private entrepreneurs—but they're far from perfect.

KUHN: Traditionally, China's media has supported the government. Now media is also being viewed as a mechanism for monitoring the government, and as a place where ordinary people's interests can be represented. Isn't that progress?

HE: Of course the role of media has changed and improved since economic reform, but the media still mainly represents the government view. Only on trivial matters does it sometimes speak for the people. It is risky, for example, for local media to criticize local officials. Upper-level supervisors do not appreciate criticism. On occasion, you may see China Central Television criticizing a local official, but you won't see much of it in the local media.

KUHN: What's the difference between a true market economy and what you call a "commercialized power market?"

HE: It's not really accurate to describe what we have here as a market economy. A better way would be to say that in China, power goes to the market. That's the starting point. If you know this, you'll understand much about China. Let's put it this way: in a socialist society, there are two ways to bring about economic reform. One way is what they did in Eastern Europe. There, power was transferred to workers' unions. In China, power went to the market. The downside of what happened here is that the power of those who have it has been commercialized. That has resulted in corruption. When a single government department has total control of everything—for example, personnel, finances, or land—it becomes a monopoly. Once government bureaus become monopolies, they cease to serve the people. Without close supervision, their services are offered for sale. The power of those who control these functions becomes a commodity. In Europe and America, it is much more difficult, if not impossible, for government officials to commercialize their power. But in China, commercialized power has resulted in corruption.

KUHN: Which of the two models is better—the Soviet approach, which destroyed the economy and is trying to construct a new one, or the Chinese approach of progressive development?

HE: No socialist country has ever found a good way to make the transition to another kind of economic system. It's too early to make comparisons between our approach and that of the Russians. The Russians have one advantage over us—their people, overall, are better educated, so they're more advanced in science and technology. The world media tell us that the Russian situation is not good. But those who have traveled there say it's not that bad. At least the people seem to have confidence in the kind of reforms they're undertaking. In China, some people feel as if they're facing the end of the world. They're panicky. Those who have money buy passports to go abroad, or they send their children out of the country. Some believe that billions of Chinese dollars went abroad in 1998. In the old days, some people who could afford it sent their children overseas to attend college. Now they're sending them to kindergarten, elementary, and high school in other countries! Those who do this prefer American and European education to our own system. More important, but less obvious, it's because they lack confidence in China's future. The Russian people say that communism ruled for seventy years and failed, and they don't want it back. The Chinese people do not yet have the same confidence.

KUHN: How big is the gap between rich and poor in China?

HE: According to recent data, the gap in China is bigger than it is in America. In America, the 10 percent who are rich own about 46 percent of the capital. In China, the rich 10 percent own about 48 percent of the capital. It has taken America two hundred years to get to this point. In China, we've had only twenty years of development, and the gap is already so big! This is the result of what I just defined—commercialized power. If nothing changes, that gap can only grow bigger. In China, some 80 percent of the people live in rural areas. These people, for the most part, are poorly educated and unable to compete in modern society. They will fall even farther behind. Retirement insurance programs are just getting off the ground in China, and education is no longer free. Those who haven't been able to save for it are suddenly faced with a heavy financial load. It's a big problem. In any society, reform means the redistribution of resources. China's reform involves everybody. If it moves too rapidly, reform could make the majority poor.

KUHN: What impact does economic reform have on ethics and morality?

HE: I have never felt that our moral degradation began with economic reform. It began much earlier—in 1949. At that time, morality was overturned. Since then, various political movements, especially the Cultural Revolution, have destroyed traditional Chinese moral principles, most of which were based on the teachings of Confucius—for example, loyalty and trust. One of the ugliest and cruelest things that happened in the Cultural Revolution was that the government encouraged people to betray one another by informing on one another. That alone destroyed much decency and virtue. The Chinese people who emerged at the end of that terrible time were not the same kind of people as the ones who saw the Communist victory of 1949. They had become a people with no shame. Once economic reform was implemented, people became obsessed with money. But the fact of reform was not the problem—the real problem was what the earlier political movements had done to the character of the people.

KUHN: So it's not the market economy that has caused the deterioration in morals.

HE: Not really. It simply provided an opportunity for people to express the lack of values that had been created earlier. Prior to reform, the Chinese people had been occupied with class struggle. Suddenly they were confronted with economic reform. The gate to the larger world opened up for the first time in decades. They realized that all the people in the world who supposedly needed to be liberated by them actually lived better lives than they did. They had trouble dealing with this. In the meantime, corrupt government officials were setting a negative example for the people. They were misusing power—and getting away with it. The people also discovered that in such a system being good didn't pay off. So they followed the example of their superiors. In China we have a saying that describes this: "If the upper beam is not straight, the lower ones will go aslant." If rulers want to end corruption in the people, they must set the example. If they ignore laws in the name of making money, the people will do the same. When officials are not punished for wrongdoing, it leaves the impression that it's OK to do wrong. That's why morality and ethics have deteriorated to such a degree in this country. Now, at all levels, people are risking prosecution to make money illegally.

KUHN: We know that personal relationships are essential to doing business effectively. How does *guanxi* work in China?

HE: Today, the Chinese people are ambivalent about *guanxi*. People who lack such relationships crave them. Once they have them, they become arrogant about them. For a while, the novel *Hu Xueyuan* was popular in China. Hu Xueyuan's business exploits were highly praised, yet he was unethical. His success came through his relationships to the courts, a local governor, and some gangsters. The era of Hu Xueyuan has not passed. Many people still rely on him as a role model for doing business.

KUHN: Some say that this is why the most successful foreign investors in China are from Taiwan and Hong Kong.

HE: Sure! They understand how the system operates in China. They know how to build a *guanxi* network. The Japanese are the next most likely to benefit. Our system tends to confuse Europeans and Americans; however, in recent years they have become smarter—they employ the children of high-ranking officials and those who already have a broad *guanxi* network to represent them. It has taken the Americans and Europeans a long time to get to this point—but they had to become smarter or lose out. The representative's job is to deal with government. For example, the Japanese have a special unit in Shenzhen whose people do nothing but talk to the government. That's their only job.

KUHN: Many people have become unemployed as a result of reform. What's your best estimate?

HE: According to official data, we have about 30 million unemployed in China. I'm sure the actual number is higher. In almost every family in every city, there's someone who lacks a job. It's a serious and seemingly insoluble problem.

KUHN: Why insoluble?

HE: I've analyzed the ages and education levels of the unemployed. Most of them went to middle and high school during the Cultural Revolution. Following the Revolution, the college entrance exam was restored and the best students went on to a college education—and to the better jobs. The ones who failed that exam are the ones who are unemployed today. They simply didn't receive a good education, and now they can't compete in the job market. They are the leftovers of the Cultural Revolution. The more our society is modernized, the more obsolete they become. In economists' terminology, these people are the structurally unemployed. They don't want to take lower-class jobs, as nannies or maids or menial workers—the only jobs they're now qualified for. The government makes available only a small amount of money for their support. It does nothing more than prevent them from starving. They exist on the fringes of our society.

KUHN: The government has many burdens.

HE: There's really not much the government can do. The problem is complicated. The government would like to see these people change their values. The people think the government should assign them good jobs; clearly some have to change their outlook. I'm more worried about their offspring. These poor, unemployed people cannot possibly support their children through college, so the cycle will repeat, and poverty will pass to the next generation. In the future, the gap between rich and poor will be a matter of education levels.

Kuhn: That's characteristic of many countries, including my own. The ultimate solution is that an expanding economy will raise the standard of living for everyone.

He: We're looking for solutions. But even if we come up with proposals, we're not sure the government will adopt them. It's highly unlikely that our suggestions will ever become state policy. In China, nobody really listens much to scholars. All we can do is our best.

Kuhn: That's a problem of scholars everywhere. Let's discuss some specific problems. Start with banking.

He: The debts owed by state-owned companies are, on average, as high as 80 percent. They borrowed money from the banks, and the money in the banks is the savings of the people. This has resulted in a major loss of national capital. The government has attempted to apply various solutions, but none of them has worked well. The stock market approach didn't work either—much of the money went to traders. That does no good for the people or for the government. There's a Chinese saying that is appropriate here: "Don't drink poison to quench your thirst."

Kuhn: Migrant workers are another serious issue.

He: A serious issue, but not a new one. I wrote an earlier book, about ten years ago, on the history of China's population and economy. I addressed the fact that over the past three centuries China's population growth has consistently outstripped its resources. In 1949, the famous scholar Ma Yinchu raised the issue, but Mao Zedong ignored it. Today the problem is worse than ever. We tell others that we can support ourselves, but we know that China is greatly overpopulated. The sheer weight of our population has done much damage to the environment. We have overexploited it to supply food. In rural areas, peasants can't have even one *mu* [0.1647 acre] of land; consequently, they're unable to support themselves, and often they head for the cities in search of jobs. In Shenzhen, many of the people who were executed were young peasants who couldn't find jobs and resorted instead to stealing and killing. Wherever they turned, they were doomed.

KUHN: How about women's issues?

HE: China's version of women's liberation started in 1949. Unfortunately, many of the programs designed to protect women soon became ineffective, and women faced serious problems, especially in competing in the job market. This is still the case today. On the other hand, some women have been very successful in their jobs—but even success has its problems. Many successful women are unhappy with the state of their personal lives. Some cannot find husbands, because men perceive them as being too strong to be good wives. China's traditional view of women is different from the West's, but this sort of thing is not just a problem in China—it happens in other developing countries.

KUHN: Have you been disadvantaged because you are a woman in China?

HE: I haven't personally encountered much sexism, but I've seen other women experience it. I've come to the conclusion that the liberation of women in China is not so much a political or economic issue as a cultural one. Traditions die hard. My own situation is somewhat unique. I don't hold a position with the government, so my opinions are entirely academic.

KUHN: My hunch is that your gloomy assessment is in part conditioned by your scholarly position. Recognizing the dramatic progress China has made since the end of the Cultural Revolution, what do you see twenty years in the future?

HE: If we cannot overcome corruption in government, we'll end up like Latin America. There, power is married to money. In China, we add one more thing to the mix—organized crime. Some local bureaus already function like the Mafia—this is especially true in rural areas. In the future, there will be stratified levels of power among the upper classes, and perhaps an uprising of migrant workers at the other end. Here we are talking about people who don't have a permanent job, who have no legal identification and no residence. These people have to move around the country to survive. As I said, this class produces many of the criminals. In cities like Beijing, Shenzhen, and Guangzhou, some 75 to 95 percent of the crimes are committed by migratory people. This problem will become even more serious in the future. I suggested to some friends that the situation is similar to one that existed prior to the Taiping Tianguo Uprising of 1851. Prostitution is blossoming, beggar groups are growing, and we're seeing the rise of new religious groups. Government bureaus are crowded; many college graduates cannot find jobs, so they are assigned to these bureaus. The situation was similar in the Qianlong era of the Qing dynasty. Hong Xiuquan created a religion then, and today we have Falun Gong. I'm just a scholar, so it's hard for me to predict what will happen in the next twenty years. Based on what I see now, I'm not optimistic. Just the condition of the environment alone makes me pessimistic. I think we may see small, local uprisings, but nothing on a national scale—the government is too strong. At the same time, many government officials simply lack the necessary qualities to govern well. They lack both managerial skill and morality.

KUHN: What is your best hope?

HE: Political reform. We need to establish a local supervisory system. All governments have at least some corruption, but in some other countries there are strong checks and balances against abuse. We have nothing like this in China. Even the selection of government officials is a problem. Those at upper levels tend to pick people who support their interests—people who listen to them. Policies from the central government are often stymied at the local level. This is because those required to implement them are often incompetent or corrupt. They are out for themselves. In making decisions about investment, they consider only local interests and ignore the larger situation. That's why some items are overproduced—consumer items, like refrigerators, televisions, and so on. The sooner political reform comes, the better. But the reform has to be complete.

KUHN: You've stressed the importance of planning. Can you give me an example?

HE: Yes. There was a time when the government tried to reduce staff. But they didn't think it through. Those who were laid off had no place to go, so they eventually had to come back. If a small reform like that can't succeed, how can a bigger one do any better, unless it's properly planned?

KUHN: So is reform futile?

HE: First, I have never viewed reform as a movement; I see it as a way of living. In other countries, reform may involve revising laws. In China, where stability is a top priority, just moving a tile might be called a revolution! At least that's how Lu Xun [China's foremost modern writer and intellectual, 1881–1936] characterized it. People are coming to realize that reform can improve the quality of their lives. It's not guaranteed, but it could.

KUHN: What will it take to really implement reform?

HE: The biggest obstacle is corruption. To make reform work, we'll need to punish corruption. Sure, some of the results of reform may be painful. People will have to understand that. It will take time to complete the process. Some people's interests may be damaged along the way. Reform, by definition, is the redistribution of interests. We must be brave. Some people will have to lose more than others do. But look at the data: Today's *unemployed* workers are not that much worse off than the average *employed* worker was during the Cultural Revolution. But they're relatively poor when you compare them to others today. When these poorer classes see others around them driving cars and taking overseas vacations, they focus on how poor they are themselves. Actually, they're not worse off than most people in China in earlier times.

KUHN: Aren't the problems we're talking about labor pains, painful but indicative of new birth—that is, the natural results of making a transition? Won't conditions improve as the reform continues and interests are balanced?

HE: Certainly a new interest balance will be formed. The question is, what will it be like?

KUHN: For example, you noted that much of the unemployment is structural in nature, because of the realignment of industries and enterprises. After restructuring, at least some of the unemployed will find new employment.

HE: Even in America, some people end up permanently unemployed. China is not unique in this respect. We should be farsighted on this issue. I have stated repeatedly that unemployment is not caused by the reform. Reform is not the problem. The revolution of 1949 destroyed the social order that had been in place for thousands of years. To restore it, China will have to pay a price. The gap between rich and poor exists in every society. There is no culture where it does not exist. The difference is that in other countries that gap has been created by many generations of wealth accumulation. In China, it has been created by the commercialization of power, and by government officials stealing from the public. The normal order has been destroyed, and the pain we are experiencing as a people is the result. As reform continues, pain will continue. It cannot be any other way.

KUHN: The historical perspective is important here.

HE: Many Chinese people don't know their own history. They don't know what happened before they were born. They know nothing about the Cultural Revolution, the Great Leap Forward, and so on. A Roman scholar once said, "One will never grow up if one does not know what happened before one was born." Anyone who doesn't know the history of China will not understand the current situation.

KUHN: As an economist, journalist, and published author living and working in China, you seem remarkably free in all that you say—a fact that might surprise most Americans. Doesn't your own freedom of expression reflect China's deepening commitment to reform?

HE: Here's how I see it. We've had twenty years of reform. Before that, the three powers—political, economic, and cultural—were all married to each other. Since reform started, those powers have been gradually separated. Now we have some freedom—but it's limited. As a scholar, I feel obligated to tell people what I have observed. I think that in every country there should be scholars who are willing to contribute their knowledge to the country without reward.

KUHN: Have you personally benefited from reform?

HE: Yes, reform has brought me many benefits. For example, if the college entrance exam had not been restored, I would not have been able to attend college. On the other hand, if you look at it from a different perspective, it was always my right to go to college. I simply had that right restored—that's all. There was nothing "normal" about the way we had to live in China from 1949 until the year reform started. In those days, people involved in the various political movements like the Cultural Revolution betrayed each other and often didn't work. As a citizen, everyone should have the right to earn a living, to own property, and to experience certain freedoms. These rights go with being born human— they are not a bonus granted by the government.

KUHN: Let's talk about management in China. Clearly, it should be separated from politics. But where does creativity come in?

HE: There's lots of room for creativity in China. In this sense, we're much better off than before reform. Reform has taken us a long way, but it will require creativity to solve the problems that it has created. If we don't address these problems, they will worsen. To solve them, reform itself must be deepened and broadened. It cannot happen in only one area. Real reform has to involve three areas: ideology, politics, and economics. So far, we have had many years of economic reform but no real ideological or political reform. In official newspapers, we still read the same ideology we've been reading for years—no matter how much the real world may have changed. At the practical level, this creates problems. If politics is to serve economic interests, then ideology is a way to mediate the interests of different classes. If things change only in the economic realm but not in the ideological or political realm, conflicts and tensions are created. We've come a long way in economic reform. Now it's time for politics and ideology to catch up. Government must take the lead here.

KUHN: Are the newly formed businesses as dependent on the government?

HE: I've talked to many entrepreneurs. For example, in Shenzhen there is a well-known financial software company called Jin Jie, and it is one of the companies that the government supports. In order to operate, they have to deal with the government. They'd rather not be dependent on the government, but they have no choice. Consequently, they're not sure about their future. In China, no company can survive without the government, because it has the monopoly on resources. Not only that, but the government makes the rules by which everyone has to do business. A given manager may no longer work for the government, but there's no way he can avoid being involved with it. Every manager must deal with tax bureaus, commerce bureaus, and banks. That means they have to maintain those relationships.

KUHN: Even in America, the government plays some role in regulating commerce. In your opinion, what is the proper relationship between government and business in China?

HE: Don't get me wrong—I'm not saying we don't want the government involved. The issue is *how* it should be involved. Government should only be involved in the businesses it has to be involved in, and leave the rest alone. That by itself would significantly reduce corruption. Society, then, might move a little closer to normalization.

KUHN: How can China effect change most efficiently? What is the most important measure to take?

HE: I've already said it—political reform. In other words, the government's relationship with business must be normalized. It should retreat from areas where it doesn't benefit business—and that means most areas.

KUHN: How will China's stock market affect its future?

HE: That's a long story. In 1998, I wrote an article about the difference between capital-in-kind and financial capital. Our capital-in-kind is underdeveloped, while our financial capital is bubbling [i.e., assets are overvalued] too early. There's a rift between the two. Do you know why America and Europe are so well developed? Because their capital-in-kind has control over financial capital. As a matter of fact, the financial crisis in Southeast Asia was a result of financial bubbles. The reason the situation in this country is not as bad is that the currency exchange rate is controlled by the state—and the state also has total control of the banks. In China, the three-way relationship between state-owned companies, the banks, and the money depositors could trigger a financial crisis. Why? Because if bank-owned capital is not high enough, the bank is technically bankrupt. In 1998, bank-owned capital dropped to three percent. According to international standards, it should be at least eight percent for solvency. So we're technically bankrupt. But of course we have our own special situation, so we don't consider ourselves bankrupt. Yet with bank-owned capital so low and debt so high, there can't help but be problems. The government has tried various measures to solve the financial problems, but so far none of them has worked.

KUHN: You were saying that the stock market is in a bubble. What are your criteria for a bubble?

HE: First of all, most people who become rich make their money in at least one of three areas: real estate, rare products, and the stock market. These are what produce bubbles. I often joke with my friends who are engaged in those businesses that what they are producing is bubbles. Granted, our bubbles in China have diminished a lot in recent years. But we will still have to pay a price, just as they did in Japan. In the process of reducing its bubble, Japan found itself in a trap. We're in the same situation. I elaborate on these issues in my book *The Trap of Modernization*. In 1993, we had to make a large-scale adjustment, because the bubble was causing the economy to malfunction. Premier Zhu tried many measures to correct the mistake. However, since the bubble problem is related to other problems, none of his measures achieved the hoped-for success. That's not his fault. The ultimate problem is the system itself. As long as we have this system, it will create insoluble problems. Even the most capable people will not be able to solve them, because they're generated naturally by this kind of system.

KUHN: Stock markets, in theory, are an efficient mechanism for the optimal allocation of resources from providers of capital to employers of capital.

HE: The stock market has its place in China for, as you said, the efficient allocation of resources. But it can devolve into a system for robbing national resources. The stock market provides a way for the government to redistribute bills and debts. Ordinary people don't know this, but they should. The problem in China is that we don't have many places to invest. It's difficult to register a company. You need to obtain permits from up to ten government bureaus—sometimes dozens! In addition, you have to pay exorbitant taxes and levies. And there's no guarantee that your company will be profitable. So people prefer to deposit their money in banks. Then, as interest rates on bank accounts move lower and lower, people begin to reconsider the stock market. So the cycle repeats itself. Unless something changes, this problem will get worse.

KUHN: Let me conclude with a personal (i.e., self-serving) question. *China's Pitfalls*, your book on social problems, is well-known both in China and the United States. You've told me that my book on investment banking is much better known in China—why is that?

HE: To the Chinese, investment banking is something new. For many people, yours is the first book they've ever read on the subject. When it was published here, it became instantly popular.

KUHN: It's nice to end on a happy note.

Internal Migration

Requiring residency registry for all Chinese citizens was not Mao's idea. It started in the Qin dynasty, the first centralized imperial government in China (221–206 B.C.E.), but how it works has been changing throughout history. In Mao's era, according to sociologist Wang Lihua, the residency registration had at least three functions: politically, it controlled population movement; economically, it provided access to consumer resources (such as the distribution of coupons for city residents to buy food or clothing); sociologically, it divided people into rural residents and city residents. The system began to change in the early 1980s, with 1984 being a turning point.

When the coastal cities of Shenzhen, Zhuhai, Shantou, and Xiamen became Special Economic Zones with favorable tax treatment, the question was how to make them attractive to foreign investors. One way was the provision of cheap labor, but where would the cheap labor come from? At that time, most people in those cities were already employed. So the pool of cheap labor would have to be peasants, who were only too willing to leave their exhausting work in the fields. Reform had widened the gap between urban and rural workers: wages in the coastal areas were higher than elsewhere, and large numbers of people began migrating from rural to urban areas, benefiting both themselves and the state.

The term "floating population" describes this surplus labor force from rural villages which has gone to work in the cities; it is estimated at about 100 million people, something less than 10 percent of the population. There are several reasons why this migrating workforce became so large so quickly. First, agriculture is hard work with low pay. Second, reform increased production efficiency on the farms, yielding a surplus in laborers. Third, the rapid growth of construction and other projects in the cities required this labor force. And fourth, government policies that had restricted people from relocating were relaxed.

Along the roads to Beijing, Shanghai, Guangzhou, and other coastal cities one can see endless numbers of peasants willing to work for low wages, which distorts the labor market as a whole. The government has no idea of how to deal with these transient masses. In the old days, the military might have been called to take them back home. Now this is impractical, if not impossible. Furthermore, the countryside can no longer absorb so many workers. The only hope is to provide for the floating population with social services, schooling, health care, and insurance.

In Mao's era, the residence registration system was an efficient way of regulating the Chinese people. There was a simple registration book called a *hukou*—five to ten pages depending on the number of members in the household—which recorded where you were born, where you had lived before, and where you were living now, and sometimes local police or postal departments kept a record of this data. You needed a *hukou* to buy food or fuel, to apply for jobs, to go to school. The residence registration card controlled every aspect of your life. If you left the place where you were born and you were unable to obtain a residence registration card in the new place, you simply could not survive. Even today, you need your *hukou* to receive whatever social benefits are being provided, such as housing for your family or schooling for your kids. The *hukou* of migrating workers are tied to their home villages, so they can move to the cities but they cannot legally stay there: their housing options are restricted, they cannot get social services for their families, and their children cannot go to school.

Nevertheless, economic reform has been gradually weakening the residence registration system. As long as you have money, you can get pretty much what you want. Moreover, some cities encourage rich people from other areas to make investments locally by issuing them a temporary residence registration card. And in the countryside, the system has collapsed, so if local people or peasants travel to a new place, it is impossible to track them.

In China, as elsewhere in the developing world, this migrating population has caused a measure of social instability. In the major cities, many apartments now have iron gates across windows and doorways. The crime rate in the large cities has surged because of the growing gap between rich and poor, and many of the criminals are migrants and some have been executed. Migrating people are largely unhappy people. Though they are able to make more money (and often send this money back to their families in rural areas), their lives are painful; they are isolated, often without relatives or friends in the city. They have no social network, and so migrants are often exploited by city people. There have been numerous reports, for example, of young rural maids being raped by their masters. In some sense the grimmest problem for the Chinese leadership is how to prevent this migrant population from turning into an antigovernment force. One hundred million rootless workers living on the fringes of society poses a serious threat to the nation's social stability.

Migrant Workers: Moving, But Not Always Up

In a market economy, labor and capital have an intimate (and not always mutually supportive) relationship. Since the reform of state-owned enterprises, untold numbers of laid-off workers and farmers from poor areas are descending on China's cities in search of jobs. At least 100 million people are on the move. It is the largest peacetime migration in human history. As seen in this segment of our PBS documentary transcript, this particularly fluid element of the labor pool has not seen the benefits that Deng's reforms promised.

WONG XIANGFEN: We out-of-towners are willing to suffer and take on dirty and tiring jobs. This is our strength. Lots of the laid-off locals complain that we are taking away their jobs. I'm actually happy to hear them say so because it means they realize we're improving ourselves.

CONSTRUCTION WORKER: Since I've come to Beijing, I feel that Beijing people have a very good life, much better than in my hometown. I wish I could live in Beijing.

MA HUILING (FEMALE CRANE OPERATOR): I've been here about three years. I got this job because my husband is an employee of the company. My province was too poor to stay in because the land is not good. So we came here to work. My shift lasts twelve hours, so I'm here almost all day.

CONSTRUCTION WORKER: It's been two months since I left home. Since I've come to Beijing, I'm tired all the time. I don't eat or sleep very well, but I have to make the best of it. There are no holidays. We even work Saturdays and Sundays. The job is very tough and tiring and the wages are too low.

FOREMAN: Some of the workers live in the parking garage now. The mealtimes are five in the morning, noon, and seven in the evening.

CONSTRUCTION WORKER: *(interviewed while standing in line for food)* Cabbage again? I've been married one year.

INTERVIEWER: Do you miss your wife?

CONSTRUCTION WORKER: I miss her. Actually I don't miss her.

INTERVIEWER: You really don't miss her?

CONSTRUCTION WORKER: Yeah, I don't miss her.

INTERVIEWER: How come?

CONSTRUCTION WORKER: I'll go back to be with her; but it's useless to miss her, so I don't miss her.

MA HUILING: I have one child. He's four and a half years old. He's back home in the countryside. I've only been able to go back once in the last three years, for Chinese New Year. I want to stay in Beijing for a few more years, to earn money for my little boy since I don't have enough for his education.

INTERVIEWER: Have you received any salary yet?

CONSTRUCTION WORKER: Not yet.

INTERVIEWER: Will you get it after the building is finished?

CONSTRUCTION WORKER: Yes, but who knows when that'll be.

DR. YU (HISTORIAN AT PURCHASE COLLEGE OF THE STATE UNIVERSITY OF NEW YORK): As long as the Chinese economy continues to develop and provide job opportunities for these rural laborers, then we'll be OK. But if the economy fails to provide jobs and a minimum living standard, it will become a social and political problem.

CONSTRUCTION WORKER: I'm not going to do this for the rest of my life. After I save some money, I'm going to do something different. I'm not coming back.

Underground Church

Alienation is the other side of hope, and it is also new. Millions of Chinese are reaching out for the new jobs and possibilities the new economy is promising. But others have lost hope. In our documentary, we followed Mrs. Gan, whose husband was compelled to work in a nearby city.

MRS. GAN: You should talk to poor people like us and understand our situation, so I feel I want to tell you about my suffering.

NARRATOR: Mrs. Gan can afford either rice or vegetables—but not both. She can't afford schoolbooks for her son. They are no longer provided free. Nor is his medical care.

MRS. GAN: Whenever the school asks for more money, my son comes home worried. He says: "Mom, I don't want to live any more, I want to die. Look at me, I'm born disabled. You didn't let me die when I was born. After graduation how can I find a job?" There's a cavity under his left shoulder; the hole is as big as a fist. He says, "If I depend on you guys, you won't have any money either. Let me die. You still have hope for me, but I'm disabled. What can I do? Mom, you have to tell me which is the best way to kill yourself." I said, "Take sleeping pills."

INTERVIEWER: Did you really say that to your mother?

MRS. GAN'S SON: I did.

INTERVIEWER: What made you say that?

MRS. GAN'S SON: Because I'm a drain on my family and they can't have a good life because of me. So I thought of hanging myself.

WOMAN INSIDE AN UNDERGROUND CHURCH: Today we face suffering everywhere, whether we're at home or at work in the markets. We ask for God's mercy.

MRS. GAN: We formed a church by ourselves, which is illegal. Churches have to be approved by the government.

NARRATOR: The Chinese Government restricts religious practice to authorized religious organizations and registered places of worship. Yet millions are seeking consolation and fellowship in an underground church like this one.

WOMAN INSIDE CHURCH: We are the lowest people in the world. Money and power, we have none.

GROUP IN CHURCH: Yes it's true.

WOMAN INSIDE CHURCH: In this society, there are many people who ridicule us as fools. God chose people like us. He lifts us from dust and feces. The fruit we bear will be just and kind. We have Jesus' life inside us. Now that we walk on this path, we want to thank the lord.

GROUP IN CHURCH: Amen.

MRS. GAN: Do you know why I believe in God? Because I'm poor. My belief in God gives me peace so that my mind is not distracted by the suffering. I don't lie. I don't know if I've sinned. I don't even know if it's right to talk to you and let you [i.e., CCTV] interview us. I don't know; I'm confused. To say this out loud is a good thing to do. What am I afraid of? That's the way it is.

Yan Mingfu: "The Whole of Society Can Be Involved"

Yan Mingfu, former secretary of the Central Committee of the Communist Party of China (CPC), executive vice chairman of the Chinese People's Political Consultative Conference, and minister of the CPC United Front, is a founder and chairman of the China Charity Federation (CCF), China's largest charitable organization. Minister Yan began his career as Mao Zedong's official Russian translator, serving Mao in his secret talks with Nikita Khrushchev. Having survived various purges and severe terms of imprisonment, especially during the Cultural Revolution, he rose to high office in the Communist Party under reform Premier and Party Secretary General Zhao Ziyang. In 1989, Yan, along with Zhao, was dismissed for sympathizing with the students in the Tiananmen Square protests. Thereafter, Yan served in the Ministry of Civil Affairs from 1992 until his retirement in 1997. His wife, who was present during the interview, is an elegant woman who speaks English and French fluently, having studied as a child at St. Joseph's Girls Catholic School of the Franciscan Missionary in China. Their daughter is a French-educated attorney who is the managing partner in Beijing for a major French law firm. I interviewed Minister Yan, with whom I have been friends for a number of years, in the CCF conference room (which is furnished with chairs and sofas of many colors, some of them clashing, since each was donated by a different company or person).

KUHN: Minister Yan, what is the purpose and guiding philosophy of the China Charity Federation?

YAN MINGFU: The China Charity Federation (CCF), I have to say, is a product of this nation's current economic reform. For a long time, the Chinese government was solely responsible for helping the poor and sending relief to disaster-stricken areas. Now, with reform, the open policy [i.e., opening of society], and the market economy, the whole of our country can be involved in such efforts. It is this new climate that made it possible for us to found the CCF in 1994.

KUHN: What's your role in the CCF?

YAN: It was actually my idea. When I served in the Ministry of Civil Affairs, which is responsible for helping orphans and distributing relief to the poor, I recognized that many nongovernment people also have a deep love and concern for these people and would like to contribute to the effort of helping them. We needed a single-purpose organization that would unite these efforts. I proposed the idea of the CCF, and the government formally approved it in 1994. In 1997, I left the government and joined the CCF as acting chairman. Later, the board elected me chairman, in which capacity I continue to serve.

KUHN: The market economy has many benefits, but one of its problems is the growing gap between rich and poor. You campaign aggressively to get the rich to recognize their obligation to help the poor.

YAN: The growing gap between rich and poor has underscored the need for charity. Back in the days of egalitarianism, it would have been difficult to get anyone to help, but now the disparities are obvious. We try to tell not only the rich but also all people about the conditions of the poor in China. In 1998, when three major rivers flooded, we witnessed a unified effort involving all economic levels across the country. The rich and the poor pulled together to help those who were devastated by the flooding. Fully half our donations came from ordinary people. Their donations ranged in size from 1 to 1,000 *yuan* [equal to about twelve cents to $120 at current exchange rates, but far more meaningful when compared to China's yearly per capita urban income of under $750]. Of course, some large enterprises made sizable donations as well. The key is to make people aware of the need. Their love and compassion will do the rest.

KUHN: You remind me of a moral philosopher who seeks to teach wealthy people the importance of their obligation to help the poor. It strikes me that this is an important role in society.

YAN: I do feel an obligation to let people know that they can't just take from society and not give anything back. A fair and civilized society is one in which everyone accepts the obligation to help those who are in distress. The more we collectively understand this, the more we are advancing as a people. Once society recognizes the obligation to help, an organization is needed to coordinate the efforts. Such an organization must be publicly accountable so that it can engender the trust of those who contribute.

KUHN: Why was charity of this type not encouraged during the pre-reform socialist economy?

YAN: If you look at the whole history of China, charity has a long-standing tradition. When the Christian missionaries came to this country, things changed. Of course, missionaries and charity go together, but the westerners also brought their gunboat diplomacy. For a long time, people associated charity with the rich giving alms to the poor and with the gunboat diplomacy of Western nations humiliating China. When the People's Republic of China was founded, this approach to charity was associated with the wealthy using their riches to deceive those whom they ruled. Charity was seen as a class issue; consequently it was eliminated and not replaced by anything that met the need.

KUHN: Let's focus on some specific projects of the CCF, such as sponsoring old people's homes. Shouldn't families be taking care of their own elderly?

YAN: Chinese society is rapidly aging. More than 10 percent of the population is now over sixty. A single-child family can end up with four old people to take care of—up to six in some cases, if both sets of grandparents are living. As people age, they are running out of people to take care of them. Many young people are either leaving the country or moving to other cities in China to look for jobs. This can leave old people stranded without support. We have to think about what can be done to help old people like these. And what about those who live in families with multiple marriages—and those who have only one or two children? These problems are beyond the ability of families to solve. They therefore become society's problems. The government has set up housing for old people in the countryside. Some installations have a capacity for thousands. But all this housing is still insufficient to meet the need. Consequently, we seek donations. The Shanghai & Hong Kong Bank has set up a special foundation to help us. Each year they spend 2.5 million in Hong Kong dollars [about $320,000 in U.S. dollars] to help finance public and private homes for old people. We also develop community services through which old people's problems can be addressed. China has learned from Hong Kong and from Western countries. We offer the services of volunteers who do the shopping, cooking, and laundry and escort people to doctors. We plan to train some social workers to specialize in looking after the elderly.

KUHN: You also do job training—for example, in operating computers, and doing housework. This seems unusual for a charity organization.

YAN: As China's economic reform continues, more and more factories are laying off employees, or even firing them. The government provides these ex-employees with some assistance, and there are various job training programs for laid-off employees. The China Charity Federation has more than a hundred member branches around the country. We focus on laid-off employees who have serious problems. For example, some have cancer and have had surgery, but their condition still allows them to perform light duties. Handicapped employees who have been laid off and the financially disadvantaged may also find free vocational training in Shanghai as a result of donations. Some receive training in computer skills, such as data entry and storage management. We've had good results in these areas. Because these people are the most disadvantaged, it should follow that society shows greater compassion for them and facilitates their efforts to become reemployed. We have such programs not only in Shanghai but also in other cities, including Guanzhou, Tianjin, and Xian.

KUHN: What is the "harelip project"?

YAN: The CCF is helping Chinese children who were born with harelips to have them repaired. It will continue until every child in China who needs this surgery has had it. That may mean hundreds of thousands of operations. We have just started and have only done a few thousand. We want our children to grow up in the twenty-first century with smiles on their faces!

KUHN: As you know, we worked together on a project that united music and charity. What is the traditional relationship between culture and charity in China?

YAN: Since we invited your wife to come to Beijing for a charity performance [piano] with the China National Symphony, we have thought of inviting others, including Arnold Schwarzenegger, to put on special events. Sports and cultural events are an excellent way to draw attention to the needs of the poor, and to raise money to help them. On the other hand, poor people are also entitled to enjoy the arts and culture as much as anyone else. Therefore we often organize events that give them access to top quality sports and entertainment. Blind people may not be able to see what's going on onstage, but they can certainly enjoy the sounds of singers and musicians. We have arranged concerts of both traditional and foreign music for the people we serve. We gave away tickets for *Madam Butterfly* to some poor students; they enjoyed it very much, and it was gratifying to see their joy at being able to attend.

KUHN: What lies in China's future?

YAN: I am very hopeful for this nation. As long as China can remain on the road chosen by Deng Xiaoping, we will move ahead. The present leadership is doing just that, and the people are following. Consequently, I believe we will make major progress in the years ahead. I hope the 50 million impoverished peasants and the millions of poor living in metropolitan areas will find a better life. The CCF is working hard to help free them from poverty.

KUHN: Let's talk about the people who are living in poverty. Has the market economy made their plight worse?

YAN: Poverty has always been with us. People in the western mountain regions have lived in poverty for generations, mainly because they face naturally adverse circumstances. With the development of the market economy, the whole country has grown at an unprecedented pace, so more resources are available for helping the poor. The number of poor people in the countryside has dropped from 250 million to about 50 million. On the other hand, there have been some casualties. Some badly managed businesses have gone bankrupt—they were not able to withstand the competition. As a result, some employees were laid off and temporarily joined the ranks of the poor. As the market economy grows and companies prosper, the unemployed will find more opportunities for work. In the long run, the market economy will do much to alleviate poverty and unemployment. In fact, it already has. Of course, I don't want to deify the market approach. It has many drawbacks, as those in the West know—but it's still the best way to keep the economy growing. The market economy doesn't prevent us from using other means to help the poor—our organization, public welfare organizations, other nongovernmental organizations. We are doing our best to create and preserve a fair society.

KUHN: You were one of the leaders of the Communist Party when you were relatively young. When did you first hear about the market economy?

YAN: It was in 1979, when I was meeting with a delegation from the Encyclopedia Britannica, that I first heard Deng Xiaoping discuss his theory of the market economy under socialism. It was not long after he returned to power after the horrors of the Cultural Revolution, and he said that the market economy does not belong exclusively to capitalism. I was really there.

KUHN: When did you begin to change your own thinking in favor of a market economy as being good for China?

YAN: It was just after Deng Xiaoping introduced his reforms in rural areas with huge success. In fact, this was the beginning of the market economy. Deng gave farmers access to the market, allowing them to compete for customers. This changed China from a nation of scarcity of agricultural products to one of abundance. It made me realize the power of a market economy, and that the conservatives were wrong about it. Later, when economic reform spread to the urban industrial and financial areas, it ran into trouble and catalyzed the return of many skeptics to power. Around this time, 1992, Deng gave a major speech while traveling in Southern China, which turned things around. It motivated the further buildup and expansion of the market economy nationwide, bringing it into full play, and China's economy was greatly expanded during this period. This clinched my belief in the market economy. I see the market economy, with appropriate government supervision, as the only road to a strong, rich society in China.

KUHN: Some say that with all the material benefits the market economy has brought, it has also had a negative impact on morality. Have greed and the competitive pressure to make money done damage to traditional values?

YAN: I have to say that the most serious damage to traditional Chinese morality happened during the Cultural Revolution. During that terrible decade, people lost sight of their ethical standards. It had a withering effect on the ethics of several generations of Chinese people. Since then we have been rebuilding our national morality. That process is not yet complete, and since it is not, some have been caught up in the blind chase after money. The restoration of morality will take its historical course; its completion will take time.

KUHN: Will you share your personal impressions of what life in China was like during the Cultural Revolution? How did you feel at that time?

YAN: The years of the Cultural Revolution should only be thought of as a crazy period in China's history. The worship of Mao Zedong got out of hand. People simply lost control of their senses. It was truly a crazy era. China survived because of its farmers; in the cities, things were a mess. Workers didn't go to work, students didn't attend classes, but the farmers continued to work very hard. It was the produce of the farmers that kept the nation going. If the farmers had followed the example of the people in the cities, China would long ago have collapsed. During that time, I was in prison. I didn't really know what was going on outside. My impression is that once the Cultural Revolution got going with its terrible ferocity, Mao Zedong tried to end it, but it had gotten out of hand.

KUHN: What kind of thoughts ran through your mind when you were in prison?

YAN: Two feelings dominated all others. The first was that I did not have a chance to express my filial piety for my mother. It was winter when I was arrested, and I noticed that my mother—a very hardworking woman from a farmer's family—wore shoes that had only a very thin lining. I wanted to buy her a pair of cotton-padded shoes. I was unable to do it. All of my family members were arrested, including my mother, my father, and my brother, because of me. My mother died before I had an opportunity to show my love and respect. The second great burden was my feelings for my wife. She wasn't allowed to visit me in prison until the end of my sixth year of incarceration. When she came to see me, I was wearing prisoner's clothing—cotton-padded pants and a black jacket. Prisoners were not allowed belts, to prevent them from committing suicide. When we walked we had to hold our pants up to keep them from dropping. My head was shaved. When I saw her, I said, "You're getting older!" She had been doing forced labor in a rural area, and it had taken its toll—she wasn't very pleased with my remark. She told me I had been "resting" all those years in solitary confinement. We can laugh about it now, but the human tragedy was appalling.

KUHN: Since your wife is here, I'd like to ask her how she felt when she came to visit you in prison and you told her that she looked old.

MRS. YAN: I felt that I really was growing old! I worked very hard in the countryside at that time. My skin was sunburned.

KUHN: How did Mr. Yan look to you?

MRS. YAN: He looked like a Buddhist priest—very young. He was sitting there in solitary confinement with nothing to do. He wasn't working, so he looked very young.

YAN: I did no work in the prison. I took care of myself, but I got very weak.

MRS. YAN: Yes, his face was as pale as a white wall.

YAN: I had even lost some of my ability to converse with people. I was alone so much of the time—in a solitary cell. I spoke with almost no one for seven and a half years. I was in prison six years before I ever saw my family. Before that, I was always alone in that cell. My wife didn't know whether I was alive or dead.

MRS. YAN: That's right, I didn't know whether he was alive or dead. I was working hard in the countryside trying to stay alive.

YAN: Well, I did get a chance to talk to someone in my first year in prison—my interrogators. That was the year I was endlessly grilled by those trying to get me to admit things I had never done.

MRS. YAN: After the first year, there were no more questions to ask him. So they left him alone. My husband would have been very happy if someone, even the interrogators, had asked him some more questions.

YAN: Someday I'll write my remembrances of those terrible times. During my final year in prison, I was allowed visitors. My wife brought me food and books, so I was able to catch up on my reading. But my wife's visits were limited, so she sent other people to visit me—my daughter and niece, my brother and my sister. This brought me much peace of mind. For a long time, my visitors withheld the knowledge that my mother and father had both died. They felt that the news would be too sad for me. Initially, my father and I had been committed to the same prison, under orders from Jiang Qing [Mao's third wife, a ringleader of the Cultural Revolution and one of the infamous Gang of Four]. She said that my father was a spy for the National Party [Kuomintang, led by Mao's archrival, Chiang Kai-shek]. My father's prison number was 67100. Mine was 67124. There were only twenty-three prisoners between us, but because of my solitary confinement I never saw him. My father died after only six months in that prison. My wife knew all this, but she hid her sorrow when she came to visit me. She said everyone was OK, and that I should live my life with strong resolution. The Cultural Revolution was not just a tragedy for our small family but for all of China. I believe that the present generation of Chinese people has a duty to prevent such horror from ever happening again. That's why we are doing so much to promote education. It was ignorance that caused people to blindly worship one person during the Cultural Revolution. That's also why we stress the rule of law today. We enact and strictly abide by certain laws. During the Cultural Revolution, people were arrested without legal justification and in many cases were persecuted to death in our prisons. We cannot let this happen again.

KUHN: What is your primary concern regarding what's happening in China today?

YAN: China is a big country with many people. Things cannot change too fast here. We need stability; we have to be patient. Political reform is lagging behind economic reform, but I have to be patient in my dissatisfaction with this process. Having just been to the United States, I can see how far behind China is. It isn't realistic to expect China to catch up with the United States anytime soon. Besides, America won't stand still and wait for us. We need to speed up our economic growth, not to compete with America but to offer the Chinese people a better living standard than they now have.

KUHN: What kinds of political reform do you feel would be good for China in the near term?

YAN: I think the present administration is streamlining the bureaucratic structure and seeking to create honest government. Much time and energy has been spent in creating intermediate, non-governmental organizations. These can deal with technical issues that were once addressed by the central government. This policy should be aggressively pursued. Right now, self-government is being broadly implemented in villages. Village leaders are elected democratically. From this experience, we will learn how to apply democratic principles on a wider basis. At the right time, democracy will move to the county government level. China is a huge land embracing many nationalities—fifty-six in all. Economic and cultural development levels vary widely throughout the country. As a result, it will take time to implement direct election at higher levels of government. At higher levels, we must learn how to strengthen the role of the National People's Congress, and also the Chinese People's Political Consultative Conference which is very important for supervising the government. It is easy for government officials to become corrupted. Not long ago, it was revealed that an entire municipal government had been corrupted, resulting in smugglers being able to smuggle goods worth some 10 billion *yuan* in a short time. The supervision of government must be strengthened. This is where both the People's Congress and the Political Consultative Conference can do more. I also believe the watchdog role of the media must be strengthened. My personal goal in all this is to do everything I can to help the poor of China achieve a good standard of living.

China Charity Federation

The following section is taken from our PBS documentary. We follow Yan Mingfu on location as he operates the China Charity Federation, from visiting flood-ravaged provinces to setting up job training in cities.

YAN MINGFU: A fair society is one where all people help those who are having difficulties. This is the sign of a progressive and civilized country.

NARRATOR: As the government retreats from many of the services it used to provide, private efforts are being made to fill the gap. In 1998, floods devastated Sichuan province. Yan Mingfu, on behalf of the China Charity Federation, personally delivered millions in flood relief.

YAN: *(viewing flood damage)* The whole thing collapsed?

MAN #1: *(pointing)* Yes, the whole thing collapsed. It slid about a dozen meters.

MAN #2: This is the part where the landslide happened. There will be more landslides in the future.

YAN: Our principle is to do as much as we can to help, even if we are only able to help a single person or a single family. If this family gets out of trouble, it'll be one less that needs help, right?

MAN #2: *(introducing Yan Mingfu to a crowd)* He is our old revolutionary and senior comrade, Yan Mingfu.

YAN: *(to flood victims)* Today we came specifically to meet with all of you and extend consolations from people all over the country.

YAN: *(at CCF headquarters)* The establishment of the China Charity Federation, as I've said, is a product of the entire system of reform in China. With the planned economy in transition to a market economy, people more and more feel that the entire society should be involved in the public welfare. For a long time, people in China associated charity only with the ruling class giving alms to the poor or with the imperialist policies of western countries. After the founding of the People's Republic, charity was characterized as nothing but a way for the ruling class to deceive people.

NARRATOR: Yan grew up in a westernized family devoted to public service. His father headed the Chinese YMCA. Yan himself became a Marxist and Mao's Russian translator.

YAN: Of course everyone thought that being Mao Zedong's translator was the highest honor. But nobody was able to predict what he would say at different times or when he would suddenly recite lines of ancient Chinese poetry or his own poems. And this was something that was extremely challenging for a translator.

NARRATOR: By the 1980s Yan had risen to the highest levels of government. In 1989, he represented the leadership in negotiations with the students demonstrating in Tiananmen Square.

YAN: We talked face-to-face with the students, but unfortunately this effort didn't work, and then the tragedy happened.

NARRATOR: Yan, with other leaders, was removed from office and though he eventually returned to government service, he never regained his former status. Now retired, he devotes his time to projects like retraining laid-off workers.

YAN: How long have you been laid off?

MAN AT COMPUTER: Two years.

YAN: What's your family living on now?

MAN AT COMPUTER: Savings.

NARRATOR: Meanwhile, as the country's largest non-governmental organization, China Charity offers all kinds of help to all kinds of people. Out of a revolving fund, it makes small loans to help people who want to start their own businesses—$750 enabled a woman in Shanghai to open a flower shop.

FLOWER LADY: After I was laid off, I went to learn a skill. I became interested in flowers, so I eventually opened my own shop. On the first day, I sold six basket arrangements and I lost money on all of them. When customers asked, "How much does a basket cost?" I said, "I just opened. I don't know how much they should cost. You decide." They gave me forty *yuan* and I said OK. Later I calculated the cost of my materials and they totaled about forty-five *yuan*. So I lost some money, but I was just starting out and I got better after that.

5 Chinese Characteristics

From Politics to Economics

After the tragedy of Tiananmen, many of us who worked in China were sufficiently unhappy with the government that we would not go back. A year or so later, in the summer of 1990, I was chairing a conference at UCLA on creative and innovative management in large bureaucracies, and I invited a senior official of China's State Science and Technology Commission to participate. When he arrived, several of my colleagues and I verbally jumped him, as if he, a government official, had given the order to go get the students in Tiananmen. It was unfair and doubtlessly inhospitable, but we needed to release our frustrations and he was a convenient scapegoat. "How can you represent a government that attacks its own people?" we wanted to know. "And as a professor"—he taught at a Beijing technical university—"how can you make your own students suffer?"

"We can only influence the future, never change the past," he answered, with surprising equanimity under the circumstances. "China's suffering is now more your fault than mine; you've abandoned us when we most need your help. Your absence gives advantage to reactionary forces." His short reply silenced the criticism and flipped me like a coin. A few months later, I returned to China, and I have been back several times almost every year since.

In those heady days of early 1989, just prior to the crackdown in Tiananmen, politics were openly discussed wherever one went in Beijing; it was the hot topic and it energized virtually every gathering. For several years after the crackdown, politics was forbidden discourse: in the early

135

1990s, I never heard a Chinese speak about politics in the presence of another Chinese, although politics would sometimes be discussed with a foreign friend in secluded circumstances, such as while driving. On these occasions, I would realize that the old fervor was still present—bubbling, as it were, below the surface, waiting, building.

In 1994, returning after a two-year hiatus, I was surprised to find that politics was no longer so interesting to my Chinese friends. They didn't seem to want to talk about Tiananmen anymore. The rage suddenly was economics. "I am perfectly happy for this government to remain in absolute control," confided one of my formerly politically active friends, "as long as they leave me and my company alone so that we can make money." The market had opened, and people had opportunities previously unimaginable. Economic gain was the new Chinese goal.

The Tiananmen movement is now seen as representing the past. The lesson that many Chinese took away from the 1989 tragedy was that politics and economics are sometimes contradictory, and when you are forced to choose between them, politics ought to come in second. Particularly in a time of reform, if you challenge the government, the consequences will be counterproductive. The students of Tiananmen, I am now told, were not being realistic. So the Chinese people have become realistic. Reform needs a peaceful, stable environment to survive and flourish.

Most recently, I have begun to sense a reemergence of political interest among these now thirty-something former students, though it is a more refined political sensibility—more sophisticated, more sensitive to gradual change, and always, above all, seeing stability as a primary good. Perhaps it is the predictable maturing of radical students into mainstream businesspeople with a vested interest in the status quo. Perhaps it is the maturing of Chinese society itself.

Political Structure

Political leadership in China is bifurcated between the government and the Communist Party. This is true at every level—national, provincial, county and municipality, towns and villages—and it is also true, instructively, in large industrial enterprises. The government is headed by a largely ceremonial president (Jiang Zemin), who is technically elected to a five-year term by the National People's Congress, but who in reality has been predetermined by the Party. Actual executive powers rest with the State Council, which is composed of one premier (Zhu Rongji), several vice premiers and state councilors. All commissions and ministries of the central government, all twenty-two provinces, five autonomous regions, the Hong Kong and Macao Special Autonomous Regions, and the four directly reporting municipalities—Beijing, Shanghai, Tianjin, and Chongqing—report to the State Council. The command of the military belongs to the Central Military Commission. Historically, the positions of greatest authority are those of premier and general secretary of the Communist Party (also Jiang Zemin), but individual personalities make their own rules—the best example being Deng Xiaoping who was "paramount leader" without ever holding either position.

The Communist Party of China (CPC) operates, in essence, a parallel governmental structure. The CPC is headed by a general secretary; the National Party Congress is the highest Party organ. The Central Committee, elected by the National Party Congress, in turn elects the Politburo and its Standing Committee, as well as the Party general secretary. Operational authority over the powerful party machinery resides with the Politburo and the Standing Committee, considered the primary source of power in China. Thus President Jiang, by virtue of his position as general secretary of the Party, invests his position as president with real power.

In past years, all real decision-making was carried out by the Communist Party, and then communicated to the government, which followed the CPC's directives without hesitation; in fact, the process was more form than substance since most of China's leaders occupied simultaneous positions in both the Party and the government. In recent years, however, although top leaders continue to hold dual positions, the government has steadily assumed greater responsibility for true decision-making and the trend is expected to continue.

It is commonly assumed by westerners that although China has embarked upon substantial economic reform, it has undergone no political reform. This is not true. Certainly, economic reform has been the priority, but political reform has been real and continuous, if slow. Consider the beginning of relatively free direct elections in rural areas (see "Chinese Democracy: Finally Progress" in the Appendix), the increasing (non-rubber stamp) power of the National People's Congress[13] and provincial

---

[13] The Constitution of the People's Republic of China establishes two national legislative bodies, the National People's Congress (NPC) and the Chinese People's Political Consultative Conference (CPPCC). The constitution (1993) states that the NPC "is the highest organ of state power" and it exercises the legislative power of

people's congresses, the enhanced role of the Chinese People's Political Consultative Conference,[14] or the term limitations (two five-year terms) on the PRC government's senior leaders. To say that more political reform

---

the state. The NPC is "elected [selected] from the provinces, autonomous regions, and municipalities directly under the Central Government and of deputies elected from the armed forces. All minority nationalities are entitled to appropriate representation." "The National People's Congress exercises the following functions and powers: (1) to amend the constitution; (2) to supervise the enforcement of the constitution; (3) to enact and amend basic laws governing criminal offenses, civil affairs, the state organs, and other matters; (4) to elect the president and the vice president of the People's Republic of China; (5) to decide on the choice of the premier of the State Council upon nomination by the president of the People's Republic of China, and on the choice of the vice premiers, state councilors, ministers in charge of ministries or commissions, the auditor general and the secretary general of the State Council upon nomination by the premier; (6) to elect the chairman of the Central Military Commission and, upon nomination by the chairman, to decide on the choice of all other members of the Central Military Commission; (7) to elect the president of the Supreme People's Court; (8) to elect the procurator general of the Supreme People's Procuratorate; (9) to examine and approve the plan for national economic and social development and the report on its implementation; (10) to examine and approve the state budget and the report on its implementation; (11) to alter or annul inappropriate decisions of the Standing Committee of the National People's Congress; (12) to approve the establishment of provinces, autonomous regions, and municipalities directly under the Central Government; (13) to decide on the establishment of special administrative regions and the systems to be instituted there; (14) to decide on questions of war and peace; and (15) to exercise such other functions and powers as the highest organ of state power should exercise."

[14] According to the Chinese constitution, the Chinese People's Political Consultative Conference (CPPCC) "is a broadly based representative organization of the united front which has played a significant historical role, will play a still more important role in the country's political and social life, in promoting friendship with other countries and in the struggle for socialist modernization and for the reunification and unity of the country." The CPPCC is a congress-like organization of diverse elements of Chinese society, which they call "the united front." It is composed of the Communist Party of China (CPC), other noncommunist parties (under the leadership of the CPC), personages without party affiliation, representatives of mass organizations and ethnic minorities, and representatives of Hong Kong, Macao, Taiwan, and overseas Chinese. The CPPCC conducts political consultations on major state policies. The CPPCC's National Committee serves for five years and generally holds its sessions concurrently with the NPC. The Standing Committee is the permanent working body of the CPPCC when the CPPCC is not in session.

is needed is surely correct, but to say that no political reform has been undertaken is surely not.

Slogans

Found everywhere, slogans are a Chinese characteristic worth analyzing. Long a mechanism of mass appeal intended to construct a collective psyche and promote common goals, slogans are now focused on making people more market conscious. Slogans are more maxims than advertising, and they beseech you, or shout at you, from building walls and factory floors; they are strung over the facades of public buildings and adorn the interiors of concert halls. But instead of proclaiming that "U.S. Imperialism is the Enemy of the People," "Workers of the World Unite," or some other dictum of Party proletariat ideology, the slogans in today's China proclaim the importance of the market, urging companies to compete, workers to serve their customers, and, well, everyone to get rich.

"Never Say No to the Market," a corporate slogan of Haier Group, China's largest appliance manufacturer, is one of my favorites. It is festooned lavishly all over Haier's corporate headquarters and factories. Haier President Zhang Ruimin (see page 241), who has lectured at the Harvard Business School, explains: "This slogan is to remind our employees that we are servants of the market, and we should always supply our best service to the market. Some employees tend to think that it is the market that needs us, not we who need the market."

Another slogan, written in bold, elegant characters three feet high, ran on for fifty feet or more as it hung from the ceiling of a textile factory, which it utterly dominated. What several years ago would have articulated something hackneyed about Marxist-proletariat ideals turned out to be "Get the South Korean Order Out in Thirty Days!"

Although the messages of the market-oriented maxims of today differ dramatically from those of the revolution-provoking maxims of Mao's era, the method of communication is the same because the underlying culture is the same. Using slogans to generate a collective psyche and forge common goals is an idea very much central to Chinese tradition. But to have these slogans now focused on making people more market-centered is to embed a subtle contradiction, because being successful in a market economy requires creative competitiveness and an individual initiative that can break the collective mold. One of the ironies of China is that public slogans, this traditional mechanism of collective control, are now encouraging people to become independent and undermine that collective control.

Yang Mianmian: "Never Say No to the Market"

Yang Mianmian, one of a surprising number of female senior executives in China, is a cofounder and the executive vice president of Haier Group, China's leading manufacturer of refrigerators, freezers, air conditioners, televisions, and various other consumer electronic products. With annual revenues of $3.2 billion in 1999 (including $1.4 billion in exports sold in 160 countries), Haier's stated goal is to become one of the world's five hundred largest companies, which reflects Chinese national pride (one of our overarching themes) as well as corporate aggressiveness. For example, Haier now has a 25 percent share of the small refrigerator market (used as hotel minibars) in the United States. I interviewed Ms. Yang, who was trained as an engineer, as we walked around Haier's modern corporate headquarters in Qingdao, adorned with all manner of corporate slogans, and as we sat in a kitchen showroom surrounded by Haier products.

ROBERT KUHN: Why is Haier's slogan "Never Say No to the Market"?

YANG MIANMIAN: This phrase is the clearest expression of Haier's corporate culture. We display it everywhere in our factories and offices. We focus on the market; we emphasize serving our customers. We think *for* our customers—we think of things that may not occur to them. If we know Chinese needs better than the Japanese and Americans do, we will do better in the Chinese market than Japanese and Americans will. In a competitive market, success depends on who knows customer needs better. Customers are attracted to those companies that know their needs sooner and are able to solve their problems more efficiently. The market is all-consuming to us, and we inculcate that sense in all our employees.

KUHN: How are new products developed?

YANG: First, we learn from the market what customers need and what problems they want to solve. Then we find the most advanced technology available and we turn it into products through a quality service system. The results are new products. For example, we are studying whether the Chinese market needs digital video disks (DVD)—since an earlier VCD technology [a lower capacity CD] is already widespread in China—and if they do, what kind of DVD do they need, and so forth. When new products go to market, we not only make profits but also obtain further information that will enable us to develop yet newer products. This enables the company to improve continuously.

KUHN: How do Haier's divisions work together for the common good?

YANG: Each division takes care of its own business. For example, the refrigerator division is responsible for refrigerator design from start to finish, provided that the products are intended to be in the market within three to five years. But products that are five to nine years out will be designed in our central technology center.

KUHN: Haier allocates substantial resources to its new product development center.

YANG: Yes, and for good reasons. On the upper level, we have a central research institute, on the lower level, we have several institutes that research basic technologies. We also have a new product exploration center that investigates new products, listens to feedback from customers, and gathers new information from international markets

KUHN: How is your central research institute organized?

YANG: Our central research institute studies how to solve problems our products may face in the market after five years; it has several centers. For example, the technology cooperation center studies advanced technologies in China, and the science and technology center studies advanced technologies abroad. Our product development center has eleven specialized research institutes. They're concerned with refrigerating storage, refrigerators, small appliances, electronic products—there are research institutes for almost everything. There's also a production-method development center, where we determine which equipment, work lines, and molds are needed to make new products. We also have an analysis and examination center, where we determine whether the performance of our products conforms to international standards.

KUHN: What are "the three Cs?"

YANG: Haier's electronic business sells computers, communications equipment, and consumer electronics products. The three Cs also denote three qualities: comfortable, confident, and content.

KUHN: Can you describe your personal management style?

YANG: I look for problems at the basic level, talking with customers and workers, and then I discuss how to solve them with higher-level personnel.

KUHN: Haier has grown through mergers and acquisitions. How do you buy companies?

YANG: First, we consider only companies that conform to our specific needs. Then we look at the condition of the target company. Is it totally dead, in its heyday, or newly born? Next, we ascertain who will run the company after we acquire it. And if we know who will assume the leadership of the acquired company, we want this person to participate in the negotiations as well. I'm deeply involved in the discussions of all issues and in the execution of decisions. We react rapidly when competing with others in buying a company. We compete on speed.

KUHN: Is Haier aggressive in acquiring companies?

YANG: We don't want to devour any company. If we decide to purchase a specific company, we have to be able to break down the barriers between that company and Haier. It's critical that the Haier corporate culture is appreciated and implemented. In the past, a company that made refrigerators couldn't possibly make television sets. Now we can acquire a television company and we can make television sets.

KUHN: Your goal is to become one of the five hundred largest companies in the world. How do you expand efficiently?

YANG: First, we have to be strong. Only when you are strong can you be big. Haier's president, Zhang Ruimin, and I agree that we should learn from the strongest companies in the world in order to strengthen our own company.

KUHN: Haier has become international.

YANG: We have companies in the Philippines, Indonesia, Malaysia, and Yugoslavia. We are one of the first Chinese companies to build a manufacturing plant in the United States [a $30 million refrigerator factory in Camden, South Carolina].

KUHN: What is Haier's corporate structure?

YANG: Haier is a collective, owned by the employees, but no employee actually owns stock. Theoretically, being a collective means that everyone has a share of the profits, but in reality all profits remain in the company to fund further development; they're not distributed. But I want this structure to change: I want to enable the workers to own a portion of the shares individually.

KUHN: Tell us about Haier's distinctive corporate logo.

YANG: In 1984, we imported a refrigerator from Germany; it was pure white, and someone suggested that we put something on it to make it look more attractive. So we created this trademark of two young boys, obviously friends, one with black hair and one with yellow hair. The black-haired boy represents the Chinese, the yellow-haired boy represents the Europeans, and the image represents the cooperation between Chinese and Europeans. The thumbs-up means that Haier wants to be number one. People can always tell a Haier product by the corporate symbol of these two boys.

KUHN: As a female senior executive, describe the role of women in China.

YANG: In Chinese traditional culture, women are seen as weak. The stereotype is that women are not capable. But the current market economy gives unprecedented opportunity to women. Some women want to prove that they're just as good as men, and they're working hard to achieve commercial success. The more pressure they face, the more motivated they are.

KUHN: How do you interact with Haier employees?

YANG: I'm among the oldest in Haier. My employees are younger than I am, so they're not as experienced. I deal with difficulties much better than they do.

KUHN: Would you mind telling us about your personal life?

YANG: I have a happy family. Four generations live together: my mother-in-law, my children, and my grandchildren. My husband was my classmate at the university. When we came to Qingdao, he went to work on train engines and I went to work on bus motors. Later I changed to refrigerators. My children are all grown up; my elder daughter has a child. I'm the most malleable, agreeable one in the family. I don't have much time to be with the family, so I accept the lowest status there. I don't get into many conflicts, because I usually listen to everyone else.

KUHN: Do you cook?

YANG: I cook sometimes. I grew up in Shanghai, and Shanghai people are very picky about their food. When I want to have a good dinner, I'll cook. And I'm a good cook—every time I make dinner, the family eats a lot.

KUHN: What do your children do?

YANG: Both my children work in trading. One works for a foreign-owned company, the other works for an import and export company. They're much luckier than my generation was.

KUHN: How did the Cultural Revolution affect you?

YANG: My husband and I graduated from college in 1963, a few years before the Cultural Revolution broke out. All intellectuals suffered; we wanted very much to do things then, but there was no chance. We were sent out to do labor—not brain labor, but physical labor. Our knowledge was useless. It was very painful. Therefore, when the Cultural Revolution was finished, we cherished our opportunities and made the best use of them. We wanted to develop ourselves and fulfill our goals. When I was at the old home appliance company, I worked for our president, Zhang Ruimin. I was in charge of importing new technologies. When President Zhang came to Haier Refrigerator, he brought me with him, and we started to build the company.

KUHN: How do you balance corporate life and family life?

YANG: The company's kitchen is my career; my family's kitchen is my life. When career and life are in conflict, I subordinate my life to my career. Only when the company's kitchen sells well will my career develop and my family's kitchen have everything. The balance between life and career is always imperfect, but I do my best. To me, happiness depends on whether or not I can do things I want.

KUHN: When you are busy with the company's kitchen, do you have time for your family's kitchen?

YANG: The ones who work in my family's kitchen usually are my husband, my mother-in-law, and my children. To me, my career is bigger and more important than my life.

KUHN: How do you compare your generation to the younger generation?

YANG: The younger generation has better opportunities, and those in my company work very hard. They never experienced the hardships we did, but we weren't as hardworking as they are.

Class

Every country has its stereotypes. In China, people tend to divide themselves into northerners and southerners. Southerners are seen as delicate, northerners as coarse. Stereotypes are traditional, but the idea of classes is new in modern China.

In Mao's China, people were equal—equally poor, sharing, as it were, the same iron rice bowl. (There were hierarchical differences in society, but people were differentiated by political stature, not economic strength.) By the mid-1980s, as reform gathered strength, a good number of Chinese were no longer poor, and a gap, the inevitable result of a market economy, began opening between them and those who were less well off—a gap that has been widening.

Class differences now appear everywhere in China—expressed openly by housing, cars, clothes, entertainment—just as they do in America. Rich people drive Mercedeses, own several houses, spend their leisure time in expensive restaurants and clubs, and send their children to study abroad, while the poor still struggle for the basic necessities of life.

Not all of the privileged children are sent abroad. The privatization of Chinese education is a new phenomenon. In Mao's era, all schools were public and controlled directly by the government. The reform in education began in the early 1990s, and in 1992 the government gave universities the right to set their own tuition. Today wealthy Chinese can use their money and social connections to get their children into private schools, which are very expensive (more than an ordinary worker's annual salary) and provide a much higher ratio of teachers to students.

Chinese take education extremely seriously, sending their children when they are very young—even at two or three years old—to special schools to learn music and art. Rich people see their children's education as another kind of investment. Good education today, they believe, means more earning power tomorrow.

Reinforcing this emphasis on education is the Chinese policy on population control. Since 1973 when China began to promote family planning, more and more families have only one child, and it is not uncommon for parents and both sets of grandparents to dote on that child, showering it with educational aids. Computers are *de rigueur* in such households, and single children in China today are called, for good reason, "little emperors and empresses" (see the Appendix).

Although the majority of Chinese are far better off today, the great disparity between wealth and poverty is an overt phenomenon, especially in coastal areas. At the beginning of reform, the government was in a dilemma. On the one hand, it wished to encourage individuals to become rich and thus take the lead in developing the country's economy—which is what Deng Xiaoping proposed. On the other hand, it also desired that China would remain a socialist nation, and social classes were not supposed to arise in such a nation. Overall, China may be richer than ever before, but the distribution of wealth is much more unequal; the vexing problem today is not the poverty level but the growing gap between rich and poor. According to official statistics, approximately 50 million of China's 1.3 billion people live in poverty, which is defined for a family as having a yearly income below five hundred *yuan*. The new, upwardly mobile middle class in China is estimated to be about 100 million people.

Economic reform has meanwhile narrowed the old gap between cities and countryside. In terms of wealth or income, the inhabitants of some rural areas are now even better off than their neighbors in the cities, and there are city residents today who want to move to the countryside because they see more opportunity there.

China is in the midst of an immense historic transformation, and there are many reform regulations that are not tightly structured. The system is chaotic, and people have become wealthy by exploiting loopholes in these regulations. Examples are the acquisition of state-owned assets or government contracts in non-competitive bidding, sweetheart loans from government banks, importing goods with lower than official tariffs, exporting goods at very low costs in order to expatriate wealth, and circulating money from inside China to outside China and then right back in again to take advantage of incentives given to "foreign" investors. The government and its academic advisors recognize these and other such problems, and they are defining policies, such as redistribution via taxation and some form of social security, to alleviate the extreme disparity between the rich and the poor—a disparity that they realize could eventually result in political and social instability. The issue is social justice: how to divide the wealth among the people fairly; how to balance the wealth between coastal and inland China; how to raise the prospects of the poor and make them self-sufficient.

In its thirty years of planned economy, China created an egalitarian culture, where the only people you ever encountered were people just like yourself. Thus, when reform arrived, to know someone among your friends, colleagues, or relatives who was obviously better off than you were made you suspicious and jealous—"red eye disease" is what Chinese people call it. It is a disease that poses a potential threat to the new social contract between the Chinese government and its people.

Yang Millionaire: Shanghai's "King of Stocks"

For centuries, Shanghai has been China's window to the West, the center of its commerce, trade, and industry. The city was "opened" after the Opium War in 1840, and held the distinction of being the most important metropolis in Asia for the next hundred years. Although Shanghai's economic and cultural influence developed before Hong Kong, many merchants and financiers eventually moved to the British colony seeking stability in the face of the mainland's many wars and revolutions. However, during the early 1990s, the development of Shanghai took off; it's now leading China's economic development and will soon replace Hong Kong as the "Head of the Dragon"—that is to say, Greater China's most important financial center. In the 1920s and 1930s, Shanghai was called the "Paris of the Orient." It was widely influenced by foreign cultures and Shanghai natives were well-known for their entrepreneurial spirit. As this most cosmopolitan of China's cities continues its resurgence, that spirit is once again flourishing. There is more to be had, more to be done, and more to be earned—and people want more. For many in Shanghai, the stock market is seen as a road to the affluence they're just beginning to taste. This risk-be-damned mentality is exemplified by individuals like Old Xiao, a retired engineer who is a passionate amateur stock trader, and the whimsically nicknamed Yang Millionaire—perhaps the first, and certainly one of the most famous of China's stock market tycoons. CCTV camera crews tracked both Xiao and Yang extensively, and below is the transcript of their part of our PBS documentary.

NARRATOR: Stock trading was first permitted in 1990. Today, 44 million Chinese have opened stock market accounts, buying and selling the shares of over nine hundred companies. From housewives and retirees to traders and speculators, buying and selling has become an infatuation.

OLD XIAO: *(at brokerage office watching stock screens)* Dong Ting Enterprise would be a good buy now.

FRIEND: Dong Ting is not really so good.

OLD XIAO: No, no, it's lifted up three other stocks.

FRIEND: Maybe you're right.

OLD XIAO: Different kinds of people come to the stock market. One is we old people. When we can't find better entertainment, we come here. It's a place for us to go when we want to get out of the house and chat with other people. We don't buy a lot of stocks. If we profit, it's a small profit. Another kind are those who come here purely for profits. They invest a lot and profit a lot.

NARRATOR: Yang Millionaire is a figure inconceivable in the old planned economy—a man famous and respected for getting rich.

MAN ON TRAIN (WITH YANG MILLIONAIRE): I've never met you but I've heard about you, and I thought you must be quite a character. Everyone else is making small investments but you are making big deals. And you have bodyguards following you everywhere. That's unheard of.

YANG MILLIONAIRE: My nickname is more famous than my real name.

MAN ON TRAIN: Yes, your nickname is "Yang Millionaire."

YANG MILLIONAIRE: Nowadays, it's a market economy. People who use their brains rule others. I think that my stock tactics come from what I learned from Chairman Mao in junior high. Mao said, "You won't know about pears if you don't taste one." This fits with the modern thinking that you measure your ability through action. You won't know if you don't try.

NARRATOR: As China moves to a market economy, the government can't keep up its old commitment to provide food, clothing, and shelter for everyone—from cradle to grave. So, facing an uncertain economic future, some risk their savings in the fascinating pursuit of profits.

OLD XIAO: I was getting older and I realized that I was losing my ability to go out and work. So, a few years ago, when Deng Xiaoping encouraged us to try the stock market, I decided to do it because I need more money for my retirement. Otherwise how am I going to afford to live?

NARRATOR: Once Xiao Hui—or "Old Xiao" as his friends call him—could have counted on free medical care, an apartment and plenty of food in his retirement. He can't expect these any longer. So even out for his morning exercise, he carries his radio to keep tabs on the market.

OLD XIAO: *(stretching outside)* In order to play stocks, you've got to have a good healthy body. The brain has to be clear. And you have to know the country's economic policy.

OLD XIAO: The stock market in East Asia went way down.

FRIEND: What about Indonesia?

OLD XIAO: Indonesia is the worst. Their problems are economic and political.

OLD XIAO: Just before I retired I was making about three hundred *yuan* a month. I wanted to play the stock market, so I saved money like crazy. I didn't do anything but save. At first, of course, I lost money because I had no experience and the market was up and down all over the place. But after a while I gradually understood more and more and started to make a little money. Now, I study the market. I read seven newspapers a day. You know, I really feel the improvement in myself. As the stock market improves, I improve. But honestly, I'm not very good at stock investing. The good traders make a hundred times more than I do.

YANG MILLIONAIRE: Hello. We should be buying soon. Is it at 2.3? See how patient we've been.

NARRATOR: Yang Millionaire embodies the short history of the Chinese stock market. He got in at the beginning, figured it out, and made a killing.

YANG MILLIONAIRE: It's the goal of my life to become the King of Stocks. But I might not be able to reach it, because it all depends on circumstances. For example, without the new economic reform policy I would have ended my days in a steel factory as a tiny screw in the communist machine.

NARRATOR: Yang had been a Red Guard during the Cultural Revolution. As a young steelworker, Yang was wrongly accused of pilfering. In disgust, he quit his job and began to look for something else to do.

YANG MILLIONAIRE: Then I read in the newspaper that the government had approved the formation of a stock exchange. I went to the market to watch and learn.

DR. ZHENG SHIPING (POLITICAL SCIENTIST AT THE UNIVERSITY OF VERMONT): It was very difficult in the beginning; most Chinese didn't even know what a stock market was. Sure, the market had existed before in the '20s and '30s, but by 1990, only very few people were still around who knew what the stock market was all about.

NARRATOR: No trading rules had been established, and prices fluctuated by region. Yang got the idea of buying government bonds where the prices were low and taking them to sell where the prices were high.

YANG MILLIONAIRE: I went to the Bank of China for advice and the answer I got was, "We don't really know because there's no regulations yet. Trade or don't trade; you have to decide for yourself." I'd read in the newspaper that the police department had established a special unit. So I got the idea to hire two of them to watch me while I was trading. If they didn't arrest me I figured it proved that I wasn't doing anything illegal. When I think about it now, it was just a silly trick. But I wanted to protect myself.

NARRATOR: Within ten months, Yang was a millionaire. But in a society still committed to socialism, it wasn't acceptable to have so much money or so much power.

DR. LU XIAOBO (POLITICAL SCIENTIST AT COLUMBIA UNIVERSITY): You've got to understand that after going through more than thirty years of a socialist economy, people in China had created a kind of egalitarian culture. In other words, people wanted everyone to be the same. If anyone became richer, others would get red eye disease—feelings of inferiority and jealousy. As a result, people like Yang Millionaire became the subject of much debate in society.

YANG MILLIONAIRE: I was trading in such volume that when I sold, the market started to go down. Zhu Rongji ordered me to be watched. He said, "In the stock market there is a really rich guy named Yang Millionaire." I was considered a bad citizen. Back in 1990, stocks were thought of only as a product of capitalism, and non-investors thought that stock trading would lead to bankruptcy. These misconceptions came from years of communist miseducation.

NARRATOR: As a young man, Xiao worked at a military air base in central China. In 1965, at the beginning of the Cultural Revolution, Xiao was accused of going against the Party. He was jailed for ten years.

OLD XIAO: The Cultural Revolution was a disaster. Oh, don't even talk about it! To what extent were people tortured? They beat people up, of course. They beat me badly. It was common at that time. People were so skinny they didn't even look like human beings anymore. They would break all your bones and knock out your teeth until you fainted. Then they would use cigarettes to burn you and wake you up again.

ZHAO QIZHENG (MINISTER OF THE INFORMATION OFFICE OF THE STATE COUNCIL): Stability is more important than anything else in China and it's what every Chinese person wants. This is what we learned from the experiences we've had this century. China is a big yet underdeveloped country. Stability is extremely important.

YANG MILLIONAIRE: The Communist Party now is different from before. In the past, they didn't have anything, but then they got the whole country. Back then they wanted all poor people to unite. Now, they don't want poor people to be united. Now they want rich people to support the nation's development. If you lose your job and don't have any money, they are afraid of you. If you go the Maoist route and try to rebel now, they won't allow it. They want stability now. And who's the most stable? The rich, of course. People who have just purchased stock want a stable society so they can live happily.

NARRATOR: People like Old Xiao are being encouraged by the government to take their savings out of the banks and invest in the market in order to sustain economic growth and maintain stability. Buying stocks is easier and far less regulated than in the United States; in fact, it's as simple as going to an ATM machine.

DR. ZHENG: People have an impression that the Chinese stock market will never collapse because the Chinese government will not allow it to happen. They think their investment may go up and down in the short run but they'll never lose the whole thing. So they feel it's like long-term savings.

WOMAN SECURITIES BRANCH MANAGER: I don't think that all this investing is a good thing because in China the stock market is still in its infancy. It just isn't as fully developed as in other countries. The regulations aren't what they should be yet, and mutual fund investment just started. Average people are simply experimenting.

OLD XIAO: Sometimes I do worry about losing my savings. When the market goes really low I can't sleep. But I don't talk much with my family about my trading. I talk more with my friends outside.

OLD XIAO: It doesn't matter if it takes a long time. You buy when stocks are low, when there is a negative opinion about playing the market. It's a revolution going on right now. Things in China can only get better. But I'm not playing the market to improve China. All the profit I make will eventually be mine.

YANG MILLIONAIRE: *(lecturing to a large audience)* Now, look at the stock market. Me, I made a million, but he *(pointing at a fellow in the audience)* lost a lot. I mean a lot.

NARRATOR: The gospel of personal profit is what Yang Millionaire preaches. He travels widely, teaching eager listeners how to make money in stocks—and maybe how to avoid losing it.

WOMAN: Should I change my stock now?

YANG MILLIONAIRE: If you want to go for the long term you should definitely change now. Last year when I gave a speech here the market was low. I told everyone to buy Da Tong at ten *yuan* a share. Now it has doubled in value. You have to have patience with your investments. You can't keep asking, "How come the price hasn't gone up yet?"

WOMAN #2: It's only been a short time since I started listening to his [Yang's] lectures. But I've already come to realize how wrong my trading in the market has been. I bought the ones that I shouldn't have bought and sold the ones that I shouldn't have sold.

OLD MAN #2: If I had traded according to [Yang's] recommendations, for sure my investment returns would have been better. I haven't made any money yet. I am stuck with my old investments that have dropped in price.

YANG MILLIONAIRE: If the price goes down, then don't sell it. If the price goes up, then you can sell. This isn't a big problem. You should figure it out yourself. Right? Someone like me who is famous all over the country has been created by the society; it isn't because of any special talent I have. Very possibly, my desire for change was stronger than others. But I was born in Shanghai and the stock market opened in Shanghai, and that's how I became who I am today. I'm simply a product of my time.

Women

Throughout Chinese history until modern times, women had always lived in the shadow of men, subservient and dependent. A cruel expression of this unequal relationship was the Chinese custom of foot binding, an ancient practice that prevented a woman's feet from growing and caused severe life-long disability. Girls' feet were bound with meters of cloth so tightly and early in life that they would resemble a "three-inch golden lotus."[15]

It was Mao Zedong who said that women "lift half the sky" and the communist revolution gave women many rights. Mao's initiative, personified by his ambitious wife, Jiang Qing, had significant impact on women in the cities. In rural areas, it was more theory than fact, however, and most women continued to be treated poorly. Their education lagged behind that of men, and there were more restrictions on their behavior. With the advent of economic reform, women began entering the market

---

[15] The practice of foot binding originated in the palace of the last king of the Latter Tang Dynasty (C.E. 923–936), at a time when normal big feet were considered alien to feudal virtue and feminine beauty, and continued even when it was banned by the Manchurians who established the Qing Dynasty (1644–1911). Before a girl turned three years old, all her toes but the first had been broken and the soles of her feet were bent in extreme concavity. Most couldn't dance and many could hardly walk. Foot binding ceased in the twentieth century with the end of imperial dynasties and the increasing influence of Western fashion. In remote mountainous areas, women still had their feet bound even after New China was founded in 1949. In 1998, the Xinhua News Agency announced that the last factory to manufacture shoes for bound-feet women had ended production.

economy and finding new opportunities and challenges. Nevertheless, the new market-oriented emphasis on efficiency eventually resulted in lay-offs, and more women were laid off than men.

Traditionally in China, women have been considered less capable than men; thus, the phenomenon of rural women leaving home is seen by many Chinese men as a challenge to the male domination of society. Whether these female fugitives are young girls seeking better opportunities or middle-aged women fleeing unhappy marriages, they are all departing to seek economic independence from their fathers and husbands. In general, economic reform has brought unprecedented opportunities to country women.

But the situation is complex. After rural women enter the market, they become cheap labor and can be exploited by the market system. Though rural women are asserting and improving their positions at home, they have become most vulnerable to the buffeting of market economics. Young rural girls generally work as babysitters or maids for intellectual or rich families in the cities, and after some time many marry local boys and settle down. Increasingly, country girls are marrying city boys—another way in which the separation between countryside and cities is breaking down.

For China's educated urban women, however, the reforms are a different game. They can become almost whatever they want to become, and it is they who have benefited most from Mao's "women lift half the sky" dictum. Though it has not been uncommon for women to be running large departments of major enterprises or government agencies or being members of congress,[16] the new phenomenon is surely women starting their own companies. Because it is so novel and untraditional, private business seems to be the playing field most equal for women and many have founded their own companies, from flower shops and furniture stores, to real estate firms and engineering services, to technology companies and Internet ventures.

Coterminous with reform, a women's liberation movement in China has been developing in China, under the guidance and leadership, as they say, of the Communist Party and the government, which established various women's associations to support the broader goal of national develop-

---

[16] Women occupy many senior positions in China—ministers of government, secretary generals, enterprise leaders, rocket scientists, senior generals in the military—for example, Mme. Wu Yi, current state councilor and former minister of foreign trade; Mme. Chen Zhili, minister of education, and Mme. Zhu Lilan, minister of science and technology. Chinese women make up almost 20 percent of the seats in the National Congress.

ment. But recently, female organizations are tailoring their missions according to the characteristics and needs of women, a position advocated for years by Chinese feminist scholars. Programs to protect rural women from physical hardships and psychological stress are an example; initiated by women themselves, these programs, while they try to get financial support from the government, are not designed or guided by the government.

Arguments about the potential benefits of divorce in China—that dissolving unhappy marriages may serve society more efficiently than keeping bound those depressed from unfulfilled marriages—is changing the relative status of women. Not only is divorce increasing in number, but also the social stigma is being mitigated. No longer must wives suffer in silence as they endure boorish, domineering, indecent, or unfaithful husbands. Women are taking an increasingly active role in open debates on relevant public policy issues, such as the ease or difficulty of granting divorces and whether the "guilty party" should be punished (see "Reflections on Divorce" in the Appendix, page 285).

The infanticide of baby girls through drowning or abandonment is a hideous practice left over from feudal society, and there is acrimonious debate on how frequently it still occurs. It seems clear that since China is still a poor country, these abominable acts have not been stamped out entirely in remote areas, though they occur far less than they used to. Certainly, the Chinese government has passed laws that forbid all acts of infanticide and has instituted programs to combat these criminal offenses. The National Coordination Committee on Women and Children, operating under the State Council, is one of a number of organizations responsible for children's welfare. Civil affairs departments are responsible for the adopting and caring of orphans. At present there are 40,000 welfare institutions, including orphanages, in China's rural areas, and hundreds of orphanages in urban areas.

Regarding the growing independence of women, one conversation I had with a young female beneficiary of the economic reforms was particularly telling. I was interviewing an assistant manager in a factory owned by Legend Holdings, China's largest computer manufacturer and a highly progressive company. She was a petite young woman in her late twenties—wide-eyed, energetic, and focused intensely on her work. She had risen quickly and was now supervising more than two hundred, largely male workers on a PC assembly line. She was delighted to show me and our China Central Television (CCTV) crews around Legend's test facilities, where, she told us proudly, the quality control was up to the highest international standards.

After discussing the basics of her job and life, I asked her what she would do if Legend failed to reward her financially or give her the promotions she deserved. She replied that such neglect would be unlikely, since Legend was an entrepreneurial company that rewarded good performance and in fact had treated her well. "But," she said without hesitation and still on camera, "if they fail to do right by me in the future, then I'll quit and get a better job." She made her point with a grittiness that one would not have expected from a young female assistant factory manager in China speaking to national television.

Her simple comment was, to me, indicative of what's happening to most Chinese people regardless of their gender. It voices the increasing confidence that ordinary Chinese feel about themselves and their country. Here was one ambitious young lady who was not only willing to walk out of one of China's most respected enterprises if her needs weren't met, but she was also unafraid to say so, right in the face of an unknown foreigner working cozily with CCTV's camera crews. For all she knew, her comments might have been on that night's evening news! I know no better personification of the New China.

Rural Women: Shifting Paradigms

Economic change often forces personal change, and the points of greatest volatility and uncertainty in a changing society always occur where categories intersect. Women from China's countryside, who stand at a crucial juncture of gender and class, have little education or experience with the complexities of urban life. In the course of producing our documentary, we spoke with a group of educated urban women who have formed a nongovernment organization to help their rural sisters adapt. Song Mei and Long Di are the older leaders of this support group. All the others are young rural women working and living alone in Beijing.

SONG MEI: Our organization is called "Rural Women Knowing All," and we are the only ones who focus on rural women in China.

GIRL: I don't need to work today; it's Sunday. My employer took her kids to school today herself so I decided to come here.

SONG MEI: Mostly we help rural youngsters adjust to city life.

TONG XIUTAO: Farming at home taught me nothing. Instead I wanted to see the world and experience life here.

CHU HAIER: It was like a dream to me to see Beijing—Tiananmen Square, the Great Wall, and the Forbidden City.

NARRATOR: On Sundays, "Rural Women Knowing All" offers workshops on the problems of living in the city without family support.

LONG DI: *(addressing about twenty-five girls)* We're going to talk about very personal issues today: dating and marriage. It may not be your problem. It could be somebody else's. By talking about it, you may learn something useful, and you'll be helping out the girls around you.

LONG DI: *(talking privately)* Normally, it's difficult for people to adapt to a new way of life and it's natural for them to lose heart. They think that they're not pretty enough or that they don't work hard enough, and they tend to lose confidence and hope.

WONG XIANGFEN: *(speaking to the entire group)* I heard a story from a girl working at a bookstore. The girl was being harassed by the manager. How can her girlfriend help her?

SONG MEI: The famous female author, Bing Xin, said, "You are a human being first, and then you are a woman." Many girls said that they had never heard this type of thing before. When they were home they were not human beings; they were something less—country girls. However, when they came to the cities, they had an opportunity to be in contact with a more sophisticated type of woman, and this change was huge.

GIRL IN DENIM: There is a deeply-rooted mentality in the village to treat boys better than girls; therefore girls' education is taken lightly. It's felt that an investment in a girl's education will be lost because they'll marry and move out. But in Beijing there's no such discrimination.

LONG DI: If a boy shows his love for a girl, but the girl doesn't want to accept it, how can she politely refuse him without hurting his pride? This question comes from someone here. Let me ask, if this were you, what would you say to him?

GIRL STANDING: *(laughing sheepishly)* Well, actually, I did write this question.

LONG DI: OK, pretend you are the boy. How would you feel if the girl said that to you?

GIRL STANDING: I would feel hurt.

LONG DI: *(to one of the few boys in the room)* How about you? How would you feel?

BOY STANDING: *(speaking casually, almost smugly)* I wouldn't think it's such a big deal. Flowers grow everywhere; I would go find another.

LONG DI: See, they'll go look for others. Why should we worry about them? *(All laugh.)*

CHAI XIUTAO: Parents in the village generally worry more about their daughters than their sons. Our parents are particularly worried that we can't protect ourselves when dealing with the opposite sex.

LONG DI: Back home, your parents probably decided whom you would marry. Now you're in the city, a new world, and you find yourself wanting to marry somebody else. How do you face the pressure from home?

CHAI XIUTAO: It's hard fighting with our parents. It's like arms fighting with legs.

LONG DI: But today's modernization inevitably separates you from your parents. Their lives were poorer than ours, which are improving every day. We no longer just want to survive; we want something more refined. Falling in love is not for the purpose of seeking a marriage partner. On the contrary, it is a process of seeking yourself.

SONG MEI: *(reflecting privately)* Economic reform brought the most changes to rural women. They are getting the chance to change their fates and lead lives very different from that of their mothers.

Guanxi

In China, *guanxi*—a special mixture of good relationships, connections, and working friendships—is particularly important for doing business. The critical role of personal feelings when people work together is an ingrained part of Chinese culture, and if you are a foreigner intending to conduct business in China it is necessary to understand how it happens. So what is *guanxi*, a term both endearing and pejorative that characterizes Chinese business and is often misunderstood by (or simply unknown to) westerners?

Simply put, *guanxi* is the reliance on relationships—on the personal experience and friendship of people who have known and trusted one another over time. The Chinese prefer to do business with people they know and can rely upon. (*Guanxi* can also be indirect; a good introduction from the right person can prevent endless frustration.) When you do almost anything in China—build a factory, for example—you must be sufficiently familiar with the members of the local government. Only then will they be willing to give you the needed support. You also need good connections with local businessmen, so that you can more easily get contracts or sell your products. All this is *guanxi.*

Here is an example of *guanxi* in action. Dr. He Zhiyi, an elegant and thoughtful professor of economics and business at Beijing University, is the founder of Golden Tech, an innovative and growing software company. His strategy is to merge and integrate a series of small software companies in order to build sufficient critical mass to enable the company to go public, raising capital for accelerated expansion. But in China, being able to go public and raise money in the stock market requires permission from the government. In fact, more than permission is needed, since there are strict quotas which are allocated to different interest groups, from provinces to ministries. Professor He told me that the key person in a certain provincial government who decides which local company is selected to go public under their allocation is a personal friend from university days and that this relationship would facilitate the process for Golden Tech. He added that in China, with the market economy so new and inefficient, personal relationships enable such officials to make better, more informed decisions. "Because he has known me and my character for so long," Professor He said, "he could feel confident that I would maintain high standards of business and morality."

Good *guanxi* is best built over time; the Western (particularly American) proclivity to conclude business rapidly is considered barbaric by the Chinese, though they are far too polite to say so to foreigners. The practice of having many meals together before doing business in China is more than relaxation; it is a vital part of the long process of building *guanxi.*

Perhaps *guanxi*'s most conspicuous expression is by the so-called princelings of China—the children of senior Party leaders who have prospered in the market economy by making good use of their connections. Much maligned for taking advantage of their positions, history may record that it was this enterprising group of young people who, in the 1980s, first brought new ideas about markets and business to China. Educated from the late 1970s at the best foreign universities, often in the U.S., these princelings were often naïve and usually self-serving, but they were pioneers nonetheless. It was because they were princelings that they had the courage and confidence to try all kinds of new things. Though they engineered many failures, they did help establish the Chinese stock and bond markets, the listing of "red chip" companies in Hong Kong, and the forming of new-style companies. No moral judgment is intended, but princeling contribution to reform, particularly in the early years, should be recognized.

The obvious criticism is that if friendships override competence, then the results can be disastrous—and, indeed, much of the Asian financial crisis in the late 1990s was said to be related to such "crony capitalism," when, for example, bad loans were made to good friends. The abuses of *guanxi*, especially when government relations are important for business, are glaring.

But when I hear reform-minded Chinese say that the elimination of *guanxi* would reflect a maturing of the market economy, I grow a little sad, because a distinguishing mark of Chinese culture would be irreparably lost. There is something pleasant about doing business with associates you know well—real people, with whom you have shared lunches and dinners, everyone eating from the same dishes, and many a laugh. There is something comforting in the confidence that you will not lose their business because of one or another minor misunderstanding—or that good *guanxi* will prevent a competitor from stealing your business with a slightly better price. In theory, *guanxi* can make bad economics;[17] in practice, it does make good culture.

The Chinese Way

A Chinese friend was trying to explain the differences between the Chinese and Western ways of thinking. "Compare your knives and forks with our chopsticks," he said. "Knives and forks are quite practical for modern food, but Chinese believe they look and work like weapons, reflecting the Western proclivity for cutting and stabbing. Chopsticks are an elegant, refined way of gathering and eating food, but Westerners believe they are

---

[17] *Guanxi* does not necessarily make bad economics in China; indeed, it can make very good economics, solidifying business relationships. *Guanxi* makes bad economics only when it replaces or substitutes for everything else, such as a good business sense, financial logic and accountability, respect for laws and regulations, and an understanding of the overall political climate.

impractical and hard to use, reflecting Chinese inscrutability." Stereotypes invade even the tabletop.

One M&A-related incident provides insight into the process of change in China. Some years ago, after I began speaking out about the importance of M&A for China, but before it became officially accepted policy, I was asked by a mid-level official in a relevant ministry to give an in-depth interview about M&A to the largest circulation business and finance newspaper. The official asked me to comment on how M&A works in the United States and how it would be helpful for China's economic reform, particularly how it might bring efficiency to industrial structure and business organizations. The interview went well, and I was quoted reasonably accurately, but one sentence surprised me. Near the end of the article, the official who had triggered the article was quoted as saying that M&A was not appropriate in China, because such freewheeling techniques were inconsistent with "socialist principles."

When I next met with the official, not knowing what to say, I found myself apologizing for having misunderstood his position on M&A. He smiled and assured me that I had misunderstood nothing and that, on the contrary, a policy change encouraging M&A was indeed essential. Was he misquoted then? I asked. "No," he answered, smiling more broadly; he had been quoted correctly.

"What am I missing here?" I asked, and what I then learned explains as much about the Chinese way of change as it explains their M&A policy.

"You have to understand that M&A is still not accepted as official policy in China," he began patiently, "so as a government official I must publicly support the current policy. However, it should be rather obvious to all readers that what you were saying about M&A made sense and what I was saying did not. You were seeing the future; I was describing the past. Even senior officials in my ministry will realize that you were more in the right in your analysis than I was, and that M&A may in fact be appropriate—and this is the way policy changes are sometimes made in China."

It is often said that the Chinese are natural businesspeople. One need only look at the predominance of Chinese entrepreneurs in various Southeast Asian countries (such as Indonesia or Malaysia), where ethnic Chinese, though a minority of the population, control a great deal of the commerce (and garner a great deal of jealousy). And yet in traditional Chinese culture, which is based on Confucianism, business is taken lightly or despised. An old Chinese saying states that all businessmen are cunning; to be a businessman, it is assumed, is to deceive people.

But by the 1990s, in the full flush of reform, it was a common joke that *all* Chinese people were going into business. "Jumping into the sea" was the operant metaphor—a phrase that captures the excitement and uncertainty of the market economy. Some say that the present-day Chinese passion for business is more circumstantial than natural. In Mao's China, for energetic, ambitious people, business was one of the very few alternatives to a career in politics. This may also explain why many overseas Chinese, from Southeast Asia to the United States, go into business—they have no interest in local politics (or they are unable to participate in it), and they cannot easily enter the companies or organizations of others, so the only career path open to them is to start their own businesses.

A seemingly baffling phenomenon in today's China is the frequent disconnect between people's apparent salaries and their obvious lifestyles. It's hard to pin down where all this non-salary income comes from. We know that formal salaries are low, whether for managers of enterprises or middle-class workers. Yet so many people have so many expensive accoutrements of modern life—automobiles, cellular phones, foreign vacations, electronic gadgets of all sorts. How can they afford these? Part of the answer is that, in China, many workers have other sources of income in addition to their normal salaries. Governmental officials and entrepreneurs often have substantial non-salary benefits and perquisites. Sometimes their non-salary compensation is much more than their salaries, even twenty to fifty times as much. In addition, many enterprising Chinese workers supplement their incomes by consulting or moonlighting in second jobs. This kind of income is called "gray income." It is not illegal, but it is not completely legal either. And since China's tax collection system is weak, it is easy for people to get away with not paying taxes on their non-salaried incomes, which are hard to track.

Zeng Jinsong: "We're Learning Fast"

Dr. Zeng Jinsong, an automotive engineering scientist, a Ph.D. from prestigious Qinghua University, is president of Innostar High-Technology Enterprises, a recently formed state-owned company with an entrepreneurial style. Jinsong, and hence Innostar, has interests in real estate, telecommunications, Internet service, import-export trading, apparel, and entertainment productions. Energetic and constantly in search of new business opportunities,

Dr. Zeng is a longtime personal friend. I interviewed him in a model apartment of his major real estate project, Technocity, located in the Asian Games Village section of Beijing.

ROBERT KUHN: What is the official name of your company?

ZENG JINSONG: Bei Chen Technocity—Northstar Technology City, in literal English. The name comes from the fact that we have two shareholders. The first is the Technology Innovation Corporation of China, which is owned by the Ministry of Science and Technology. The second is the Bei Chen Group, a large real estate development company owned by the Beijing People's Municipal Government [not the central government]. Each has its own specialty.

KUHN: So the company you lead is state-owned?

ZENG: Yes, 100 percent. Here's how I see state-owned companies. There are two basic kinds—"fixed" and "new." In one sense, they're all the same; in another, they're very different. Traditional state-owned companies utilize the old-style, fixed managerial style. They report to upper-level political leaders, which means that the operating business executives and managers don't have the authority to make decisions. The start-up state-owned companies, like our own, have adopted the new managerial style. More and more such companies are springing up around the country. They are much more vigorous, taking the market seriously and driven by its needs. It has been only about twenty years since the economic reform started, so we're not very experienced. We're exploring, learning, and practicing. I try to learn all I can from people with more experience. But we're learning fast.

KUHN: How do you make decisions?

ZENG: All decisions are based on the market. If we don't adjust quickly, we lose out. We invite experts to analyze ideas before we implement them. We look at potential competition—both legal and illegal. We consider the possibility of piracy of our products, such as electric meters or apparel. We seek to defeat piracy by taking advantage of economies of scale. We produce more products at a cheaper price. Pirates can't compete with that. I try to be as thorough as possible. We make decisions and then report what we've decided to our bosses. Because they also use the new approach, they have no difficulty accepting our decisions.

KUHN: How much freedom do you have when it comes to making decisions?

ZENG: Freedom means different things to different people. Some think that freedom means doing whatever they feel like doing. I disagree with this definition—it's too risky. Freedom is relative. To be responsible, I have to accurately gauge market conditions and correctly discern the opportunities they present. I'm not free to be irresponsible. I've worked in this company for ten years, and my boss has been my boss for the same length of time. During that period, we've earned each other's trust and confidence. We have a mutual understanding, and within that I have a great deal of freedom. When I analyze a project, I think of the risks involved; then I try to devise an appropriate strategy. The better it works, the more freedom I'll have next time.

KUHN: What kind of business is Innostar doing?

ZENG: Our mandate is threefold. First, the construction of the Beijing High-Tech Innovation City, approximately 200,000 square meters, with a total investment of 2.2 billion *yuan*. The second mandate is to operate this large development efficiently. We intend to turn our "Technocity" into the largest comprehensive service center for the new technological industrial sectors in the whole country. This is a huge investment and it has to work. Our third mandate is to look for new projects. Because the two shareholders are in different fields, they can take advantage of each other's strengths to invest in new business areas. For example, one can provide real estate and the other technology to develop new plants and projects.

KUHN: Your company, though relatively small, is quite diversified.

ZENG: Chinese enterprises, in my opinion, have not developed to the point where they can operate in highly specialized ways. Because of the short history of economic reform, we have to remain nimble and diversified. We should explore any business opportunities that come up. We may find some things that are a good fit, that would benefit our core businesses. In the future, of course, specialization will be the way to go.

KUHN: What other businesses are you exploring?

ZENG: We've entered the communications industry. Currently, we are a government-certified Internet service provider (ISP). We are exploring international telephone communications using the Internet. We test electric meters. We're in the apparel business. We're also in the entertainment and fine arts business. We have organized some concerts, including ballets. We put on the Grand Unity New Year's concert in the Great Hall of the People at the end of 1998.

KUHN: What do apparel and concerts have to do with your core business?

ZENG: Apparel can help us establish brand name identification, which can elevate and improve our image, motivating customers to want to do business with us. If you have a good public image, people will want to cooperate with you. Being involved in the arts can also enhance our public image. We've worked with the Radio Broadcast Symphony Orchestra, the China National Symphony Orchestra, and the Central Ballet Troupe. The Unity Concert we sponsored was done entirely for public relations purposes—to influence the public. We invited performers from both mainland China and Taiwan to participate. Our board praised us for the positive results the concert produced. The government was supportive, too. What we're doing helps us get used to the market economy. There's progression from a planned economy to a market economy.

KUHN: You stress brand identification.

ZENG: Brands build credibility. People are familiar with a brand's product quality and price—and they know what to expect from it. It's very important for Chinese enterprises to earn this kind of brand name recognition from their buying public.

KUHN: As the general manager of a new state-owned enterprise, what's the biggest problem you face?

ZENG: Opening new channels for financing. There are too few alternatives. I understand, from a macroeconomic viewpoint, why tight controls must be placed on the financial system. But I'd like more options when it comes to financing—that is, long or short-term debt. The nature of the projects we're doing should determine the financial structure of our borrowings.

KUHN: What are your dissatisfactions with the state-owned enterprise system as it presently exists?

ZENG: The current Chinese economic system is still under development; it's a time of research and testing. Those who run it are asking themselves hard questions, like what kind of business environment do we really want? No matter what choices are made, there will always be new challenges. Personally, I'm satisfied with this system; I'm trying to work within it to get my specific needs met for this enterprise. Others may not be satisfied, but I am.

KUHN: Do state-owned enterprise have any advantages?

ZENG: We have harmonious relationships with various government departments. It's also relatively easy for us to work with other state-owned enterprises similar to our own. That makes it easier to find business partners.

KUHN: If you were a manager of an old-style state-owned enterprise, could you create new businesses, such as ISP, apparel, concerts, and so forth?

ZENG: It would be difficult. In such enterprises, the managers grew up with traditional industries, and they tend to stay the course. Many of them are not familiar with the arts, ISP, apparel and the like. Sudden changes would be disconcerting. They'd rather work with known quantities. It's hard for them to think in terms of repackaging themselves, changing their image, doing something completely new. Many do not realize the importance of advertising. A notable exception is the famous Maotai Liquor manufacturer. And the old traditional state-owned enterprises are all having difficulties at the moment. They're busy enough trying to work through old problems without being concerned about trying something new.

KUHN: Your relationship with the government makes it sound like you're still operating in the context of a planned economy, rather than a market-driven one.

ZENG: Not really. Even in a market economy you have to have administrative bodies. We see them as a societal resource. By cooperating with administrative bodies, your operation benefits. It's better supported. The government is the institution supporting societal development as a whole. The more taxes we pay, the more effectively the government can do its job. A strong government represents a strong support system for business. It's a benevolent cycle. By demonstrating that we have a good relationship with government, we enhance our image in society. That in turn fosters our own development as a multifaceted company doing business on a large scale.

KUHN: Isn't this an image of a governmental business?

ZENG: Your term "governmental business" is not a complimentary one, is it? You have to consider the system we live under. We're a socialist society with special Chinese characteristics. In that context, the term "governmental business" is not necessarily pejorative.

KUHN: Be that as it may, you do seem to be projecting the image of a governmental business.

ZENG: I have to say that we're taking advantage of this image in certain ways. We want to make people feel that we're under the leadership of the government; this gives us a certain credibility, since they know the government is keeping its eye on us. We're never far from its oversight—we actually want to project this image. But though we accept the government's oversight of our business, market forces also drive us.

KUHN: So how do you really see yourself, government or business?

ZENG: I see myself as an entrepreneur who is running an enterprise. I have a certain range of administrative power, and I have clear-cut responsibilities for this operation.

KUHN: As the general manager of such an enterprise, can you talk about your annual salary?

ZENG: My yearly salary is capped. Some of my subordinates make more money than I do. The board determines my salary, and I determine those of my subordinates, based upon prevailing market standards. My own monthly salary is approximately four to five thousand *yuan.*

KUHN: Do you have any other benefits in addition to your salary?

ZENG: Some. The company provides me with a car, and I'm allowed better accommodations than others when I'm on a business trip.

KUHN: Since you are in such a high position of responsibility, what would happen to you if your enterprise were to perform badly?

ZENG: It's not clear. If it can be determined that the bad performance was due to my dereliction of duty, I would of course be removed. In such instances, criminal charges could actually be brought against me, according to current Chinese law. Consequently, I'm under great pressure to do my job well. But our performance may not be tied exclusively to my decision-making; market forces also play a role. The economic environment is constantly changing. If poor performance is due to such factors, I might be excused. But there's really no way for me to know.

KUHN: Conversely, if the enterprise turns out to be very profitable?

ZENG: My superiors will give me even greater support and approval. It's not clear whether any material rewards would be involved. So far, I've never received a bonus.

KUHN: If your enterprise doesn't do well, how much would you stand to lose personally?

ZENG: I don't think I'd lose that much economically, because I don't make that much in the first place. But if I lost this position, I certainly wouldn't be able to drive around in a company car.

KUHN: How do salary structures of the old-style state-owned enterprises compare with those of the new style?

ZENG: Those in the new style who make large contributions will have higher incomes. This practice is nontraditional. The salary difference could be quite large.

KUHN: Are the higher salaries and financial incentives of the newer-style companies a driving force in bringing about innovation?

ZENG: Yes! Your words are very incisive—incentive compensation is indeed a driving force, especially when linked to profit and performance. People in the new state-owned enterprises are constantly coming up with new ideas and concepts. In the old-style enterprises, it's often a matter of seniority. The directors of the old-style enterprises tend to seek ways to preserve the status quo. They're oriented to security. Our retirement and welfare systems are as yet far from perfect. The pension income of retired factory directors is usually very low, and they become quite poor when they leave their position. No matter how well they do while they're on the job, retirement is still a bleak financial time for managers of state-owned companies.

KUHN: What kind of corporate culture are you trying to create for your enterprise?

ZENG: I want to foster the enterprising spirit within the company—to bring everyone's initiative into full play. I want to create a learning environment, in which everyone is constantly upgrading his or her skills and knowledge. We keep raising our management standards. I try to be really involved; for example, I play basketball with my employees.

KUHN: With the perspective of time, could you talk about what happened in Tiananmen Square on June 4, 1989?

ZENG: I know this occurrence has been talked about a great deal outside China. It was a very important event in the history of China and has affected our economic, cultural, and political development. The issue cannot be avoided. I believe there were many causes for what happened, but I'm not able to offer you a comprehensive analysis. Everyone got involved—there were students talking with students, with troops, with the government. I'm sure everyone has an opinion about it. One common denominator was that everyone wanted to see a better China.

KUHN: Obviously, there were differences, large ones.

ZENG: The differences were just in how people thought we could make China better. Not everyone agreed, of course. The result was more and more confrontation. The government and various authorities wanted to see a peaceful solution. The demonstrators knew this and wanted to press their advantage to gain concessions. In China, peace and stability are paramount. There was immaturity on both sides. No one had any experience in anything like this. They didn't know how to handle it. Frankly, it took some time for me to understand what had happened. When the confrontation occurred, blood was regrettably shed. It didn't end the way it was supposed to end. Things like that weren't supposed to happen in this country. They must be avoided in the future. Everyone knows now what has to be done to prevent it from occurring again. After the Tiananmen event, everyone committed himself or herself to economic development. There were still differences of opinion, but everyone agreed that violence wasn't the answer. We realized we needed to create new models to cope with contradictions and confrontations. It's possible that Tiananmen even played a positive role in the history of China. From 1989 to the present, China's economic situation has drastically improved.

KUHN: What actually happened on June 4? Could you go back and fill in some of the details?

ZENG: Sure. On June 4, 1989, I had just graduated with a Ph.D. from Qinghua University and entered an orientation program at this company. Work time had been reduced, and everyone was talking about the students gathering. Most enterprises closed temporarily, as did ours. My boss, the general manager, thought our young people should leave Beijing for their own safety. It was not a good situation. Emotions were running high. Work had come to a stop and the military was in the city. We weren't sure where or how it was going to end.

KUHN: What were you doing personally?

ZENG: I spent my free time with my classmates. Some of us demonstrated in the square, others just stayed on the streets. We talked with the military face to face. We learned that they didn't have much of an idea of what was going on. Communication between the central government, local government, local officials, and ordinary people was not the best. Even though the military had been in Beijing for some time, it was clear that they didn't have a clue what to do. They really didn't understand the situation. From the students' point of view, no violence was necessary. We were peaceful. We thought we were right, and that our ideas, if implemented, would improve the nation. That's how I looked at it. We did not feel we deserved the treatment we got. We meant no evil, only good. We thought our ideas would accelerate the development of China. Things got out of control.

KUHN: What are your candid reflections now?

ZENG: We have to ask the question: if Tiananmen Square hadn't happened, would economic development in China be where it is today? Probably not. The history of China shows that each time a big event like Tiananmen occurs, it takes a long time to get back to a peaceful state, and everyone has to concentrate on returning things to normal. Tiananmen was no exception, and the result, after Deng Xiaoping's southern trip in 1992 was accelerated economic reform. Of course we all felt that the way Tiananmen was handled was inappropriate. No one wanted to see it resolved the way it was, and I believe that each side has done much thinking in retrospect. I think I understand what happened better now, not simply because I have matured, not because of my position with this enterprise—but because I understand more about the nature and history of the Chinese people. What happened on June 4 was the result of immaturity on both sides. Everyone involved behaved inappropriately. I think we're all aware that this must never happen again.

> *As mentioned before, Zeng Jinsong is a personal friend. More importantly, he's a prototypical example of China's new generation of entrepreneurs—a dealmaker who works smoothly within the system, not opposed or against it. His company, Innostar, might best be described as a nexus for Zeng's incredible portfolio of talents and relationships. For the PBS documentary, our CCTV camera crews followed him around as he made his deals. Following are excerpts from the actual transcript.*

NARRATOR: Zeng Jinsong does whatever it takes to make the deal. That means having connections, pull; the Chinese word for this is *guanxi*.

ZENG JINSONG: For what I do, *guanxi* is extremely important. Because China is still a developing country, all resources—money, materials and talent—are scarce, and the laws enforcing fair market competition are loose and incomplete. So things are not fair.

ZENG: *(touring his massive real estate project, then under construction)* In the back will be elevators, and in the front will be escalators.

IMPORTANT WOMAN: Why don't you put the stairs here?

ZENG: Smart idea, smart idea.

NARRATOR: Zeng Jinsong is one of a new generation: he's not interested in selling any particular product—he looks for good opportunities.

ZENG: Now is the opportunity for us to take advantage of an immature market and find what will be successful for our company. I believe we should jump at whatever business opportunities present themselves.

NARRATOR: Jinsong's lifestyle includes an expensive apartment and private school for his son—but his salary is only about $8,000 a year. That's the way it works in China.

ZENG: *(outside the Great Hall of the People in Tiananmen Square)* What time will they arrive? They better hurry. They have to rehearse, then do their hair and make up.

ZENG: *(on stage, greeting artists)* Nice to meet you.

WOMAN SINGER #1: Long time, no see.

NARRATOR: Jinsong's company sponsored, and Jinsong himself produced, the grand New Year's Eve Unity Concert, where for the first time musicians from the mainland, Taiwan, Hong Kong, and Macau came together to play both Western and Chinese classical music.

WOMAN SINGER #2: I'm so sorry. I just flew in from Hong Kong this morning. I got up at five, so I'm very tired.

ZENG: Involvement in the arts is a means of creating a good public image. We would like to see our concerts attract more and more people and at the same time give us a stronger image in society. I believe this is a very important element in adapting to a market economy. The second reason we do this is so that we can develop a closer relationship with the government. In China, almost all decisions are still made by the central government. In other words, the central leaders and the heads of the ministries have a huge influence in the economic area. So through these events, we foster closer ties with the state.

ZENG: *(inside the Great Hall of the People in Tiananmen Square, frenetically directing pre-concert activities)* I need more programs here. Send them over right now! *(To a high-level guest in the vast audience)* How are you? I'll ask them to send more programs over.

ZENG: *(reflecting after the Unity Concert)* In terms of freedom, I think it's all relative. For me, more freedom exists right now than ever before. After all these years, I've learned how to make my ideas accepted. Personally, I'm satisfied with the current system. My only concern is how to work within this system and find the direction that best fits my development.

6
Odyssey and Media

Finding China

Growing up as I did in a mostly Jewish, mostly middle-class town on Long Island in the suburbs of New York, China might as well have been Mars. It wasn't on my mental radar, I never imagined ever going there, and besides the occasional *National Geographic* special and regular Chinese food (all New Yorkers like Chinese food), my exposure to the nation and its culture was nonexistent.

My grandparents came to America in the first decade of the twentieth century in that great wave of Eastern European immigrants. With big dreams but no money or knowledge of English, they found themselves in the slums of Manhattan's Lower East Side—an area that continues to be a magnet for new immigrants today. The Lower East Side is now home to hundreds of thousands of Chinese who share the hopes and struggles of that earlier immigrant generation. By the time Chinatown had really taken root, however, my parents had already met, married, and moved their family to suburban Long Island. (After World War II, my father had borrowed a few thousand dollars and started a successful clothing manufacturing business. My family wasn't rich, but we were comfortable and I had every educational opportunity.)

My circuitous road to China began in Boston, when I attended MIT's Sloan School of Management in a program for mid-career executives. Although I had an earlier doctorate in anatomy/brain research from UCLA, I had been working in various business ventures but had never taken a business course: no economics, no accounting, no finance. And so

173

I went back to school, at age thirty-five (and at the same time reestablished my science life as a research affiliate in MIT's psychology and brain science department).

While at MIT, I wrote my first book on the use of scientific methodology to study corporate strategy. That led to other books on strategic management, creativity in business, deal making, and investment banking. By the middle 1980s I was, in the evenings, adjunct professor at New York University's Graduate School of Business Administration (now Stern School of Business), and during the days an independent investment banker and consultant. In 1989, I was approached by The Geneva Companies, the leading merger and acquisition firm working with private businesses, to give a keynote speech about deal making, an invitation that would lead, about three years later, to my partners and I acquiring the company and my becoming president.

It was at this same time that I took my first small step towards Mars— towards China, that is—though it wasn't my idea at all. Dr. George Kozmetsky, cofounder of Teledyne and former longtime dean of the business school at the University of Texas at Austin, has been something of an academic and professional mentor to me. He's in his eighties now, but continues to be among the sharpest and most active individuals I know. When he retired as dean in 1983, he presented me to the search committee as a candidate to replace him, and, while I wasn't selected (I was shortlisted on the final three), in the process we became extremely close.

George is a brilliant visionary, pioneering the development of business incubators, and generating synergy among business, academe, and government; he's the winner of a National Science Medal, and he was prescient enough to have been one of the first backers of Michael Dell. He also happens to be close friends with Dr. Song Jian, then State Councilor and Chairman of China's State Science and Technology Commission.

In early 1989, Dr. Song asked George to invite to China a small group of investment bankers and financiers who could help the Chinese science establishment transform their research institutes into market-sensitive enterprises, leveraging their technology for entrance into the world of commerce. George gave me a call; he mentioned that since I was an investment banker who had been trained as a scientist I might be less threatening to the wary Chinese scientists than the typical suspender-attired, Wall Street MBAs—how could I turn George down?

Of course, my prior impression of China had been quite stereotypical: I imagined dour, humorless proletarian masses wearing identical uniforms and working in huge steel mills or on pre-industrial farms, and a constrained, homogenous society built on totalitarianism and tyranny. Despite my rather narrow perspective on the country, I did have a secret dream—one that I'd developed in summer camp as a child, and one that I couldn't fulfill without visiting China.

I wanted to play Ping-Pong with the Chinese.

Ping-Pong had been used as a diplomatic icebreaker back in 1971, shortly before President Richard Nixon and Secretary of State Henry Kissinger went to China in 1972, but my reasons had nothing to do with the furtherance of diplomacy. I just wanted to play Ping-Pong. I had played well as a preteen and then briefly in college, and although I hadn't picked up a paddle in years, I had a strong desire to find out firsthand just how it felt to play with the best. And in Ping-Pong, there was no question at all—the Chinese were the best in the world.

Ping-Pong Entrepreneur

My first look at China didn't do much to dispel my initial beliefs. The old Beijing airport was dingy, with rickety turnstiles operated by stone-faced guards in green Mao jackets. And though the architecture and furnishings at the Daiyutai State Guest House where we were lodged were elegant in an old-world European sense, the entire compound was walled off from the rest of China, which seemed uniformly austere and gray.

As special foreign guests, we weren't supposed to leave the compound unaccompanied, but I knew I'd have to ignore that rule. After giving my scheduled lecture, which had to do with entrepreneurship, new-venture financing, and the nature of risk, the time had come to pursue my ambition. I begged off of the officially obligatory visits to the Beijing Opera and the Great Wall and furtively wandered the Beijing streets to no avail: there were no Ping-Pong tables on the main avenues, where I had naïvely expected to find them. (There *were* funny signs in English: "Bus Stop for Foreign Experts" was one I thought especially hilarious. What did that mean? Were no Chinese permitted to board those buses? What about foreigners who didn't know much about anything? Were all foreigners assumed to be experts? The Chinese are still struggling with their English translations: in the passport control area of the Shanghai airport, there is to this day a prominent suggestion box labeled "Accusation Box." A sign bought by our TV crew at a street sale in Beijing instructing people to

"Flush the Toilet" in proper Chinese, was translated, to the endless amusement of my colleagues, as "Mang Out After Shit.")

Clearly, I needed an accomplice to pull off my Ping-Pong caper. Now, the State Science and Technology Commission had assigned to me, as translator and chaperone, a bright, energetic young man in his early twenties named Zhu Yadan, whom we called Adam. Adam was fluent in English and not at all intimidated by the strange group of big-shot investment bankers.

Every time I saw Adam, I told him that I wanted to play Ping-Pong, to which he would respectfully reply that the schedule had been determined by the authorities and no deviations were allowed. I kept bugging Adam until he decided, being a polite young man, that it would be easier to avoid me than argue with me, so whenever he saw me coming he would head off in the opposite direction. Finally, frustrated, I ambushed him in the expansive lobby of the Daiyutai Guest House and made my considered plea: "If you won't take a risk to satisfy someone who has traveled eight thousand miles to help your country free of charge, there's absolutely no hope for entrepreneurship in China."[18]

The next day, while I was attending a lecture in a large public hall, Adam came up to me and whispered, "Wait ten minutes, then walk slowly out the back and look for a small black car. But don't follow me now."

After the requested ten minutes had elapsed, and feeling more like a spy than a would-be Ping-Pong player, I ambled out into the rear parking lot, trying (and no doubt failing) to appear inconspicuous. Remarkably alone, I looked around but saw no one. There was an old car—its grayishness more the product of age than color—but no sign of life.

Assuming I had missed a signal in my first undercover role, I walked over to the dusty vehicle, and saw that it was occupied: there were two strange men bent over in the front seat and a third—Adam—huddling furtively in the back seat. The back door swung open and Adam pulled me into the car as though I were being kidnapped. Off we hurtled to Chinese People's University, in the northwest sector of Beijing, where waiting for me, to my horror, were three of the top Ping-Pong players in the country and one of the national coaches. To make matters worse, a hundred or so students had gathered to witness the Beijing debut of this American "champion."

"Do you know Jack Smith [not his real name, which I don't remem-

---

[18] The Chinese government did pay for our group's transportation and accommodations, which were very nice indeed.

ber]?" one of the Chinese players asked me, with a smile full of good fellowship. "He's your number one player. Last year I beat him 21-4."

Well, the best I can say is that I wasn't a complete embarrassment; Ping-Pong diplomacy was not rendered forever dead. The Chinese players rather kindly allowed me an increasing number of points per game—first five, then eight, then eleven. All the Chinese students were rooting for me, and like Rocky Balboa I began believing in myself.

I turned to the translator, and to the assembled students, and said loudly with mock menace, "Please tell my Chinese friend that in the next game I'm now going to get thirteen points."

To which I got a swift reply: "Please tell my American friend that in the next game he's now going to get *zero* points."

My opponent then announced broadly to the student spectators that if I got as many as three points, he would crawl under the table to shake my hand.

I could not believe what this fellow could do with that little white ball. He had a serve—I kid not—that barely bounced on my side of the table before instantly reversing itself and skipping back to his side of the table, seemingly defying the laws of physics while effortlessly eluding my awkward lunges.

However, the story ends as *Rocky* did: I lost, of course, but I had my dignity. Remarkably, I did get those three points—one of which I actually earned—and under the table he crawled, to the unbridled delight of the audience.

Later that evening, I took Adam and the Chinese Ping-Pong players to dinner at a local hotel and found myself caught up in the intoxicating atmosphere of the pre-Tiananmen political fervor. Here were young people yearning for the freedoms we take for granted—not just freedom of expression but the freedoms to decide how and where to live one's life. There was a heated discussion as to how far the students should go to effect fundamental change in Chinese society.

Some months afterward, I learned that Adam joined the students in Tiananmen Square, and although not one of the leaders, was targeted for disciplinary action. Just before he was to be detained, and while he was serving on an official delegation to the United States, Adam chose to stay in America. Without means or relatives in the United States, he moved to Philadelphia, working at multiple menial jobs while struggling to earn an MBA degree. For years, until he graduated, he came home to a cold, damp subterranean storage room of a grocery store where he labored.

Adam kept in touch with me, always his vivacious, perceptive, sparkling self, and in 1994 we began to work together. Today Adam Zhu is my full partner in all my China-related activities. What is particularly interesting to me—and indicative both of the Chinese love for China and the changes that have taken place there—is the depth of his commitment to supporting his homeland and to facilitating the broad development of the country. He now has the skills necessary to be a highly successful American investment banker, with all the financial and personal perquisites thereof, but has chosen to work with and for China, to help build the country and improve relations between China and the United States. Though he was in Tiananmen Square during those fateful days, and though he later disobeyed official directives, Adam is highly appreciated by many leaders in the PRC government; two high-level ministers remarked to me that Adam is among the finest examples of the new generation of young Chinese professionals.

Adam Zhu: Son of the Revolution

> *As I've mentioned, when I met Adam, he was in his early twenties. He had been assigned to be the translator for our small party of investment bankers and financiers, and although he was clearly a representative of the government—and, officially, the Party watchdog—we all became fond of him, due to his remarkably gregarious personality. He told me a little bit about himself then: he was from a small village in the north of China in Manchuria, and he and his parents had experienced great suffering during the Cultural Revolution. Despite the tragedy he faced, he caught up in his education and excelled in college, eventually finding his way to Beijing and obtaining a job with the State Science and Technology Commission. It wasn't until much later that I heard his complete—and remarkable—story, which by that time included participation in the Tiananmen protest, a flight from potential questioning in China, the hard-won beginnings of a new life in the United States, a rededication to helping China, and a great desire to promote U.S.-China relations. Following is his firsthand, stream-of-consciousness account.*

My parents were medical doctors tending to the needs of farmers in Hunan Province in the south of China. When the Cultural Revolution came, as educated people, as professionals, they were of course among the first to be persecuted. They were taken away to reeducation, and I was sent up north to Manchuria to live with my grandmother, who was widowed and alone. I was just a baby at the time, two months old! And I stayed with Grandma until I was ten and a half. My parents came to see me only a couple of times each year. I called my grandmother "Mama."

The village Huoluling (Stove Hill) where we lived was very small, just thirty-six households. Everyone knew everyone else. In fact, you could say that I really had over a dozen mothers. Because we were so poor my grandmother couldn't afford milk for me (there was no such thing as baby formula at that time in China). Instead, I was passed around to whichever woman had recently given birth, so that I could share in her baby's milk.

When I was ten years old, I was finally sent back to my parents, back to the south. They were living in Xintian, a small city in Hunan—of course, anything would be large compared to the village where I grew up. They were working at a hospital; my mother, a surgeon, is a serious and tough professional woman. After the ten-year nightmare of the Cultural Revolution, she appreciated and treasured the opportunity to practice her profession again. As a result of her outstanding performance, she was soon appointed president of the hospital. Women in senior executive positions are actually not so rare in China, where many women run companies, or are government officials, or have high-ranking Party positions. That's one of the good things about Mao's reforms, and it's one of the reasons why women from mainland China are stronger and more independent than women from Taiwan and Hong Kong. Mainland Chinese girls are tough.

As for my father, he was also reinstated when the Cultural Revolution finally ended. He later went into politics and was appointed director general of the Civil Affairs Bureau of Xintian County. Different from my mother, my father has an optimistic and ebullient personality; he always keeps a smile on his face. He was later elected vice chairman of the County Congress.

Well, because my grandmother's village was so small, I really had no education at all. My parents were worried that I wouldn't be able to keep up with the other kids in school. They got me a tutor; they wanted to inject me with four years of education in six months.

You have to understand what I was like at the time: I was ten, I'd never seen a city, and I was suddenly living with people who were total strangers—even though they were my parents. When I first arrived, my parents wanted to make friends with me, so they asked me what I wanted as a gift—they

were making forty *yuan* a month at the time, which was more than my entire village made, probably. I remember what I told them. "I don't want
toys or books. I just want a meal. I'd really like some roast pork."

I was very, very skinny. In Manchuria, we were all malnourished—all
we ever ate was *congee* [a thin porridge], and it wasn't even rice *congee*; it
was sorghum [a rough grain that grows in the North of China]. Sometimes
we would have a little potato . . . not often. We would forage whatever we
could from the fields.

When you can't find enough to eat, education can't be a very high priority. Anyway, there wasn't really a school—all we had was a housewife
teaching the neighborhood kids. That's what they called school. So I
couldn't really read; I didn't know math. All I was really good at was per-
forming, because I acted in Red Young Pioneer propaganda plays. All those
who saw my plays thought that I was a talented actor. Some even told my
Grandma that I should move to a big city to pursue an acting career.

My parents wanted me to make something of myself. My mother is from
a well-to-do family—they had a Chinese medicine business. Her father operated several herbal medicine stores, and all of his nine children were doctors, either in Western or Chinese medicine. Anyway, my mother hired a
tutor and basically forced me to learn. She put a great deal of pressure on
me, and I resented it. It was already tough enough learning to call my
mother "Mom." She tried her best, but it wasn't a very healthy relationship.

Still, the pressure worked. The tutor was good, I studied hard, and I
soon knew enough basic stuff to join the kids my age in school. My first
semester, however, went badly; I was the worst in the class and everyone
knew it. But by the second semester, I was starting to catch up. By the
third, I was at the top of the class. And then I skipped two grades. Can
you imagine it? I went from zero to grade five, and then I skipped two
more. I went to college when I was fifteen years old. (They had special
programs for students who were young and talented.)

I didn't do that well in college during the first two years, partially because I was so young. I don't think I was mature enough yet. However, in
the third and fourth year, I studied hard and did tremendously well. I
knew if I really wanted to make it to Beijing, which by then had become
a strong ambition, I had to do well academically. So I went back for my
master's degree, at the Harbin Institute of Technology. Getting into graduate school then was not easy; admissions were extremely competitive. I
was pleased that my efforts paid off.

I had already been very good at literature and languages; my father was quite pro-Western, so he had made me read a great many English books. He gave us Western names: "Adam" is my real name—it's not a translation—my father actually chose the English name for me; my sisters' names are Annie and Abby. In fact, that was one of the dastardly crimes he was charged with during the Cultural Revolution: our names!

My father paid a steep price for his pro-Western orientation; he and my mother were sent out to the deep country during the Cultural Revolution, to toil on a work farm. He was frequently beaten and kicked. At one point, because he was so outspoken and refused to submit, the radical political cadres were going to kill him, beat him to death, but my mother saved him. She grabbed two knives and threatened the Red Guards, and they let him go. My mother was like a woman warrior.

That's probably where I got my stubbornness. I have a strong personality. Like my father, I can smile on the outside—I can be very friendly on the surface, but beneath, I can be very tough. If I want something, I'll get it, no matter what it takes!

When I was thirteen years old, I told my mother that someday I would live in Beijing and then in New York. I barely even knew where Beijing was, much less New York, but I told her that was what I would do when I grew up. I'd heard about New York from some of the Russians who were around at the time, and from some of the Catholic priests I had met.

I was already a member of the Communist Party by the time I was eighteen years old, which is very young. I was in the "special student" program, and since I had done the propaganda plays when I was a kid, I was promoted quickly. I became a standing member of the student union, and so on. Unfortunately, if you're a Party member, you have to take the toughest job when you graduate, to show how committed you are. And because the Harbin Institute of Technology was affiliated with the Ministry of Aerospace Industry of China, my job was supposed to be at a launch site, which was located far out in the middle of nowhere, because rockets are launched only where there are no cities. The launch site would be either in the northwest or the southwest of China, but I said to myself, "No way, I have to go to Beijing!"

The problem is that, in China, you need residency papers—called *hukou*—to go anywhere. If you don't have a *hukou* to live in Beijing, the police will arrest you and send you away. So I told the authorities, "I don't care what job you give me—just give me a job in Beijing." Because I was a Party member, they considered my request and found a job opening at the China Aeronautic and Astronautic University (CAAU) in Beijing.

They told me I could teach English there. It was not a particularly good job, but at least I could get my *hukou* to go to Beijing.

So the dean of the Foreign Languages Department of CAAU came to interview me, and he thought I was a good candidate. He told me that if I came to his college, he would send me to the U.S. for further training. Even though I knew that this was only a "bait" promise, I told him I would take the job. In reality, I didn't have any intention of working there. I packed my luggage, took my papers, and went to Beijing—but I never showed up at the college. I didn't report to the dean or the college. And everyone became very angry; they made a big announcement, sent my luggage, my personnel files, and my *hukou* back to Harbin.

But I had a plan. I knew that the only way I could stay in Beijing without a *hukou* was if I worked for a foreign company. At the time, the China Schindler Group—one of the first big Chinese joint ventures, a company that made elevators—was recruiting an office manager. They needed someone who spoke English, some French, and so on. Because it paid five hundred *yuan* a month, there were over a thousand people in Beijing applying for the position. Remember, my mother was a doctor, and she was making only seventy-five *yuan* a month. Five hundred *yuan* a month was a great deal of money then.

I was staying with the family of a friend from Harbin. I had no luggage, no *hukou*, no clothing even; but they took me in, and let me study for the tests. (I was very appreciative; the mother became my godmother and she remains so to this day.) There were actually six different tests: English writing, spoken English, French, Chinese writing, office administration, and computer applications. And I scored number one, out of a thousand applicants.

I received the offer of the job—but it was a bit of a dilemma. My *hukou* was gone. True, working for a foreign company, I could stay in Beijing, but I was effectively an illegal alien. If I got married and had kids in Beijing, they couldn't go to school there. There were other problems as well. Now, the only way I could get my *hukou* back was to find a powerful person to support me. I took the job at Schindler, but I was also thinking about my next generation, my future kids, and I knew I had to do something.

Then I heard that the State Science and Technology Commission (SSTC) had formed a new office called the Sparks Program Office. The Sparks program was designed to take simple technologies designed by Chinese research institutes and commercialize them for the development of industry in rural areas. A friend heard they were recruiting a new team for this office. So he put me in touch with his friend, Dr. Ren Yuling (currently a standing member of the National Congress and the mayor of Beihai City in south China), who was a director general with SSTC and a senior member of the Sparks Program Team. My name had been in the evening newspaper as the highest-scoring applicant for this Schindler position, so I was sort of famous—even though I had all these problems back in Harbin. I met Dr. Ren and told him my story. Dr. Ren, who spoke English and French fluently, told me that he appreciated my personality and respected my courage and determination. Of course, the Schindler offer helped establish my credibility. He agreed to help me after just our first meeting, for which I am forever grateful. (He made the decision to recruit me, and he was extremely nice to me. SSTC paid four thousand *yuan* to CAAU to "buy" me from them. Five hundred dollars! That's how much I was worth then!)

I was very appreciative and did my best to assist Dr. Ren in his work at Sparks, which was an important national program. His wife, Dr. Zhang, a senior scientist at the Chinese Academy of Science, and his two beautiful daughters also became my good friends. And then I began to make a lot of friends, helped along by the introductions of Dr. Ren and my godmother. Actually, I made so many friends, and was spending so much time with powerful people, and was so confident and outgoing, that a rumor started about me. It began circulating that I was the grandson of the former head of the Joint Chiefs of Staff of the Chinese military. Because we had the same last name—"Zhu"—everybody was whispering that I was his grandson.

Six months later, I found another wonderful opportunity that would completely change my life. The opening was at the technological innovation division of SSTC, and with the help of my godmother, I was able to transfer there as an international liaison officer.

As an important part of my job, I was responsible for serving as translator and guide to foreign VIPs—including Dr. George Kozmetsky's group, which is where I met Robert Kuhn. My personality served me well in this position, because I was naturally open, friendly, self-assured, and determined. Westerners thought that I was the "most Western" Chinese person they had ever met.

One of my colleagues at the technological innovation division, an intern, was a vivacious fellow named Zeng Jinsong, who had a recent doctorate from China's top science school, Qinghua University. Like me, he was a young upstart who had been a student leader in college—he has since gone on to become an extremely successful businessman, running a new state-owned company called Innostar High-Technology Enterprises.

Now, remember, this was all happening in the late 1980s, a time when many students were talking about the need for change and reform in China, and since they assumed that such change and reform would need to begin with the government, it was a time of brewing trouble. Because Jinsong and I were both young, idealistic, passionate, naïve, and very energetic, we soon found ourselves swept up into the excitement of this emerging movement. We were driven by a dream of a better, more democratic China. (I was particularly motivated because of the terrible degradations and deprivations that my family and I had suffered during the Cultural Revolution.)

We began helping out the students in every way we could: using our office's photocopier to make posters, providing them access to fax machines and computers, even bringing them food (boiled eggs, bread, ice popsicles) when they began their famous protests in Tiananmen Square. Considering that we were working for the government, these were very dangerous acts. But the danger was part of what made it exciting. I actually went down to the Square itself, to join the protests, even though if I had been seen by a coworker or supervisor, I would have been fired, and probably arrested. I was actually there, in Tiananmen, when the crackdown occurred—when the tanks started rolling into the Square. Jinsong was smarter: he stayed away.

My godmother had warned me not to go, because like many of the powerful people in Beijing, she knew in advance that the government would likely take forcible action. She was scared to death. But I ignored her, I think in part because I believed I was invulnerable: I had survived starvation and growing up without my parents; I had gotten to Beijing as I had always dreamed; I had managed to get a good job—and recovered my *hukou*, too. I couldn't imagine anything bad really happening to me! So as the tanks were moving in, I was riding a bicycle on the avenue, wearing a jean jacket with a bright red band around my head, looking just like one of the students.

I barely got out of there alive.

After the crackdown, the Party began to investigate within the government, because there were some prominent officials, even Party members, who had spoken up on behalf of the students. The Party inquisitors wanted to know whether there were other, secret supporters of the protesters hidden within the various ministries and commissions—which, of course, there were many. I had not been hidden and the investigations were inexorable. I realized I had to get out of there, as quickly as possible.

I had been making preliminary inquiries to business schools in the United States, since I figured that an American MBA would be valuable no matter what career path I would pursue. Advising me was Professor

Kenneth Tolo, then associate vice president for academic affairs and research (and, by 1990, vice provost) at the University of Texas at Austin, who also had been part of Dr. Kozmetsky's delegation. But now my timetable had to be accelerated.

I knew that a delegation of Chinese high technology representatives had been invited to visit Silicon Valley in the U.S. After Tiananmen, of course, it had been postponed. I decided I had to get the trip going again; it was my only opportunity. So I talked to people at Teledyne, a U.S. technology company co-founded by Dr. Kozmetsky, using all the contacts I had from being the liaison officer for Dr. Kozmetsky's mission. Somehow, I managed to get the delegation going again. And in December 1989, I came to the U.S. with six Chinese government officials. We visited Tandy, Apple, Teledyne, and a few other companies.

After we finished all of the official meetings, when we were in Los Angeles, I called an American, Ms. Elenora Lefkoe, whom I had met in Guilin back in 1985, when I was working as a tour guide (summer intern). She was an evangelical Christian, a Baptist; she had spent a lot of time talking to me about the Bible. Timorously, I told her that I was thinking of, basically, remaining in the U.S. to avoid possible punishment. Immediately, she said she would come with a car to pick me up. So, nervously, I packed my one bag and met her at the agreed-upon hotel. And that was that. I had no money, no job, and no close friends; but I was in America.

After I made my departure, I had to make an official report to the leader of the delegation, I had to tell him that I was not going back. I wanted to be as honorable as possible; in fact, I left all my money in my room. Frankly, I loved China—it was my motherland—and it was only because of the then-present distress, and flashbacks of the Cultural Revolution, that I was forced to leave. The delegation leader made it subtly clear that he sympathized with me, but he still had to bring back a story to the government. He listened when I told him what I was doing, and then he wished me good luck. I was worried about my parents and my sisters—but the Chinese government was really lenient; they didn't harass my family at all, for which I remain most thankful.

I immediately contacted Professor Tolo who graciously intervened to quicken the lengthy and formal admissions process, putting his credibility on the line for me. I was encouraged that I would be given special consideration at both Penn State and Temple University. But even assuming that I would be accepted, I first had to earn enough money to afford the tuition, and that meant going to New York.

I called a girl whom I had gotten to know when she was an exchange student in China. Her name was Cathy, a Stanford graduate, and she was living in Manhattan. She loaned me the money to fly out there ... so in this strange way I actually fulfilled my childhood dream of going to Beijing and then to New York!

But New York was not what I had imagined. The only job I could get immediately was as a delivery boy at a Chinese restaurant in uptown Manhattan—I had promised Cathy that I would pay her loan back right away. I shared a basement apartment in Queens with three other people who also worked in various Chinese restaurants. However, things went wrong. On my third day in New York, very much a wide-eyed immigrant, after work at around midnight, I was robbed at a subway station by four young African-Americans. This incident shocked me. I lost not just the precious twenty-some dollars in tips that I had earned that night, I lost my innocence and, at least for a time, my love of New York. I was scared and felt terribly vulnerable. My plan to make money in New York before going to business school was dead, and I decided to leave. Two weeks later, with the help of friends, Mr. and Mrs. David Ludwig, businesspeople whom I had met in China through Dr. Ren, I took Amtrak to Philadelphia, where Temple University had offered me admission.[19]

I spent the next four years working in various odd jobs in Philadelphia— as a delivery boy, a busboy, and then, while attending classes, as a handyman and stockboy at a small grocery warehouse (owned by a Chinese family) adjacent to a deteriorating housing project on Fairmont Avenue in North Philadelphia and conveniently close to Temple. Every day I had to get up at 5:30 A.M. to stock the frequently robbed grocery store and, other than attending classes two or three days a week, I worked nonstop there until 6:30 P.M., before rushing off to my second job as a delivery boy at a Chinese restaurant (Wok & Tofu) in downtown Philadelphia, where I had to ride my bicycle through dangerous neighborhoods and snowy winters, not returning home until after midnight. It was only then that I could start to study for my MBA courses, until I could no longer keep myself awake. I still remember how my eyes would tear whenever my bicycle would skid in the snow and all the dinner deliveries scattered on the muddy ground— I had to reimburse the restaurant out of my meager tips for the cost of the

---

[19] I am much in debt to William Dunkleberg, then dean of The Fox School of Business and Management at Temple University and now chief economist of the National Federation of Independent Businesses.

lost food. And, if I were a little late, many people wouldn't even tip at all; I'd look longingly into their eyes, pleading, virtually begging, for something. Then trudging home, I had to sleep, for the first seven months, on a floor mattress down in the dank basement of that grocery warehouse, which no doubt contributed to my continuing health problems.

In spite of all the hardships, I was lucky to have met some wonderful people who kindly lent their helping hands when I was down and out. It was their care and love that brought me strength and hope. I will never forget the Shou family: Susan, Charlie, Kim, Tom, Nghi, Howe, and Luck for being there for me when I was broke and panicked; it was the lowest point of my life. I still remember the first day I arrived in Philadelphia. It was a Saturday afternoon. I was standing in front of a travel agency in Chinatown anxiously looking for possible hirers. I desperately needed a job because I only had fifty dollars left in my wallet. It was Tom who picked me and took me to his store to work as a stockboy. Of course, he didn't know how much that job meant to me. Two months later, after remarkably being accepted into the MBA program at Temple University (the result of strong support by Professor Tolo), my tuition was due. If I didn't register and pay the tuition on time, not only would I lose my admissions, I would also automatically lose my legal status (F-1 visa) in the U.S. Becoming an illegal alien would be the worst thing. But where could I get the eight thousand dollars? I felt so helpless and hopeless. However, God sent his angels. The day before school started, Nghi (Tom's brother) and his wife Alice told me that they would like to help. When I nervously took the ten thousand dollars from Nghi's hand, I cried, I cried very hard. They barely knew me! Moreover, they were hardly rich. The Shou family were Cambodian refugees, a Chinese family who had lost everything there in the war and whom the American government had accepted in the early 1980s. Ten thousand dollars must have been a big part of their savings. But they could see that I was terribly worried; Nghi and Alice looked into my eyes and told me that they trusted me. These warm memories always bring tears to my eyes.

But I never stopped dreaming of finding a way to go back to China, my home. I never renounced China, you know, I never asked for political asylum. I also never associated myself with dissent groups. That meant the door would remain a little bit open.

Of course, there were always officials arriving from China on economic, scientific, and political missions. So I started quietly offering to help them out—driving them around and showing them the sights, that sort of thing. I made myself so useful to the visiting delegations that I was eventually given the chance to ask forgiveness from the government for what I had done. I wrote a letter to the Chinese Embassy in Washington, D.C., apologizing for my actions. Since my old passport expired (my diplomatic passport was valid only for two years), the embassy issued me a new passport. That meant I was granted freedom to go back to China, and visit my family and friends. Oh, I love freedom!

As an investment banker, I work with clients from all over the world. However, China is always my top priority, because China is what made me who I am today. Moreover, China is changing so fast, they need people who can change with it. There's a place for me there now. I understand China and I understand the U.S. and I believe I can make a contribution to good relations between these two great nations and peoples. I've had so many lives, and every one of them has taught me something. That's experience the new China needs.

—Adam Zhu

Eating Tofu

In China, I'm called "Doufu Wang," the tofu king, a crown I wear with honor. Tofu is largely what I eat when in China; I order the white gelatinous mass at virtually every meal. Originally, the reason was health; I'm a bit of a fanatic. I figure that a Type A personality absorbing unceasingly high stress and rarely getting enough sleep had better eat right and exercise regularly. Now the reason includes taste: I actually like the stuff.

Tofu is a soft, white, seemingly bland, high protein, custard-like substance extracted ingeniously from soybeans. As cheese comes from milk, so tofu comes from soybeans. The protein from soy is complete; having all eight essential amino acids is unique for a vegetable and helps generate tofu's mystical aura. Tofu is often cut into cubes, then boiled, broiled, baked, steamed, grilled, marinated, fried, or frozen. It can be eaten whole, smashed, blended or mixed with a million other things to create an endless series of multifarious incarnations. To some people, eating tofu is a spiritual experience.

Tofu contains certain enzymes postulated to convey protective or even curative health benefits. Studies suggest that tofu may shield against various cancers and other diseases, but the ever-changing lore of supposedly magic foods is almost always exaggerated. Nonetheless, tofu is an excellent source of protein and good-quality fat and it is certainly less harmful than many of the processed and cooked meats served in China to an honored dinner guest.

Varieties of tofu in China rival varieties of cheese in France. My favorite restaurant in Beijing is *Huai Nan Doufu Yan* (South Anhui Tofu Banquet), which offers dozens of different types of tofu dishes. It is actually operated by Anhui Province, where tofu is said to have originated sometime in the Han Dynasty, 206 B.C.E.–C.E. 200 (archaeologists have found early depictions of the preparation of soymilk and tofu). If you go to this restaurant with a regular, you will be treated to numerous off-the-menu tofu surprises. What's fascinating is just how different all these tofu dishes taste and feel. It's not just diverse sauces and flavors that characterize the unlimited varieties but the startlingly dissimilar textures. Tofu exhibits remarkable range in tactile sense; from the shape and consistency of soft-boiled egg yolks to grain-like shards that taste like toasted wheat to long sheets of "tofu skin" that could credibly pass for ravioli.

There are other vegetarian restaurants in China, some associated with quasi-religious orders, where tofu mimics traditional foods; one can order "salmon," "ham," and "lobster" that are made entirely of tofu and can give a fair imitation of the real thing. Certainly, these ersatz dishes look the part; visually, the synthetic can be indistinguishable from the original. Taste, too—if one overlooks texture—can be a close approximation, especially for those foods with a dominant and particular flavor such as smoked ham. Texture is what usually exposes the imposter.

I've developed a theory about Chinese food in China, which I like to proclaim provocatively and hope no one is offended: Taste is Inversely Proportional to Price. My mathematical formulation—as simple as the law of universal gravitation but probably not as important—is that the lower the price of food the better its taste and vice versa. I discovered this natural law empirically on my second trip to China, on consecutive evenings at two distinctly different dining experiences.

The first was a banquet hosted by a vice-minister in a large ornate room of deep red carpeting and dark wood walls, tucked away in a private area of an expensive restaurant. I'm not exactly sure what was served, but most of the courses were varieties of animal meats overpopulated, it seemed to me, with clusters of bones to which clumps of gristle, fat, cartilage, and hairlike appendages were attached. It was more than my delicate, uneducated palate could assimilate and so my surgical skills were called to action.

After each course, after I had struggled to pick and find whatever unalloyed meat I could dissect out, I'd look down at my plate and discover that whatever had been brought to me a few minutes earlier had now grown in size, so that the residue sat there in a mound several times larger and more prominently than before. I had surely eaten some of the meat, and so the unexpected expansion seemed right out of the New Testament with the loaves and fishes. My discomfort was compounded when I cautiously looked around at the plates of my Chinese dinner companions. Maybe the recollection of the mind's eye undergoes simplistic distortion over time or the retelling of this story layers in exaggeration, but even now I can see an endless circle of neat, clean-wiped plates.

The next night I was invited to the home of a young assistant professor at People's University; he was one of the Ping-Pong champions who had kindly let me win a few points on my first visit to China. (I remember him furtively showing me an undeveloped roll of film hidden at the rear of his tiny freezer, proof, he said, of his participation in Tiananmen Square—exculpatory evidence, I think he meant, when the verdict on Tiananmen would eventually be reversed.)

"Home" is an exaggeration here. It was barely a room, no larger than a master bedroom closet in a modest suburban house, where he and his wife lived on campus. There was literally no place to move; we had to eat while sitting on their bed. The cooking equipment was in the hallway and the bathroom was thirty yards down the hall. The food was spectacular: fresh, crunchy vegetables and rich, crusty grains redolent of garlic and other spices stir fried in a large wok. What a contrast to the previous dinner!

Tofu has a fascinating history in China. Legend has it that tofu was invented by monks commanded to sustain the health of an elderly emperor. For generations thereafter, tofu became part of the Chinese diet. Most were so poor that they could not afford meat; all they could eat were vegetables, grains, and tofu products. Over the past two decades, as standards of living have risen dramatically, meat products have come to symbolize upward mobility and high social status, while eating tofu has come to be considered antiquated and agrarian and, well, downright low class and embarrassing.

Initially, until my gustatory idiosyncrasies became known and accepted, my hosts were ashamed to serve me tofu. Chinese are exceedingly polite, especially to foreign guests, and if they had served tofu they would have felt, I later learned, as if they were insulting me, treating me, so to speak, as if I were a farmer. The insult would have been amplified because they would have assumed that I would have thought that they wouldn't spend the extra money for meats. In fact, when I would assertively ask for tofu, the assumption was that I was being excessively polite in not wanting my hosts to order the much more expensive meat dishes. I was not being polite at all. Not me, not when it comes to food. I was frustrated and starving. I didn't like any of the meats and I loved all of the tofus.

More recently, as my reputation as "Doufu Wang" grew, I've had to face the opposite problem: once hosts were advised of my proletariat appetites, they would order mainly tofu at banquets—for all the guests, so as not to offend me. Such cuisine constraints caused quiet displeasure among the other diners. Their disappointment was acute since banquets were the only time that these government employees could indulge in eating expensive (even exotic) meats. We finally found the balance and the routine is set: several tofu dishes are ordered for me and everyone else has whatever they like. (Often my hosts order excessive amounts of tofu—that nobody else eats—and when they politely keep ladling it onto my plate I feel compelled to overeat, thereby neutralizing, I suspect, any potential health benefits.)

Here's how I got in trouble trying to combine my love for tofu with my fledgling attempts to learn Chinese. To establish rapport (and deflate my overblown image) in China, I like to announce, in reasonably understandable Chinese, that "When I am in America, I eat tofu every morning"—a statement of fact that I thought would surprise my new Chinese friends or associates, establish a social bond, and distinguish me from other foreigners.

For the longest time, I thought my Chinese friends were smiling in appreciation of an American who eats tofu daily or, less complimentary, they were amused by my poor pronunciation (I never let my random tones and mangled grammar inhibit me from practicing Chinese). Finally, a good friend, the kind who will whisper that your fly is open or your breath less than fresh, explained to me what I was really saying. It so happens, I now know, that in colloquial Chinese, the expression *chi doufu* ("eat tofu") means to have sex, more specifically to take advantage of young girls. What I had been saying, to all whom I would meet, was that every morning when in America..., well, you get the point.

Curious about this expression, I asked about its derivation and was told that the softness of tofu suggested the softness of young girls, an etymology that is neither politically correct nor, I recently learned, historically accurate. Mr. Zhang Ziyang, a noted poet, director, and senior executive at China Central Television, filled me in over lunch of dongbeicai (Northwest or Manchurian food—characterized by large amounts of hearty, flavorful dishes presented without concern for visual elegance).

It seems that around the sixth century, tofu was an expensive delicacy and thus could not often be eaten. However, during funerals, the custom was to "enjoy" the occasion, especially if the person had lived into "old age" of at least sixty years. Tofu began to be eaten during funerals and thus it came to be said that people were using tofu to "take advantage" of the deceased. The phrase "eating tofu" was gradually transformed into "taking advantage" in general, and after that, expectedly, "taking advantage" took on its contemporary sexual connotation.

When hearing of this sixth century historical analysis, a senior government official, momentarily diverting himself from our politically sensitive conversation, enthusiastically offered an alternative, indeed dissenting view. Tofu was cheap, he began, and since the word "cheap" in Chinese (pianyi) is represented by the same character that also represents the word "advantage," the cheapness of tofu became, as it were, a pun, and was thus transformed into "taking advantage." Furthermore, since tofu was soft and made no noise when one ate it, so if one "took advantage" of a young girl and she was quiet about it (i.e., didn't reveal it), she also "made no noise." Thus both verbal pathways combined to construct the comic equivalency between eating tofu and taking advantage of a young girl. This alternative view, I might add, was offered rather passionately, reflecting Chinese fervor for their history and culture. Chinese people, it seems, take their tofu stories, like their tofu dishes, quite seriously. I feel much at home in China.

Beijing Conference: Media in the United States

In January 2000, Zhao Qizheng, the minister of the Information Office of the State Council of China, and I organized and co-chaired a three-day closed conference on "Media in the United States." It was held at the fashionable Palace Hotel, near Tiananmen Square, and at the Information Office headquarters, reasonably nearby in central Beijing. Chinese participants included three ministers and eleven directors general from the Information Office; media leaders of seven provincial and major municipal governments; senior executives and editors of (among other media) China Central Television (CCTV), China Radio International, China National Radio Network, People's Daily, China Daily, China Today, Beijing Review, and the Xinhua News Agency; and the chairmen of communications and journalism departments at Beijing University, Qinghua University, and The Chinese People's University. American participants came from Dow Jones Company, Discovery Communications International, the John F. Kennedy

School of Government at Harvard University, the University of Massachusetts at Amherst, and the United States Embassy in Beijing. The presentations were frank and factual and interaction was substantive and lively.

The very fact that a conference on the media could be held between senior American and Chinese officials is itself remarkable testimony to the changes in China. Indeed, the original suggestion for the conference came from Zhao Qizheng, who is a close associate of President Jiang Zemin, and from Zhao's newly appointed deputy director general of the International Communication Bureau, Yang Yang, who is a graduate of the Kennedy School at Harvard.

One has to appreciate that all the Chinese media, from the beginning of the People's Republic, have been considered mouthpieces of the Communist Party, with a duty to report and present news and information that support the Party's control of society and view of the world. Social stability and national pride—the two great thematic drivers we stress for understanding China—are the underlying motivation for China's traditional view of the media, in addition to the government's need to keep itself in power.

Yet the world changes, and the government of the PRC knows that China must change with it. The explosion of information from all sources electronic, from satellite television to the Internet, cannot be escaped, in spite of reactionary and generally inept attempts to restrict access. (A case in point was the government's campaign a few years ago to keep satellite TV dishes out of the hands of ordinary citizens; the prohibition failed because, in some cities, the primary purveyors of such dishes—the local sales organizations—were either the army or the police.[20] That's the market economy!)

The current Chinese government takes a realistic view. Premier Zhu Rongji, for example, has stated that the media provides a vital service as society's "watchdog," criticizing the mistakes and excesses of government. Premier Zhu has made it known that he is a fan of CCTV's acerbic investigative news programs, which like to expose corruption and other abuses of power. With such a huge governmental apparatus at federal, provincial, municipal, and local levels, it is impossible for the Chinese leadership to control the widespread corruption, the outright incompetence, and the cases of

---

[20] In one of President Jiang Zemin's most courageous acts of reform, he called on the army to give up (or sell off) all of its multifarious, though hardly coordinated, business interests. It is estimated, unreliably, that the People's Liberation Army operated some fifteen thousand enterprises generating annual revenues of about $10 billion. One, reportedly, was Beijing's five-star Palace Hotel, the site of our conference.

bureaucratic tyranny (or lunacy)—all of which have a corrosive, dragging effect on economic reform. Only the media can root out such omnidirectional, pervasive problems. When told that CCTV news is now 30 percent negative and 70 percent positive about China's current state of affairs (a remarkable shift from yesteryear's perennially Pollyanna media), Premier Zhu is reported to have said that 49 percent negative and 51 percent positive would be fine by him. Although the Chinese central government would like to see the media focus more on the failings of local government than question the policies of the central government (as would, for that matter, the American and any other government), the genie of increasing freedom in the media will have a beneficial effect on all of China.

Conference topics included:

"Seek Truth From Facts"[21]: On the importance of keeping news, opinion, and advertising scrupulously separate, and why believable content is the key to success. (Karen Elliot House and James McGregor, president and vice-president of Dow Jones International)

"Strategies and Operations of Television Networks": Why reality-based programming must be both accurate and entertaining and why sensitivity to local differences is essential. (Dawn McCall, president of Discovery Communications International)

"How Media Influences Public Opinion and Politics in the United States": The meaning, import, power, and problems of freedom of the press, and how it is expressed differently in different countries and cultures. (Prof. Thomas Patterson, director of the Shorenstein Center on the Press, Politics, and Public Policy, John F. Kennedy School of Government, Harvard University)

"Content, Programming, and the Psychology of Television Audiences": How sophisticated theories and models are used to understand audience habits, and how media positioning and programming articulate with those habits. (Prof. Leslie Davis, Department of Communications, University of Massachusetts at Amherst)

"International Information Programs, U.S. Department of State": How government and media interact in the United States; the independence of American media. (Paul Blackburn, minister-counselor for press and cultural affairs, United States Embassy in Beijing)

---

21 "Seek Truth From Facts" is a famous quote from Deng Xiaoping, which he used to epitomize a more pragmatic approach to ideology and China's development. Ms. House chose Deng's aphorism to characterize her vision of the media.

"United States—China Coproductions": Our television documentaries—"Capital Wave" (Chinese) and "In Search of China" (English)—as a case study of sensitive co-productions, and why documentaries must be truthful to be believable.[22] (Robert Lawrence Kuhn, executive producer, and Adam Zhu, producer)

Roundtable discussions dealt with attitudes and approaches to China in the Western media, media coverage of China in the United States, media coverage of the United States in China, and how American and Chinese media can promote mutual understanding. Both sides were frank— sharply so at times—reflecting each other's growing confidence that an honest exchange of values would be appreciated. When bluntness is delivered with a smile and accepted with sincerity, progress can be made even on what appear to be intractable issues.

I structured the roundtables as a simulation game. For the first session, I had the American group form a virtual consulting company that was being hired by the Chinese government to help improve the image of China in the United States; for the second, roles were reversed and the Chinese became advisors to the American government. As consultants, each side was not to question the policies of its "clients," but simply to advise them on how best to "spin" the stories. Though no instant answers appeared, by forcing each side to help the other accomplish its goal, each side gained greater insight into the other's positions and sensitivities.

The Americans said that it would be futile—and financially disastrous— for the Chinese to launch a commercial magazine in the United States with the editorial purpose of improving China's image (as the Chinese had thought would make sense). The Chinese told the Americans that the American policy of thwarting China's national interests is the root cause of anti-American feelings in China, and that no cosmetics or communications technology can mask anti-Chinese words and deeds. Human rights, Taiwan, and Tibet were brought up by both sides to bolster their opposing positions.

The Americans told the Chinese that they shouldn't feel so discouraged about American attitudes toward China, because even though the approval ratings of China might be less than desired in the United States,

---

[22] We were gratified that the Chinese conferees liked the excerpts we played of our English version, even the "negative" story of Acheng, China's first major bankruptcy and its human tragedies (see page 84). The professors of communication and journalism from Beijing and Qinghua universities said that they would like to use the full documentary as a textbook example in their classes.

the approval ratings of the media (10 percent) and the U.S. Congress (6 percent) were even worse. A Chinese senior editor asserted that absolute freedom of the press erodes objectivity and encourages subjectivity; he was met with the rejoinder that a free press is self-correcting, that limiting press freedom is contrary to the First Amendment of the U.S. Constitution, and that such a cure would be worse than any possible disease.

Several Chinese pointed out that Chinese know America far better than Americans know China—and that this is perceived by many Chinese as a slight. The Americans agreed with the observation, but asked the Chinese not to take it personally, since China is not as important to American life as America is to Chinese life—and furthermore, to our detriment, Americans know relatively little about any foreign country.

As both sides became bolder, the Americans complained about the restrictions on foreign journalists in China, such as the waiting period (often ten days) for a permit to cover a story that might well be needed overnight, and noted that such annoyances were similar to those imposed by totalitarian, repressive regimes—North Korea, Cuba, Iran, Iraq—and that such rules made it virtually impossible for a foreign reporter to do his or her job legally. There were various stories of pro-Chinese foreign journalists infuriated by such cavalier treatment, who consequently became progressively more hostile in their reporting.

To its credit, the Information Office promised to address such concerns. In fact, Vice Minister Yang Zhengquan made a believer out of the Americans with his candid opening and closing addresses, both of which acknowledged the necessity of change, and also because he attended every meeting and took copious notes. After the conference, we were told that summaries of the American presentations were being disseminated to operational people.

Not all of the Chinese who attended were completely approving, of course. One editor of an English-language publication said that American conferees were like the nineteenth century missionaries—well intentioned, certainly, but inevitably followed by gunboats sent to enforce the interests of their countries. The threat of economic sanctions (seemingly an annual affair in the U.S. Congress), the Chinese said, were the modern equivalent of gunboats.

One leading Chinese professor said that he agreed with what Tom Patterson said about freedom of the press, it was just that if such freedoms were suddenly allowed in China precisely as they operate in America, the country would fall apart. Professor Patterson pointed out that even when the "rules" of news media are the same (i.e., freedom of the press), when they are played out in different cultures or countries (e.g., England vs. Germany), the forms and expressions are also different, thus adding to the variety of human experience (see Professor Patterson's commentary which follows, page 198).

The director of the Center for International Communications Studies at Qinghua University stated that 95 percent of the Chinese people had positive attitudes toward Americans, because their image of America is gained strictly from movies and popular culture, but the 5 percent who resent America's patronizing attitudes and heavy-handed criticism are the decision-makers of Chinese society and must be reached. Most of the Chinese stated afterward that they agreed with most of what they had heard and that it opened up their thinking. Both sides agreed that modern media has great leverage in molding opinion and influencing policy, and that more such conferences should be held in the future.

Yet there continues to be uncertainty and internal confusion in the Chinese government's media strategy. Just weeks after our conference, new rules forced foreign magazines to remove their names and logos from the Chinese editions of their publications, and the atmosphere was darkened further by the government's questioning the legality of many magazine joint ventures. Foreign publishers had been viewing the Chinese market as a dream—low production costs, growing advertising revenues, and an enormous and increasingly literate and information-hungry public. Suddenly, the dream was a nightmare. The Hearst Corporation, in quiet defiance, left a blank where their *Cosmopolitan* logo would normally appear, instead of using the non-euphonious but officially licensed name of *Trends Lady*. Though Chinese officials have accused foreign publishers of abusing their partnerships by, for example, publishing more than one title under one license, the fundamental issue, of course, is government confusion and conflicting views about how to deal with media and an increasingly astute population.

Most Western observers believe that this, too, shall pass, as China's senior leaders are beginning to see media as more than the mouthpiece of the Party. Furthermore, as reform deepens, the Chinese media, like other industries, must learn to compete in the marketplace. Government subsidies will no longer be handed out so freely, and financial success in the market means acceptance by the people, so if newspapers, magazines, and radio and television stations continue to lose money, they will have to change their ways to appeal to the public. What Chinese media want from their American counterparts is advice on how to build profitable media operations. All of this is to the benefit of the Chinese people, who will be getting more of what they want. As with all peoples, what they want is the truth.

Thomas E. Patterson: Communication In and With China

Professor Thomas E. Patterson is director of the Shorenson Center for the Press and Media at the John F. Kennedy School of Government of Harvard University. He was a featured speaker at the Beijing Conference on Media in the United States.

"Let's sit down and talk about it." This American aphorism is less a proverb than a principle. It expresses the American belief that the differences between people and nations can be resolved through frank and open discussion. And it was trust in this belief that brought us—a small but diverse group of Americans—to Beijing in January 2000 as guests of the Information Office of the State Council of the PRC. Over a period of three days, we discussed with our Chinese hosts the U.S. media system's legal, political, and commercial foundations.

Effective deliberation rests on common understandings as much as it does on overlapping interests. In politics, people and nations sort themselves out on the basis of separate interests and values. That's a given. But people cannot talk meaningfully about their differences if they have radically opposing perceptions of reality. To understand why the Chinese and the Americans frequently misunderstand each other, consider an example that arose during our conference on the U.S. media.

Some congressional right-wingers had claimed that China was plotting a takeover of the Panama Canal, which the United States only a few weeks earlier had returned to Panamanian control. The allegation made headlines in the United States because it was an irresistibly good story. It is doubtful that any informed American journalist took the allegation seriously, but absurdity is nearly always the stuff of lively reportage. The official Chinese press, however, did take the story seriously, using it to reinforce an alleged American bias against China. On the final day of our conference, one newspaper featured a front page story that, in the context of the Panama Canal allegation, accused the United States of "China bashing."

One can only assume that millions of Chinese believe much of what they read in their morning papers, and accordingly had a lowered opinion of the United States. Yet the deeper reality of the incident is its foundation in a cultural misunderstanding. Out of their own experiences, Chinese journalists had naturally assumed that any major claim in the press about a foreign government reflected their own government's official view. Thus, in reading about the Panama Canal allegation, they assumed that the U.S. government was behind it or at least believed it. In the United States, however, all sorts of opinions—some of them quite zany—are aired all the time through the media. The congressional right-wingers who alleged a China conspiracy had opposed the official policy of handing over control of the canal zone to Panama. Their views did not in any way reflect the official position of "the government" or "the White House," or even of the majority in Congress.

America and China are on opposite sides of the world geographically. Culturally, they are often wider apart. And these differences are compounded by the fact that the Chinese and American cultures are both steeped in myth, which can blind attempts at mutual understanding. "Americans who think about the problem of unifying the world," the political scientist Harold Lasswell wrote, "tend to follow the precedent set in their own history." Our myopia is sometimes so severe that it's laughable. In 1940, U.S. Senator Kenneth Wherry soberly exclaimed, "With God's help, we will lift Shanghai up and up, ever up, until it is just like Kansas City."

But cultural blinders can be overcome, and people and nations can draw closer together if "they sit down and talk about it." We—the American and the Chinese representatives—came away from our three-day conference with a fuller awareness of the formidable challenges to productive dialogue and of the need to meet again to continue our discussions.

We also drew broad lessons from the meeting. One lesson was that, if the United States and China are to communicate effectively, each must take into account the belief system of the other. Americans embrace the values of freedom, democracy, and individualism. These values shape Americans' interpretations of China's actions, whether the issue is Taiwan, Tibet, or global trade. China cannot change that perspective. It derives from Americans' historical experience and way of life. To accommodate it, China must take it into account when communicating with the American people. By the same token, the United States must recognize China's cultural distinctiveness (e.g., Chinese history, pride and national stability) when addressing China.

A second lesson is that cultural differences shape media systems as much, and in all probability more, than the legal underpinnings of those systems. The media system in China is opening rapidly as a result of economic change, new communication technology, and political liberalization. It is estimated that there are more than 30 million Chinese who have access to the Internet. "Private" newspapers have sprung up in virtually every Chinese city. Even the state press has changed significantly, as the government has trimmed its subsidies, forcing government newspapers to reach out to advertisers for revenue. And as the boundaries of open expression have been extended, demands for even greater openness have increased.

Would the adoption of something resembling an American-style press law result in a Chinese media system resembling that of the United States? The question was of great concern to our Chinese hosts, who worried that press freedom would create political instability and shower the nation with crass entertainment programming.

Press law, however, never operates in a vacuum. It interacts with cultural influences to produce a distinctive media system. Although all of the world's open societies provide for a free press, their media systems are remarkably varied. The Japanese system is not at all the American system, just as the Italian system is quite different from Poland's. The range of media systems in open societies is nothing short of extraordinary. They range from the nearly chaotic to the thoroughly orderly, from the shamelessly commercial to the deeply public.

In short, press freedom serves primarily to create a hospitable environment within which political and social variations within a nation can find *their* unique expressions. It is not yet certain but increasingly probable that China's media system will open ever wider, a process that will include the liberalization of the nation's press law. The result will not be an "Americanization" of the Chinese media but, instead, a distinctive Chinese system that reflects the values and interests of its people.

Co-production

Certainly my most memorable experience in China was as originator and executive producer of the documentary, "In Search of China," excerpts of which are featured throughout this book. Actually, we produced dual documentaries on economic reform, one in Chinese and one in English, both coproductions of China Central Television (CCTV) and our K² Media Group (KMG). Each version had its own specific objectives. The eight-part television series "Capital Wave" was a milestone in Chinese television, for several reasons: it was the first true United States/Chinese co-production on business, the first nationally broadcast documentary series focusing on mergers and acquisitions, and it featured extensive interviews with CEOs of major American corporations. "In Search of China," our PBS special, uses China's remarkable economic transformation as the metaphorical lens through which international audiences might view the equally remarkable transformation of Chinese society, warts and all.

The coproduction is emblematic of those happy coincidences when independent groups have similar ideas that can best be implemented together. I had proposed the series on mergers and acquisitions to CCTV in late 1997, and in their response I learned that Li Qiang, a young creative director in CCTV's Economics Department, had proposed a similar idea, but that the CCTV leadership was not comfortable with their own internal understanding of such new thinking. One has to remember that until recently M&A in China had been considered either a characteristic of capitalist economies inappropriate for China or the last-gasp medicine to be administered only *in extremis* to a dying enterprise.

The timing of our proposal was fortuitous but not accidental. Earlier in 1997, several of China's senior leaders had begun to speak positively in formal speeches about "capital" and the progressive role that mergers and acquisitions could play in restructuring China's economy. It was as a result of this policy change that Li Qiang (who was getting a Ph.D. in mergers and acquisitions at Chinese People's University) had independently proposed a series on M&A. So when the CCTV leadership introduced us to Li, it became the task of Adam Zhu, who was to become the producer of the series, to take the lead in developing a coproduction partnership between our American team and the CCTV team. This was a true collaboration, with the parallel objectives of giving Chinese audiences current and comprehensive insight into the problems and progress of Chinese enterprises and companies, and bringing to international audiences the challenging impact of a changing economy—the story of people striving and struggling with economic reform.

I set five criteria for the dual documentaries—economic honesty, reporting integrity, creative insight, startling stories, and artistic excellence—and I required "buy-in" from both Chinese and American teams. I am often asked whether there were conflicts between the production teams, and how difficult it was to harmonize them—the assumption being that divergent economic, social, and political views between countries would generate journalistic and artistic discord. There surely were significant creative battles, but these fights had no correlation with the nationality of the combatants. It was just as likely for an American producer to argue with an American editor or a Chinese producer to criticize a Chinese director as it was for disputes to arise between Americans and Chinese. At heart, all of the participants were committed to their craft, and good craftsmanship thrives on tension, conflict, and thoughtful resolution, not on simplistic style, constrained structure, and forced agreement. My appreciation, and often sympathy, went out to Adam Zhu, our fearless producer, for being the one whose responsibility it was to resolve those conflicts. Whenever I would ask him about some new, seemingly vexing problem, he would often answer with a worldwide and time-honored expletive: "Artists!"

But how would we deal with the sensitive area of editorial control? This was a bigger issue. In our contract with CCTV it was agreed that each side would have veto power over the material in the other's final cut, in order to preclude embarrassment. Technically, this meant that while CCTV could not decide what would be in the final cut of the English version, they could object to our showing anything they did not like. Conversely, since we insisted on parallel clauses, we had, technically, the same right to veto what CCTV would broadcast over their own national channels. (I am unaware of a similar arrangement in a CCTV co-production and I am amused at the potential spectacle of an American exercising veto rights over a CCTV program broadcast in China.) CCTV lived up to its end of the bargain, and in March 1999 Adam and I flew over to Beijing to view and edit the final version of the eight-part documentary on M&A to be broadcast on CCTV. We made many contributions, through many nights, particularly regarding the use of American-related merger-and-acquisition examples.

I was more concerned, of course, about CCTV's interest in evaluating the final edit of our English-language version, especially since we would be presenting some rather strong stories about China's problems. I was reassured by a conversation that Adam overheard at the Beijing press conference announcing the Chinese series. A mid-level CCTV executive was telling his staff that he would have to approve the English version, when his boss, a senior CCTV executive, interrupted to ask him why he thought he had the competence to do so! The point was apparently made; as it turned out, no advance screening was ever demanded, and no veto of any kind was requested.

The issue of editorial control was sacrosanct at KMG and central to the project. In a meeting with a senior Chinese media official, I remarked that if our documentary appeared 100 percent positive about China,

American (and international) audiences would believe zero percent of it. On the other hand, if the documentary were, say, 90 percent negative, the same audiences would believe the 10 percent positive part of it to be true—my percentages were an exaggeration to be sure, but my point was how to understand the psychology of Western audiences.

Of course, the documentary is far from 90 percent negative—I assured the fellow that it would be nothing like that—because China's reform is far from 90 percent negative. But we would have no concern about the ratio of "positive" to "negative," I told this astute senior official; rather "we would strive to tell the truth as best we could using a diversity of verité stories that honestly represented contemporary China." The most effective propaganda, ultimately, is truth—though in any complex situation, explored in any medium, "truth" is always an elusive goal.

I reinforced my views by citing an article that I had read in *China Today*, China's primary English-language newspaper, about the "bias" of the American media toward China. I said to this senior official that although I probably agreed with much of what the writer said, his arguments were so trite, generalized, stylized, homogenized, pre-packaged, ham-handed, and screechy, that I found myself mentally arguing with him as I read his simplistic analysis, and I wound up mentally defending American media more than I ever had. I became progressively angrier with each purple-prosed sentence, so that I ended up quite in the opposite place from where the writer had intended to take me.[23]

---

[23] Following are some delicious excerpts from this article, "U.S. Media Bias to China," an usually long opinion piece in *China Today*, April 5, 1999. We are told that the author, Li Xiguang, is a journalist with the Xinhua News Agency of China and, at the time of his writing, was a research fellow at the Kennedy School of Government at Harvard. "...But after a final analysis of the American press and politics, I find that the U.S. media seem to have several reasons for calling Chinese spies: the Cold War mentality the U.S. media harbor needs a spy to fill the vacuum left by the demise of the Soviet Union.... Old-fashioned people in the United States are not ideologically and psychologically prepared for the dramatic progress China has made economically and politically.... Also the media need the figure of a spy to make a profit. The acquittal of their president in the case of Monica Lewinsky has left newsrooms without a strong seller and the public without a compelling story. Spy stories are simply golden apples falling from the trees. What kind of story could be spicier than a spy story after a sex story in the U.S. today—particularly when the spy is Chinese? Conventional wisdom says that a country ruled by a Communist government is threatening and ready to steal.... Positive stories [about China] upset the public and do not sell. So by the control of the means of

Who Could Have Thought It?

In June 2000, Adam Zhu and I were meeting with Minister Zhao
Qizheng and advising the Information Office of the State Council in
preparation for a major Chinese cultural exhibition in the United States
to coincide with President Jiang Zemin's visit in September 2000 for the
opening of the United Nations. With tours planned for New York, Washington, Los Angeles, San Francisco, and Chicago, the exhibition is intended to be the most significant, high visibility presentation of Chinese
culture ever mounted in America. Highlights include viewings of the
most important artwork ever allowed out of China; fashion shows fea-
turing Chinese supermodels wearing elegant and startlingly modern,
Chinese-designed clothes; concerts of classical Chinese music; and other
gala events. (Adam played a major role in organizing the exhibition; he
arranged for about twenty major American corporations to be cospon-
sors; he met personally with the CEOs—China is now that important—
and arranged their participation. In the process, he earned the nickname,
awarded by both sides, of "Super Agent.")

Adam and I very much enjoy speaking with Minister Zhao. We like exploring the contrasting though parallel perceptions of Chinese and Americans: for example, the Chinese perception that the American media is
biased against China, and the American perception that the Chinese
media acts as the government's "mouthpiece." Minister Zhao often
stresses the long history of cooperation between America and China, particularly during World War II when thousands of Americans gave their
lives to fight for China's independence from Japan.

On this occasion, he then referred to the Korean War, just five years
later, when America and China suddenly found themselves bitter enemies. Again, Minister Zhao articulated the contrasting perceptions of each
side: the Americans believed that they were fighting for Korean freedom;

---

communication, the media will avoid the dissemination of any information that
might run counter to their business interests. To the media executives, every story
has a price tag. If an event [occurs] which will enhance the image of China and improve U.S.-China relations, a question will be raised among the editors: Can we afford to cover the story . . . ? In another sense, the FBI needs [foreign] spies to spy
[i.e., to justify its own spying by monitoring emails and faxes] . . . . A Chinese saying goes, 'A whorehouse needs a virtuous shop sign to sell well.' For the anti-China
hardliners [in the U.S.], the shop sign is the spy [allegations against China] and the
meat they are going to sell is their new missile defense system."

the Chinese believed that they were fighting to protect their motherland from a foreign invasion force approaching their borders. He said that it would be impossible for Chinese and Americans to come to consensus about the Korean War and so we should agree to put this issue to the side. What we should do, he stressed, is to make sure that war never again becomes a means to settle disputes between us.

Before he could continue to develop this theme, I interrupted, almost jumping out of my chair, and told him of a fascinating television production on which Adam and I were working. The story began about three years before when we were invited by China Central Television (CCTV), the national network owned and tightly controlled by the government, to meet a famous Chinese director. Li Qiankuan, head of the well-respected Changchun Film Studio and chairman of the China Film Foundation, had made several important Chinese motion pictures, including the award-winning "Founding Ceremony of the People's Republic of China." He was a true artist, with his own vision of things; he had shown a willingness to push artistic boundaries; and he maintained the confidence of China's senior leaders (he was even a member of the People's Congress).

Mr. Li, who works with his wife Xiao Guiyun as co-director, told us that it was his dream to produce a definitive television series on the Korean War. He believed that the United States and China would become partners in peace and engines of prosperity in the twenty-first century and thus it would be instructive to look back and reflect upon the one time in history we were enemies at war.

Director Li, as he is known, envisioned a truly epic work—thirty episodes of forty-five minutes each, over twenty-two hours on the screen. The series would tell the inside story from all sides—Chinese, American, Russian, North Korean, South Korean. It would be the largest budget in CCTV history; it would involve tens of thousands of extras; the Chinese military and the city of Dalian offered major assistance; MacArthur's Inchon landing would be staged when it actually occurred (September 15); battles would be taped in the rugged terrain of Manchuria, just across the border from North Korea, in the frozen snows of dead winter; many American actors would be involved and 25 percent of the production would be shot in English.

"The 38th Parallel" (the working title) would be broadcast on CCTV Channel 1 at 8:00 P.M.—the most prized primetime spot on the most watched national network in the world (300 million television households!)—six days a week for five weeks. CCTV also hoped to engender international distribution for the non-Chinese world, which had not been common for their productions.

The script, Director Li claimed, would "respect history and offer an authoritative assessment of history." It was written by a highly respected Chinese writer, Zhang Xiaotian. It would tell the inside stories of what really was happening in China, Russia, and North Korea. The Chinese would reveal their innermost, highest-level deliberations; Russian archives had been tapped; scholarly American books were being scrutinized.

CCTV's internal proposal stated that this "first-class television production" would be "based on historical evidence and secret documents released in the past fifty years by China, the U.S. and the former Soviet Union . . . and will reproduce the profound significance of war . . . . The start will be the outbreak of the war on June 25, 1950, and it will end with the signing of the Armistice Agreement on July 27, 1953. It will cover all the major events relating to the war . . . offering full and objective depictions."

There was the promise of vivid personal portrayals of all the protagonists—influential figures and ordinary soldiers—in all the warring countries. CCTV's proposal concluded that "'The 38th Parallel' will have a strong sense of historical retrospection and enlightenment . . . sending shock waves around the world . . . and have worldwide repercussions." I was impressed how well the Chinese had done their homework, how seriously they wanted to produce a monumental work of artistry and sensitivity, and how much they sought international respect and impact.

Moved by the spirit of Director Li's vision, though weary of opposing opinions and potential pitfalls, we decided to assist in the production. I was especially concerned about the as-yet-unseen script. After decades of propaganda and vituperation, and with CCTV being the government-controlled transmitter of managed news, how could the script be historically accurate, much less "balanced"? I am a great believer in artistic freedom, but a demonized America or a cartoonish characterization of Americans I could not countenance and would not be associated with. I was apprehensive about one line in that CCTV internal memorandum about "The 38th Parallel": "It will reflect the concern of all peace-loving people with distinguishing justice from evil." Though not well translated, that sentence caused a twinge. I wondered: how would the Chinese filmmakers seek to "distinguish justice from evil"?

I was somewhat reassured by their repeated intent to "respect history" and to infuse the series with personal stories of both American and Chinese characters—Director Li said that "a soldier in war is a soldier in war."

I was cautiously pleased when I offered that our team might provide rewriting suggestions for the English-language scenes and we were enthusiastically encouraged to do so. I took scrupulous care in highlighting all changes we were recommending in their script, since this was CCTV's production, not ours, and our role was as advisors and assistants, not coproduction partners. Nonetheless, I remained troubled that I would be aiding a production with which I would no doubt have conceptual disagreements, perhaps profound ones.

There is no way that a CCTV production on the Korean War (essentially the government view, however enlightened and artistic) would be the same as, say, a Spielberg-DreamWorks production of the same events, but I believed that the Chinese not only had a right to portray their views, but also that their stated desire to be honest to history, to explore the personal emotions and tragedies of war, and to show to the world their artistic sensitivity were all worthwhile objectives. After all, Oliver Stone had every right to portray his idiosyncratic image of President Kennedy's assassination, even though Stone's view was contradicted by virtually every reputable historian of those events. Furthermore, I felt our participation could make a difference, and thus facilitate communication between China and America. We would receive no fee or payments, just a promise to consider an English-language version that might be derived from the same footage.

Just after committing to provide our assistance, CCTV's production of "The 38th Parallel," for which they had committed so much and worked so long, came to a sudden halt. We were not told details of why this massive series was abruptly stopped, but clearly the directive came from well above CCTV in the Chinese power structure. Perhaps the Chinese Foreign Ministry was involved; perhaps the governments of other countries. All we knew was that CCTV kept lobbying for permission to make "The 38th Parallel" and they kept getting turned down. To CCTV's credit, and reflecting a strong Chinese sense of fairness, the CCTV executives felt badly that we had done work in good faith, were not paid, and now would not have anything to show for our efforts.

But CCTV was persistent. It took about two and a half years of quiet inter-ministry diplomacy before they got the green light—actually, the better traffic light metaphor would be a "blinking yellow." There was no on-high decree of permission or formal blessing. As we sensed the situation, it was more an easing of a decision to block than an affirmative decision to encourage, as if the distributed selection process of the market economy was being allowed to make its slow way into the Chinese media.

So CCTV would be making "The 38th Parallel" on its own, and thus CCTV itself, not the Chinese Government per se, would be responsible and take the consequences. Orchards or onions, CCTV would get it either way. We did find it interesting that not long after we began pre-production, the historic meeting between the leaders of North and South Korea, the first in fifty years, took place in Pyongyang.

We had many days of serious casting; we arranged for Director Li and the CCTV team to work with a major Hollywood casting agency and they auditioned over a hundred American actors for about twelve major roles.[24] There are about eighty American speaking roles and hundreds of American extras. Over ninety scenes will be shot in the United States, though most of the English language scenes taking place in Korea or Japan will be shot in China.

Recently, when Director Li was in Los Angeles (to scout locations, cast the American actors, and plan the production), he was also a featured speaker at a major forum on the entertainment and media industries in Asia. He told me that when he mentioned the Korean War production in his speech, a number of American media executives asked him privately why he had wanted to take on such a controversial subject at such a sensitive time in China-U.S. relations. His answer was simple: "I am an artist," he said, "and artists seek challenges." Director Li told me that he figured that the expected controversy would spotlight the production and that "The 38th Parallel" would surprise Western critics.

Minister Zhao was pleased to learn of this Chinese-American cooperation in producing the Korean War epic series and he marveled at its historical irony. How impossible such a cooperative production between Chinese and Americans would have seemed even a decade ago, he said, and how symbolic it is of progress in China-U.S. relations and in the cinematic artistry needed to explore this complex and sensitive subject. Minister Zhao said he wanted to get photographs of the Chinese crew filming "The 38th Parallel" on location with American actors in Los Angeles. He planned to label these photos simply, "Who Could Have Thought It?"

---

[24] Several thousand American actors applied to the call, from which the casting agency chose over a hundred for formal auditions. Many well-known American character actors have been selected (MacArthur was the most difficult role to cast). In the spirit of full disclosure, the lead American role, a fictionalized reporter named Kinsky, modeled after the real war correspondent Marguerite Higgins, is being played by Daniella Kuhn, the author's daughter, whose previous credits include *Patch Adams* and *Traffic*.

Driving by Tiananmen Square.

Robert Kuhn signing *Dealmaker*
at Beijing Xidan Book Tower, China's largest bookstore.

Homesick migrant worker.

He Qinglian, controversial reporter and author.

Yan Mingfu observing devastating flood damage for China Charity Federation in 1998.

Yan Mingfu as Russian translator for Mao Zedong in the 1960s.

我们回去好好研究研究

Yan Mingfu trying to persuade students to leave Tiananmen Square in 1989.

Working together to support charity. Wang Guangying, vice chairman of the National People's Congress (center); Wan Guoquan, vice chairman of the Chinese People's Political Consultative Conference (second from right).

Haier co-founder and executive vice president, Yang Mianmian, and Haier icon.

Haier slogan: "Never Say No to the Market!"

Yang Mianmian cheering a Haier tug-of-war.

On location with CCTV crew at Haier world headquarters.

"Foreign bosses" in the early
20th century.

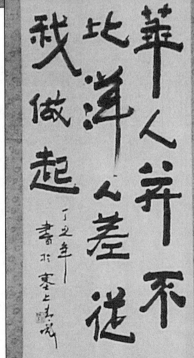

華人并不
比洋人差
我做起

丁之年
書於
寒上嘉成

"Chinese are not inferior to foreigners
—and I can make a difference."

Old Shanghai in the 1930s.

The Bund in Shanghai today.

Old Man Xiao Hui with his ever-present radio, listening to stock market reports.

Old Man Xiao at a brokerage branch in Shanghai.

Yang Baiwan: stock market pioneer and celebrity also known as "Yang Millionaire."

"Yang Millionaire" teaching other investors.

Feminine beauty with small feet in ancient China.

Support group: "Rural Women Knowing All," with group leader Long Di (right).

Deal making at dinner. Dr. Zeng Jinsong is in the middle.

Dr. Zeng Jinsong, president, Innostar High-Tech Enterprises, organizing New Year's Eve Unity Concert in the Great Hall of the People.

Senior leaders on stage with conductor Chen Zuohuang (third from right) and pianist Dora Serviarian-Kuhn(center) after a concert.

Dora Serviarian-Kuhn following a concert in Beijing.

Opening the media conference in Beijing, January 2000. The American delegation is seated in the front of the room.

Madame Zhao Shaohua, Secretary General of the State Council Information Office, addressses the media conference.

Chairing the media conference: Yang Zhengquan, vice minister of the State Council Information Office, and Robert Kuhn, with Deputy Director General Yang Yang.

Before the closing dinner at the media conference, from the left: Paul Blackburn (U.S. Embassy), Eugene Martin (U.S. Embassy), Minister Zhao Qizheng, Robert Kuhn, Ora Namir (Israeli Ambassador to China), Yang Yang, and Adam Zhu.

CCTV President Zhao Huayong (third from right) and Nina Kung Wang (center) discussing media developments in China.

CCTV current president Zhao Huayong, left, and former president Yang Weiguang, right.

Kevin Pu (left) and Robert Kuhn reporting on U.S.-China coproductions to CCTV president Zhao Huayong (right).

At the studios of *Film and TV Sync Sound*, our daily, prime-time television magazine on CCTV Channel 8.

Planning co-productions with CCTV vice president Zhang Changming (center).

Capital Wave and *In Search of China* director Li Qiang (right)
brainstorming with Adam Zhu and Robert Kuhn.

Signing the co-production projects *Capital Wave* and *In Search of China* with Wang Wenbin, managing director of CCTV's Economic Department in December 1997.

Press conference for premiere broadcast of *Capital Wave* on CCTV in April 1999.

President Liu Diyi of Beijing Television (third from right) with (from the right) Wang Liguang, Kevin Pu, Nina Kung Wang, Adam Zhu, and Ringo Wang.

Zhang Ziyang, writer, poet, director, and managing director of CCTV International Department, with Nina Kung Wang, Chairlady of Chinachem Group.

"Ganbei" ("bottoms up") with Wang Liguang, noted composer and managing director of Beijing Television Newscenter.

Co-production planning with Beijing Television.

Minister Zhao Qizheng and Robert Kuhn.

The Korean War television series production team (left to right): Zhang Xiaotian (screenwriter), Xiao Guiyun (director), Li Qiankuan (director), Robert Kuhn, Adam Zhu, Prof. Guan Runlin, Zhao Yanguo, Daniella Kuhn.

The Korean War set in Los Angeles: Li Qiankuan (center with beret) and Xiao Guiyun (third from right) directing "Kinsky," (Daniella Kuhn, standing left), a fictional American reporter, at a White House press conference with President Truman at the podium and Secretary of State Dean Acheson by his side.

Director Li Qiankuan with Daniella Kuhn, during a break in shooting President Truman's Christmas Ball at the White House during the Korean War.

The Korean War: President Truman being told of the North Korean invasion of South Korea. Directors Li Qiankuan and Xiao Guiyun are on the left.

The Korean War: President Truman (center) meeting with Secretary of State Dean Acheson (second from left) and General Omar Bradley (left).

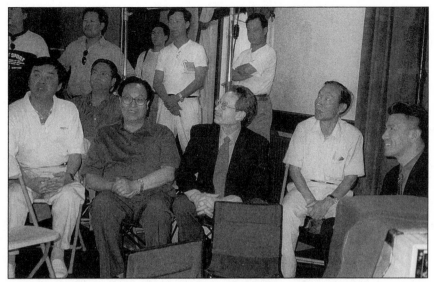

Minister Xu Guangchun of the State Administration of Radio, Film, and Television (second from left), visiting the set of *The Korean War* in Los Angeles, with Consul General An Wenbin (second from right) and Feng Ji (left), CCTV executive producer.

The Korean War director Li Qiankuan (left) introducing Robert Kuhn and Adam Zhu on the set with Minister Xu Guangchun (seated center).

Science and Technology

Song Jian: "Revitalizing the Country by Science and Education"

The Honorable Dr. Song Jian is vice chairman of the Chinese People's Political Consultative Conference and president of the Chinese Academy of Engineering Sciences. For fourteen years, from 1984 to 1998, Professor Song, as chairman of the State Science and Technology Commission, was the top science and technology leader in China and, from 1986 to 1998, as a state councilor, one of China's senior leaders. Professor Song, a distinguished and cultured scholar of dignity and charm, initiated many important programs, including the Strategic 863 High Technology Research Program, the Torch High-Technology Development and Commercialization Program, the Sparks Rural Science and Technology Promotion and Application, and China's first environmental projects. It was he who originally invited me to come to China, and I count him among my special friends. This material has been adapted from a talk he gave in April 1999 at the American Association for the Advancement of Science, in Washington, D.C.

In the past half-century, especially in the last two decades, China has advanced considerably in economic development, much to the credit of science and technology. For twenty years, China's GDP grew at an average annual rate of 9.8 percent. Compared with 1978, its GDP in 1998 increased by 6 times, agricultural output by 3.2 times. Per capita grain yield was 302 kilograms in 1978 and 410 kilograms in 1998, despite an increase of 250 million in the already huge population. During this same period, meat consumption increased from 9 kilograms per capita to 35 kilograms, and seafood consumption grew from 5 kilograms per capita to 30 kilograms. Electricity consumption increased from 266 kwh per capita to 935 kwh, more than a threefold increase. In brief, a shortage of food and other necessities no longer threatens people's daily lives. Hunger and cold have been eradicated throughout the country.

People take these definitive improvements in living standards seriously, because they had experienced protracted fear of starvation for centuries. In the past two thousand years, China suffered 1,056 major floods, which often washed away every trace of life. There also occurred 1,026 grave droughts, which parched the land and led to famine in most provinces. In the twentieth century, two disastrous droughts occurred, in the 1930s and the early 1960s, each resulting in the death of 20 million people. The most serious flood in the past forty-five years took place along the Yangtze River in 1998. Two million people battled on embankments day and night for two months and narrowly escaped a terrifying disaster. There has been a literary phrase used since ancient time in the Chinese language, "Starved bodies are strewn all over." And the long-standing idiom for greeting a friend is "Have you eaten?" instead of "How do you do?"

Most Chinese people are fond of history. They take pride in the long continuous civilization of the nation. Folks like to identify their genealogies. For example, many people know that Confucius was born on September 28, 551 B.C.E. Every Confucian descendant knows he is of the eighty-sixth or eighty-seventh generation offspring of the great man. People believe that history recorded the soul of Chinese people and indicated the destiny of the nation's future.

During the hundred years between the Opium War of 1840 and 1945, eight developed countries invaded China. Our country was defeated bitterly time after time, and was forced to cede territories and pay huge indemnities. Beijing, the capital of China, was occupied three times by invaders. Hong Kong was lost in 1842. In 1860, allied armies of France and Britain broke into Beijing and killed tens of thousands of people. The invaders looted and burned down the Old Summer Palace, which had been the only architectural example of the Gothic style in China—it had been designed by an Italian missionary painter and architect, Giuseppe Castiglione in 1720. Today, China keeps the ruins untouched as a symbol of shame. In the first half of this century, Japan invaded and occupied over half of China, killing 25 million people. To this day, the Chinese people cannot help giving out a plaintive cry over the century-long humiliation.

Fifty years ago the fate of China changed, with the founding of the People's Republic. The country has stood up since then. Hong Kong came back in 1997 and Macao became the second Special Administrative Region of China in 1999. The whole nation is joyful and welcomes the recovery of these two regions.

After the ten-year turmoil of the Cultural Revolution, Deng Xiaoping proposed, in the late 1970s, that the country could no longer afford disorder and chaos, and that the whole nation should turn to economic development immediately. Raising productive forces of the society, improving people's lives and strengthening the national economy were to be given the utmost priority. Deng decreed the abandonment of all the rules and ways of thinking that fetter the emancipation of productive forces. Following the above policy, governments of all levels and people of the whole country turned to economic development and tried every way to raise capital for investment. A tide of economic energy emerged throughout the country. Everybody was spurred to work to increase their incomes. New companies evolved everywhere. As a result, there have been twenty years of rapid economic and social development. After Deng passed away in 1997, new leaders of the country adhered to his basic policy, seizing every opportunity, speeding up development, persisting in reform, and maintaining the stability of the country. We have announced that these policies shall remain unchanged for the next fifty years.

What the Chinese people have learned from the past two centuries of modern history is that for China, which is such a populous nation, there is no alternative but self-reliance. The Chinese people must spare no pains in eradicating poverty and assuring themselves a decent life. China should make friends worldwide, pursue mutual understanding, and seek cooperation. But China cannot rely upon anybody else. God will not help those who do not help themselves.

Most people support another guideline formulated by Deng—that we must immerse ourselves in work and bide our time. The mentality of most Chinese scholars is "Don't bother much about what others say." In the past hundred and fifty years, people have been humiliated, beaten, starved, and killed, houses have been destroyed or burned, wealth has been stolen. The nation has experienced all kinds of suffering. Now we should do what we feel in our hearts to be right, and what fate dictates. You will be criticized anyway: you will be damned if you do and damned if you don't. Fortunately, nowadays killers and robbers are few. A famous Confucian teaching says, "Feel happy on hearing justified criticism from friends, and kowtow to those who indicate your shortcomings or mistakes." China has [much room for improvement] and a long way to go to build a modernized country. We should listen with care to well-intentioned advice.

China's science and technology policy is closely related to and originated from the country's background of history and economic status. In early 1950s when the People's Republic of China was newly founded, its science and technology policy focused on national defense. In less than twenty years, China, an extremely poor and backward country destroyed by thirty years of war, succeeded in mastering atomic energy and space technologies independently. At that time, Nikita Khrushchev of the Soviet Union, China's big brother then, refused to offer help. Most of the accomplishments were led by Chinese scientists returning from America and Europe. Among them were the founders of China's atomic energy and aerospace undertakings. The Chinese science community still feels grateful to the scientists and graduate institutions of America and Europe for having trained excellent scientists for China.

Since the reform and opening up of the country began in late 1970s, China's science and technology policy has shifted its focus to economic development. This was a significant turning point. Raising the skills and productivity of peasants and workers is quite different from developing sophisticated science. What's more, 80 percent of our population lives in the countryside. Peasants were used to a millennium-long, self-sufficient, small-scale family economy. A doggerel was popular among some peasants after the people's communes were disbanded:

> Raising a swine for the spring festival,
> Keeping two chicken to exchange for salt;
> Planting crops to feed family mouths,
> Holding a cow to plough a plot;
> With a firepan in my hut,
> I'm happy next only to God.

But with the opening up of the country, peasants soon realized that the old way of production would never make people rich.

In the 1980s, China's scientific community initiated and implemented a series of major nationwide projects to change the way of agriculture production in the countryside and to improve the technology and performance of industry.

The Sparks program and the Harvest program were launched to disseminate scientific knowledge and new technologies in rural areas. Thousands of scientists, agronomists, and engineers were invited to serve as magistrates of counties and mayors of small cities. About a million engineers and technicians went to the countryside to help peasants cultivate crops with new techniques, rear animals, and establish small-sized enterprises. Many new industries emerged, with millions of village and township enterprises created each year. More than seventy thousand Sparks program items have been developed in 85 percent of rural counties. Over 27 million village and township enterprises have been set up. They have absorbed 130 million peasants [who have become industrial workers] without leaving their homes. In 1998, the output value of village and township enterprises accounted for a third of China's GDP, with an annual increase of 20 percent.

In 1988, we launched the Torch program, to develop high and emerging technology industries. As part of this program, fifty-three science parks were established in coastal and provincial capital cities, further encouraging scientists and engineers to set up small and medium-sized enterprises. In the past decade, sixty-five thousand enterprises of various forms have been established by the Torch program, which have recruited 3.15 million young employees with good educations. Electronics, telecommunications, new materials, biotechnology, medicine, and aquaculture have grown to become major industries, with sales amounting to $6.7 billion in 1997, growing at about 50 percent a year. Today, personal computers, electronic telecommunication equipment, new materials, biotechnology products, pharmaceuticals, and new agricultural products are widely available in China's domestic market and are being exported to world markets.

In order to lead the development of high tech industries, the central government made a decision to allocate special financial resources to support high tech research and innovation in academic institutions and universities. China's science community acclaimed the decision and dubbed it the "863 Program," since it began operations in March 1986. Since then, it has shown gratifying results in approaching the world's frontiers in many disciplines. It is of no less importance than the Torch program, training tens of thousands of young scientists and engineers who will become leaders for further development of China's high tech industries in the new century.

China's Natural Science Foundation, which was founded in early 1980s, is now responsible for supporting scientists in basic research. A consensus was reached only in the late 1980s that basic research is the primary source of knowledge for high tech industries and the cradle for nurturing the young scientific elite. In 1997, the government decided to provide additional funds for building and improving selected facilities of basic research. Some new projects, such as a four-meter telescope for astronomical observation, a more powerful synchrotron light source, deep-drilling geological exploration, and a nationwide monitoring system for seismologists and environmentalists, are now underway.

Fundamental reform has been carried out in five thousand R&D institutions that were wholly dependent on government funding in the past. They have become market-oriented, seeking collaboration with companies to raise funds. At first, most scientists felt dreadful at being forced, as it were, to "jump into the sea" of business. But things changed rapidly within a few years. Almost all research institutions soon improved their budgets, increasing salaries of staff and [improving the] performance of their institutions. After twenty years of effort, China's science and technology system has basically made the transition and adapted to the market system.

On moving into a new century, a heated debate is going on in the government and the science community about what and how China's science and technology strategy must change to meet the challenges confronting the country. This debate must be ended before the tenth five-year plan starts in 2001. Whatever the outcome, the following basic situations should be taken into account as decisive factors for any policy making. Acting upon the suggestions of the science community, the Chinese government has made this strategy its highest priority: "Revitalizing the country by enhancement of science and education." As early as the beginning of the last century, intellectuals called out with grief and indignation that only science and democracy could save China. After experiencing century-long twists and turns, the nation has finally succeeded in making science and education its top initiative.

China's endeavor to develop modern science started only in the middle of the twentieth century, three hundred years later than in Western Europe and two hundred years later than in America and Russia. The Chinese people finally came to realize that the pride of an ancient civilization couldn't save people from poverty and backwardness. The only choice for the country was to do its best to catch up, develop science and education, and improve our democratic system. Only then will our next generation be able to live a decent life and stand side by side with people of other great nations.

The still-increasing, huge population has long been a problem troubling the Chinese science community. If the birth rate of the early 1980s were to have remained unchanged, with three to four children per family, China's population would be doubled again by the middle of the next century—a disastrous population explosion in its truest sense. Fortunately, the Chinese government accepted the suggestion of scientists and successfully carried out a tightened policy of family planning. In 1998 the total fertility rate dropped to 1.8—that is, on average each couple has 1.8 children, lower than the critical value of 2.1. Given the standing stability of the country, China's population will stabilize at 1.6 billion between 2030 and 2040, and decline afterward if people then want to do so. Economists and sociologists are greatly relieved.

The addition of 400 million people in the coming three or four decades suggests that China should put biotechnology at the top of its science agenda. To raise the productivity of agriculture, husbandry, and aquaculture and to assure the necessary supply of food will be the highest duty for China's science community. We have noticed that some thinkers have been advocating a "nonmaterial economic growth" or "more bytes and fewer atoms" [i.e., more information and fewer material things]. This may seem plausible for highly developed countries, but it is not so for developing countries like China. After all, food and material production continue to be prerequisites for survival and progress for any society. With a still increasing population, it is a long-term task for the Chinese science community to build up and strengthen our R&D capacity in agriculture-related disciplines.

While major efforts are devoted to developing the information industry worldwide, I hope I will not be interpreted as being opposed to the main trend. In this new century, information technology will be spread to every corner of human life and become the pillar for social development and progress. There is no doubt about it. What I want to emphasize is that, at least in China, scientists and engineers engaged in information science and technology should not forget to contribute to improving the productivity and supply of material goods, thus eradicating the poverty of the world's underprivileged populations.

China's strategic target of development for the first half of the new century is to make the country a medium-developed one. The plan is to increase per capita GDP ten times, from $780 today to about $7,000 or $8,000 in 2050. Accordingly, investment in all kinds of infrastructure— electric power, transportation, housing, irrigation systems, and other engineering constructions—must be increased at least tenfold. Significant improvement must be made in aviation, railway, highway, and water transport, not to mention educational, cultural, medical, health care and other facilities. Compared with fifty years ago, China has made remarkable progress. However, in comparison with developed countries, the fifty years' endeavor seems like a brief prologue of a long play. Industrialization has just taken off in China, and its climax will not appear until the middle of the twenty-first century. Therefore, building up the capacities of engineering science will continue to be one of the most important tasks for the country. That was the reason and purpose for the establishment of the Chinese Academy of Engineering Sciences five years ago.

Amazing progress has been made in the world's basic science in the twentieth century. After the brilliance of physics, biological science has come to the spotlight. The Chinese science community strongly asked its government to increase investment into basic research. We claim that China should build up its own edifice to shelter "the goddess of science," who will provide people with an unfailing supply of truth and knowledge. Despite limited funds and strained conditions, Chinese scientists in basic research have done a pretty good job in the past decade. The government accepted the request and expressed a willingness to strengthen the support for basic research as one of its long-term goals. However, the total revenue of the central government is still small—only $70 billion, which is less than the budget for science alone allocated by the United States federal government.

In its 1999 budget, the Ministry of Finance announced an increase of funding for science of 9 percent, but in fact the increase was only $100 million. Therefore, in the near future, Chinese scientists cannot expect to afford "Big Science" projects, such as seeking extraterrestrial civilizations, observing quasars, or simulating the Big Bang. But they are not frustrated and will not lose heart. They strive eagerly to make achievements in mathematics, condensed-matter physics, geology, the creation of genetically modified animals and plants, DNA sequencing for rice, neuroscience, artificial intelligence, ecological science, and in many fields that do not demand large investment. As for Big Science, it is a long-standing policy to encourage Chinese scientists to take part in selected international projects, in line with the common trend of globalization.

For two decades, Sino-U.S. cooperation in science and technology has been extremely beneficial to both science communities. Thirty-three cooperative agreements or memoranda have been implemented in a variety of scientific fields. Remarkable results were attained in exchanges of public health data, and plant and animal species. There has been extensive cooperation in high energy physics, seismology, geology, paleontology, oceanography, natural disaster prevention, water resources, environmental protection, biodiversity, and other areas pertaining to sustainable development. In spite of some occasional twists and turns in Sino-U.S. relations—through no fault of scientists, I might note—we cherish the very friendly cooperative ties between our two communities. Scientists believe that science cooperation serves to improve mutual understanding between peoples, and thus comprises an essential part of bilateral relations between the United States of America and The People's Republic of China.

The Internet

It is estimated that Internet users in China will reach 40 to 50 million by 2005 and that China will become the second largest Internet market in the world, after the United States. Yet the Internet presents a unique paradox for China's leadership, a virtual litmus test for weighing national pride against social stability, an axial clash between our two overarching themes. On the one hand, the government recognizes that free access to information is absolutely essential for technological advance and competitive success in world markets; on the other, they quite naturally fear the potentially disruptive consequences of such free access. The Internet is an unbounded, uninhibited means of communication; information on the Internet is true, false, beautiful, ugly, serious, silly, useful, useless. Everything imaginable is on the net, and it is virtually impossible to filter any of it out.

Hence the dilemma: restrict information and retard technological progress? Or remove restrictions and relax social controls? For a while, it was reported, some Chinese officials sought to create a "Chinese Intranet"—a wholly enclosed national system firewalled off from the freewheeling Internet that courses crazily around the rest of the world. Wiser heads prevailed: Chinese science and technology would have been severely impeded, and in any case such a firewall would have been impractical to build, impossible to maintain, and easy to breech, as new Internet technologies continue to provide new and varied transmission and delivery mechanisms. The Chinese government still feels that it must find ways to block those websites that are politically disruptive or pornographic or smack too much of foreign influences—an unending, thankless, hapless, and ultimately unsuccessful endeavor. With increasing avenues of access, lines of communication, and distributed routings, the technical task of blocking will become progressively more difficult; the technology of the Net will finally overwhelm the power of any government to restrict it.

But I think the astute Chinese leadership already knows this; their primary motivation is to build China, not just maintain power for power's sake, and so they recognize the importance of the Internet for China's development. They hope only to delay the Internet's destabilizing influences long enough for China to emerge as a civil society with a sufficiently high standard of living so that all its people will have a stake in maintaining social stability.

Chinese policy regarding foreign investments in its burgeoning Internet industry is in constant flux, reflecting the changing realities of the Internet and (no doubt) conflicting opinions among Chinese senior leaders. First, the government was to keep its hands off ("Let the market decide"), then came a sudden switch prohibiting any foreign ownership whatsoever; then—under pressure by WTO entry requirements—up to 50 percent foreign ownership of any Internet-related company would be allowed; then came rules restricting loosely defined "state secrets" from being distributed through Internet news services or chat rooms, and forcing the release of commercial encryption codes (thereby enabling government snoops to eavesdrop on e-mail and other data transmissions). All the while, various ministries and agencies jockey for jurisdictional and policing authority.

The snooping, I feel, is more intimidating bluster than practical threat. How many bureaucratic snoopers would have to be hired, by a government that is already bloated and must downsize, just to monitor all those e-mails? Chinese Internet policies are (to be charitable) confused and chaotic, reflecting the core characteristics of the Internet itself, and may well have changed between the time I write these words and you read them.

In the long run, I have little doubt that, provided China's reform continues, foreign companies will be allowed to invest directly in Chinese Internet companies, if only because this is what the Chinese companies themselves want. They want to access the best strategic thinking, financial capital, and operational expertise in website development, and all these are assets of foreign Internet companies. In the short run, the Chinese government will probably continue to vacillate on this particular issue—for two reasons. The first is political: if foreign companies own equity in Chinese Internet companies, it will be harder for the government to control content and intent. The second is economic: the Chinese government wants to protect its fledgling, domestic Internet industry. Without protection, they fear, Chinese Internet companies stand at a disadvantage against foreign competitors, which are larger, more experienced, armed with much more capital, and unconcerned about national borders.

Fanso: An Internet Startup, Socialist-Market Style

Despite the uneasiness of China's leaders toward the unbridled connectivity represented by the Internet, China's future, like that of the rest of the world, is global, interconnected, and immediate—and driven by high tech companies that are able to compete internationally. This future is going to be forged by ambitious young people without a communist past to remember, who already see their lives as wired and worldwide, and who are not intimated by anyone, especially large American companies. At Qinghua, China's leading science and technology university, we found four enterprising young students, including one woman, who had created a startup Internet company in a makeshift computer lab on the roof of their dorm. We followed them for months as they struggled to finance their company and build their dream.

WEN XIAOYAN: Look at the number of hits our site's had today.

LU JUN: Strange, much less than normal.

NARRATOR: The company is called "Fanso" and it's trying to find its niche in China's burgeoning Internet market.

LU: The name comes from English: we are Net Fans, So we do it [Fan-So]. We just thought it was fun. We made our name up just like that, nothing deep. We know it's very unlike traditional Chinese culture, but there is no deeper meaning.

TONG ZHILEI: We are the new Internet generation in China and this is our character.

EMPLOYEE: Our website is now composed of news, computer info, entertainment, books, games, and sports.

LU: Let's check out the NBA scores on the Web. Chicago got beat badly.

CHEN XI: It's very difficult to predict the future of an Internet business. But boldly speaking, our company will be the biggest web service provider in China within five years. We will be world famous!

TONG: Can we sell e-mail accounts?

CHEN: We don't have e-mail accounts.

TONG: We will have e-mail accounts.

CHEN: But that's not going to make us any money.

TONG: Let's sell customers' information.

TONG: Are you sure we can sell it?

WANG: It won't be a problem.

NARRATOR: The first real test to see if Fanso will fly is provided by the university, which has invited real investors to come listen to the students' pitch.

FACULTY HOST: *(Qinghua University presentation room)* On this sultry afternoon, we're here to attend the Business Plan Competition at Qinghua. College competitions give birth to many high tech enterprises in America. They have a slogan: "If we dream, everything will be possible."

LU: Every single member of our team has a dream to excel. Not just to work hard and become one of the best entrepreneurs in China, but also to become one of the best in the world, the second Bill Gates. We have excellent people and products. Now we need only one more thing—capital.

TONG: Getting real investment is going to be difficult. There are all these legal and financial questions we were not prepared for. We learned a lot about our own company through the process, and we modified our business plans.

FANSO WEBMASTER: Our room is the messiest on campus.

TONG: *(remembering our CCTV cameras)* You're damaging the image of the Chinese.

LU: Life on the Internet now is freer than real life and it will be more so in the future. Only two years ago there was no Ethernet in this building and now all of us have online access in our own rooms. We can go to domestic and international websites. This was unimaginable in the past but now it's real.

NARRATOR: The Chinese government blocks websites it deems politically sensitive or pornographic, although any savvy user can get around this. And as traffic on the Internet grows, website policing will become even more difficult.

ZHAO QIZHENG (INFORMATION MINISTER): The laws are not perfect yet. But the reason for blocking some websites is to prevent those sites from spreading anti-China speech and anything else that would have a negative impact on Chinese society.

LU: Of course we hope to have more freedom. But the government has to protect its interests. Circumstances are different between China and America. China has its own culture. I know that freedom is very important in American culture. But some information, I mean the kind of information our government limits, is simply unsuitable for Chinese culture. I believe even the American government limits information on the Internet. The FBI must be monitoring information.

NARRATOR: Through their university, Fanso was introduced to the Qing Chuang Group—a young venture capital fund set up by the Beijing city government.

LU: *(meeting with the venture capitalists)* We want to establish an entity that doesn't exist yet, which will enable communication between merchants and consumers.

TONG: This is what we call customized service. For example, you spend a lot of time searching for info. You won't have to do this on Fanso. It'll search for you. It'll supply everything you need.

FEMALE VENTURE CAPITALIST: Foreign Internet services have developed this technology for several years. They are quite perfect. If they come to China, with their strong marketing strategies, how can you compete with them?

CHEN: Americans are not as smart as Qinghua students. And foreign companies don't have a fair chance to compete with us. They'll have problems with local customs. And they'll have to convert from English to Chinese, which will cause major communication problems.

TONG: *(reflecting privately)* In the end, we didn't strike a deal with Qing Chuang. If we were only looking for money, we could've found that a long time ago. We were looking for investors who were more capable than us in many ways, such as management, finance, and getting more investment in the future.

WEN: If we can really get going and make up for our initial losses, in a year or two, our growth will be spectacular.

NARRATOR: It's now three months later, and the students have finally found startup funds from a Hong Kong investor.

TONG: *(in Fanso's new offices)* We have forty-nine people now. Some of them are full-time employees while others are part-time students. We'll offer the full-time employees shares in the company soon; this will make up for their small salaries.

TONG: Each core member of the company has only been paid eight hundred *yuan*. I've used up all my savings, and now I'm borrowing money.

LU: I should get paid a lot as CEO. More than if I worked at a foreign company.

TONG: *(kidding)* I would get about a thousand dollars a month if I worked for a foreign company. Are you going to give me that much?

CHEN: And if I were working for a foreign company, I'd be making a lot more too.

TONG: We have contacts with some foreign investors and we think they're good. And we expect around $10 million. After we get the second round of foreign investments, we will consider going public.

NARRATOR: In September of 1999, the Chinese government issued a strict warning against that kind of thinking: there was to be no foreign investment in Chinese Internet companies. China's Internet policy is in constant flux.

TONG: The speech had a really big impact. We value international investors because they're more experienced in this type of investing. They can give us more support and better advice. And we believe that nobody can stop the opening of China.

Cui Xinshui: "Launching Satellites Most Efficiently"

Professor Cui Xinshui is a senior scientist and manager at China Aerospace Corporation, a government company that launches satellites for China and other countries (including the United States), where he is responsible for the guidance systems of rockets. We were granted special permission to film in the closed Aerospace Museum in Beijing—rarely given, we were told, even to CCTV—and to interview Professor Cui. Because of a scheduling conflict, I did not conduct this interview myself (but I did help prepare the questions); the interviewer is Li Qiang, the director of our television documentaries, and the interview took place both in the Aerospace Museum and in Professor Cui's office where he was working with his graduate students. I have included without rebuttal Professor Cui's indignant denial of Chinese spying as presented in the Cox Committee Report on China Espionage (to the U.S. House of Representatives Select Committee on U.S. National Security and Military/Commercial Concerns with the People's Republic of China), chaired by Rep. Christopher Cox. My intent was not to assess accuracy, allocate blame, or continue the debate (for which this book is the wrong forum), but to portray the depth of emotion in China regarding any derogation of Chinese science—accomplishments that are a source of great pride to all Chinese people.

LI QIANG: Describe your career in the aerospace industry.

CUI XINSHUI: I started in 1960, doing research on our initial development of rocketry. Around 1965, we started situation analysis for the first generation long distance weapons. Around 1970, we started making rockets for space, getting the fundamentals ready for satellites. In 1974 I participated for the first time in the launching of a reusable rocket—and if it hadn't been for the Cultural Revolution it would have happened earlier. From the single-satellite rocket, we developed the multiple-satellite rocket; then the wraparound rocket, which is powerful enough to carry large-sized satellites. In the 1980s, I was part of our country's first long distance rockets project, with targets in the Pacific Ocean. In 1988 I participated in the development of large-sized rockets—the Chung II Kung LM-B. I took part in its first launch, in 1992.

LI: What was your part in these launches?

CUI: I was in charge of the guidance system, which ensures flight stability and a correct trajectory, or orbit. The precision of China's rocket launches has been very high, especially the Chung II Bing LM-C rocket, which has been 100 percent precise. This is the rocket that launches the Motorola satellites [for a global communication system called Iridium that required many satellites, but is now defunct]. So far, every launch has been successful, including more than ten launches of the first Star-class rockets, which are very dependable. Our success in launching satellites into their precise orbits is also very high. Internationally, our efforts are of first-class quality; our clients are completely satisfied. Such precision is dependent on our guidance systems; their design is world-class. Relatively speaking, they are better than similar systems in foreign countries.

LI: Describe China's launch site.

CUI: It's high above sea level, and the climate is poor. Each time we go to the launch site, no matter what our job is there, we must have a medical examination. All of us have to be in good health to have a successful launch. I have no big health problems; I'm just a little overweight. I usually stay at the launch site for a month, then come back home for awhile, and then return to the site. We're taken care of nicely. I'm often away from my wife, but she's used to it by now.

LI: What is your salary?

CUI: My monthly salary envelope says eighteen hundred *yuan*. When I started after college, I got fifty-six *yuan* a month; after a year it went up to sixty-six.

LI: How was your personal life during those times of hardship?

CUI: When I graduated from college, we were assigned a job. Often there was no reason given, and our personal wishes were not considered. That was the system then. It was a coincidence that I was assigned to something I wanted to do. Compared with that in foreign countries, our quality of life was not great, but our country still treated us decently. We devoted our whole hearts and efforts to this project, so we barely thought about the comforts of life. Everyone's quality of life was pretty much the same. We weren't thinking about upgrading our personal circumstances.

LI: It seems that China's original motivation to develop its aerospace industry was nationalism, but now it's economics.

CUI: China's aerospace industry was originally intended to develop our country's national science for defense, especially while we were isolated. Now, because of reform, we have to enter the international market, so we've transformed our aerospace technology into a commercial service as well. We've expanded our launching service for foreigners, and this strengthens China's stature as an aerospace nation. We want the success rate of launching our low-cost and dependable rockets to be high, and then we'll receive economic benefits for our country and for our people, including myself. Actually, my personal income has grown considerably.

LI: What about China's technological future?

CUI: China is a big country and will become an important aerospace nation. We have our own grand plans. We are going to expand our reach into space and other aerospace areas. We need to develop our economic power. As our country becomes rich, so will our people.

LI: Why does China rely on its own technology?

CUI: During the Cold War, the West blocked us from getting information, and the Soviets restricted our access as well. We had to do everything ourselves. We worked very hard do develop our aerospace industry. After the reform started and we were opened to the world, the world started to understand us. But we have a principle: we rely on ourselves to develop our aerospace technology.

LI: What position does China have in the worldwide aerospace market?

CUI: Our aerospace industry is among the best. We started late, but we've made tremendous progress. The success rate of our launches has been excellent. We trail only the U.S. and Russia. We have a large domestic market, and we need satellites for our domestic communication. There's also a large demand internationally. Labor costs less in China, so launches are cheaper here; therefore, many countries want to work with us. Whoever launches satellites most efficiently will get the business. Our future prospects are bright. If we have enough economic strength, we should land on the moon, too.

LI: I would like to ask about your family. What do your children think about your work?

CUI: I have two daughters. Both are working, one in computers, one in medicine. They have opinions different from mine. They see that I work very hard every day, even on holidays. I seem silly in their eyes. But they always watch the launches on TV, and then they see that their father's job is honorable and meaningful after all.

LI: Is China developing a space shuttle?

CUI: Yes, because China is an important aerospace country. As an aerospace scientist, I hope that our country will develop a space shuttle, go to the moon, and even farther out into space. We have the technology, but we need the funding. When we have enough economic support, it will take very little time to launch our own space shuttle.

LI: We have so many problems in China, like inflation, unemployment, and other economic pressures. Why are we devoting so much of our effort for space shuttles?

CUI: The government sees science as a primary productive force for energizing the whole national economy. We're proud that our technology helps build the nation. Yet we need to get through this transition period of reform. After our economy has improved, we'll spend more money on the development of aerospace. The space shuttle is not distant in our country's future. Our country thinks it's important, and we've made tremendous preparations for it. The space shuttle will mark China as an important country. It will inspire our people.

LI: How were you affected by the Cultural Revolution?

CUI: It was the same for everyone. We were sent to work on the farms, too, but our minds were concerned only with how to fly our rockets. Regardless of whether we were on the farm or in the mines, we were always pondering these questions. My job was farming. Every day after laboring—it was planting rice, for me—I was exhausted. But while I was lying in bed, my mind was free to think about our rockets. And since our colleagues were all together, we discussed these things—but only during the breaks from our labor.

LI: Although politicians in some countries try to keep their citizens separate, the communication between scientists should be free. When you attend international meetings, do you feel free?

CUI: I often attend international meetings on aerospace technology—in America, Russia, France, and Japan. Technology does not have a nationality. When we exchange ideas, we learn from each other; Americans learn from us, and we learn from Americans. This is normal. It not only increases knowledge but also strengthens friendship. But when the Cox Report accused China of stealing technology from America, it was complete slander and poisoned our relationship.

LI: Give us your assessment of the Cox Report, which received widespread publicity overseas.

CUI: I was outraged. The Cox Report is a total lie. It stated that our technical advances in aerospace were stolen from the United States or other countries. It totally underestimates the Chinese people's ability to develop our own aerospace industry, which was entirely the result of our own hard work. You must remember that during the times of economic hardship and international isolation—when the Western countries cut us off and when the Soviet Union was ignoring us—we were highly motivated and depended entirely on ourselves. China had already developed the technology for our missile guidance systems in 1984—work that we had begun in 1965. We even use different designs on our satellites and missiles. Our guidance-system technology was developed entirely by us. The fact that it's so precise proves that we thoroughly understand the technology. And it's impossible to upgrade the guidance precision of missiles with the technology of rockets. They're totally different. We developed each ourselves. The guidance system we applied on missiles is for missiles. As for rockets, we already had the knowledge, so we didn't need to steal it from the U.S. Cox wrote that we built our guidance systems with U.S. technology and that China rejects foreigners. We're very friendly to foreigners. His statements are false.

LI: Do you use the Internet?

CUI: Sure. But after the Cox Report, many websites in America were closed. We think that's unfriendly.

LI: The salaries in aerospace have been very low compared to private industry, and many people in technology became rich after the planned economy changed to the market economy. As a scientist who has sacrificed for his country, do you have any complaints?

CUI: Of course, I thought their quick profits were unfair. But I also thought about my work, about which I'm truly enthusiastic. Every time we have a successful launch, I'm gratified. I've always felt like I was pursuing a major goal. We didn't dream of anything extra. My attention wasn't on economic matters as long as my life was OK. I'm well aware that many people gave up research and moved into a business career. Everyone has his own purpose. We're all working to improve our country's economy, so it doesn't matter.

LI: What are your personal plans?

CUI: I've reached retirement age. But I still would like to devote my capabilities to the aerospace industry, for which I have great hopes. Our aerospace technology will improve continually, because our country thinks it's important. Thus I've been teaching the young generation— the Ph.D. students doing research. They're very devoted, and their development is progressing quickly.

LI: What do your students think about the future?

FEMALE STUDENT: The aerospace technology of China will enter the top level in the world in twenty years. I hope we'll be able to collaborate with other advanced countries, like America, on a friendly basis. In our working environment, females and males are treated equally. In some aspects, females are even treated better. We're equal at work, but women get more benefit in some aspects of daily life.

MALE STUDENT: Space technology should be a means of peace, not a tool of war. It should benefit humanity. The world should unite to explore space. And we should use space technology to facilitate the development of various other industries—this will be good for everybody, not just the Chinese.

Liu Chuanzhi: "Turning Our Technologies into Merchandise"

Liu Chuanzhi is the chairman and chief executive of Legend Holdings, China's largest manufacturer of personal computers (PCs)—desktops, notebooks, TV set-top boxes. With over two billion dollars in annual revenues, Legend's sales revenues in 2000 were 50 percent higher than that of 1999, which were 98 percent higher than that of 1998. The company also makes servers, workstations, motherboards, software, and printed circuit boards; distributes computer products from industry leaders such as Cisco and Toshiba; and provides systems integration and support services. Though China is targeted by the world's leading PC companies—Compaq, IBM, Dell, Apple, Hewlett-Packard—Legend is number one in China, with a 20 percent share of the world's fasting-growing PC market. Legend, a new-

style state-owned company, sells PCs about 15 percent cheaper than its foreign competitors and maintains a nationwide force of two thousand distributors and a network of four hundred service centers. In April 2000, Legend announced that it would split into two parts—a traditional manufacturing company and a newer one that will focus exclusively on Internet-based services and e-commerce products. Legend is making an aggressive commitment to the Internet: Internet access devices, Internet connection services, specialized portals, servers and solutions for Internet service and content providers (ISP and ICP), B2B distribution, and e-commerce solutions for three main industries (finance, telecommunications and taxation). In June 2000, Business Week magazine selected Legend Chairman Liu Chuanzhi as one of the "Stars of Asia" and Legend Holdings as the eighth best information technology company in the world.

ROBERT KUHN: Let's start with Legend's background and history.

LIU CHUANZHI: Legend was founded in 1984, with an investment of two hundred thousand *yuan* [about twenty-four thousand dollars] from the Chinese Academy of Sciences. At the beginning, there were eleven people working in a small house. Now we have public stock in Hong Kong and our ADRs [American Depository Receipts] are traded in New York. [Legend's market capitalization was about $800 million in July 2000, down from almost $2 billion earlier in the year.]

KUHN: How do you account for such success at a time when most state-owned enterprises are moribund?

LIU: It has to do with Legend's background. The Chinese Academy of Science is composed of the best research institutes in the country. In the past, they made some of the most advanced scientific machines in the world, but they didn't do anything with them. Later, as the market economy developed, values changed. We started to think about turning our technologies into merchandise. Previously our achievements were evaluated by our list of publications and scientific awards. Now our achievements are evaluated by how many products we sell and how profitable we are.

KUHN: What is the core of Legend's business strategy?

LIU: We went through several stages, each time adapting quickly to the market. We started by assembling foreign computers, but in 1990 we made the decision to build the Legend brand. By totally focusing on the Chinese market, and by providing value and specialized service to our Chinese-speaking customers, we gained a competitive edge. Our market share went from 0 to 7 percent in 1996 and to 20 percent today, and we're number one.

KUHN: Recently, you've begun to focus on Internet-related businesses.

LIU: The Internet and information technology sectors are growing rapidly, and it's essential that we cater to them. We're actively developing new products and introducing new services. [Legend achieved early success with its two Internet-focused products—the Legend Conet computer, which facilitates Internet logon; and the Living Room computer, a small, inexpensive set-top box with which you can surf the Net on your TV.]

KUHN: What's your personal background? Science, business, or both?

LIU: Science. I used to be a computer hardware designer.

KUHN: You went from computer designer to successful businessman. That's unusual. How many of Legend's eleven original founders are still with the company?

LIU: Nine of them are still here, in that they're considered employees, but they're actually retired. They resigned to give their positions to young people.

KUHN: Many important positions are held by young people, some even in their twenties. Is a youthful leadership related to Legend's success?

LIU: The computer and information industries require original thinking, unfettered by years of status quo thinking. But I think Legend's success is partly accidental. Why do I say so? For example, if a capitalist—say, in Hong Kong—gives a lot of money to someone and asks him to start a company, ten years later the company may or may not be successful. But in America, people like Bill Gates might start with little money but develop a very successful company. Why? Because Bill Gates owned the company personally, and enjoyed complete decision-making power. In China, Legend is owned by the state. It's very difficult for a state-owned business to develop in such a dynamic, demanding market. How can Legend attract the most capable, creative people? Think about it.

When Legend makes a big profit, most of this profit will go to the state. In China, privately owned companies are more advanced than state-owned companies. Logically, Legend should be much more developed than private companies, because it is backed by the best high tech institutes in China, but Legend is not as developed as it should be. I think the system is the issue.

KUHN: What's the ownership structure of Legend today?

LIU: In 1994, the Chinese Academy of Science gave the employees of Legend 30 percent of the shares. So the employees of Legend own 30 percent of the company. This farsighted decision played a very important role in Legend's development. As I said, the old founders of Legend retired from their important positions to make way for those more attuned to current technologies and market management. But that wouldn't happen in other state-owned companies. There, if you retire, you lose all benefits of your position, which are only your current salary and all the perquisites of senior management. But since Legend's founders were given shares, they still have income. The better Legend does, the more money they make; so the founders were happy to give their positions to younger people who will make the company more profitable.

KUHN: So Legend gets two benefits from its stock allocations. First, you reward the founders for their contribution, and second, you can move them aside to make room for younger and more creative people.

LIU: Both are very important.

KUHN: Were 30 percent of Legend's shares given to individual employees or held under a collective umbrella?

LIU: A collective unit. It's called the Employees Share Committee, and it's the owner of the shares. But the financial interest in these shares is allocated to individuals each year. The formula works like this: 35 percent of the interest derived from these employee shares goes to the twenty most important retirees. Another 20 percent goes to the twenty most important current employees. And the remaining 45 percent goes to the rest of Legend's employees.

KUHN: Do you own any Legend stock personally?

LIU: I own the right to a financial interest in the shares, but not the shares themselves.

KUHN: Does this mean that you have the right to any dividends declared on the shares but not the right to sell the underlying shares?

LIU: Right.

KUHN: The compensation for Chinese CEOs is much lower than for American CEOs, yet your contribution to the success of your company may be greater. How do you feel about that?

LIU: I'm a product of the generation of the 1960s. Just after I graduated from college, the Cultural Revolution started, and so my first ten years were totally wasted—and even the next ten years, while reform developed slowly, were not terribly productive. In essence, for twenty years I had nothing important to do. So in 1984, when we were asked to start the company, I was very happy. I just wanted to do things. I didn't even think of making money. Four years later, in 1988, there were about a thousand employees working for Legend. My entire motivation was my responsibility for those people. Now, as Legend has become the biggest PC manufacturer in China, I feel proud to be contributing to our national industry. As for money, even Bill Gates, who makes so much money, is donating his wealth to charity, and he says he'll give much more when he's older. My income is enough for me to live a good life, so I don't really worry about money.

KUHN: I understand. But how do you motivate the next generation?

LIU: I want to explain. What I just said suits me and people of my generation. I don't want to apply it to younger generations, and it can't be applied to them. My generation is very devoted to the country, but our attitudes don't fit in with the market economy. As far as the younger generation is concerned, their incomes should correlate with their contributions.

KUHN: Part of your job as CEO is to attract investors like me to buy Legend's stock. And if you will permit me, I will speak bluntly. As a potential investor, I'm really not concerned about how much you want to contribute to China. I'm concerned only about how closely your interests in the company are aligned with my own. I'm interested in the price of the stock, and I need to believe that you're just as interested as I am. That's why I'd want to know how much Legend stock you own. I'm not just curious. I want to be sure that we're both on the same side of the table.

LIU: You're absolutely right. I agree with you completely. In fact, when I consider whether Legend should invest in a private company, I want to know how much stock its CEO owns and how much he cares about the company. But I'm a state-owned corporation's entrepreneur, so my situation is different. I can't care about my own compensation too much, or there will be problems. It's the Chinese way.

KUHN: I understand. When I read in the newspaper that you own significant stock, that's when I'll invest in Legend.

LIU: I hope you say this to the key leaders of my country. Song Jian [see page 209] is open-minded, but others need to hear it. This is the first thing I wanted to say. Next, although my salary is not as much as my equivalents in other countries, it is relatively high in China. But when foreign institutions or even local Chinese companies consider buying Legend stock, they also want to know how much stock I own. It's very important, I do agree.

KUHN: Other companies, including foreign companies, attract young talent by offering them high compensation, including stock options. How are you able to keep the best young people at Legend without such offers?

LIU: First, we try to give them the same salary they could get in another Chinese company, or at least half of what they could get at a foreign company. More important, we offer them good opportunities to show off their talents. In most foreign companies operating in China, the top positions are held by foreign nationals, not by Chinese. But at Legend, Chinese young people find that the top positions are available to them. The top executives of six Legend companies are in their mid-thirties.

KUHN: I look forward to buying your stock.[25]

Legend Employees: "If the World Didn't Have Imagination, What Would the World Be Like?"

"Michael," the only name he gave me, is the twenty-six-year-old vice director of new business development at Legend, who is re-

---

[25] In early 2000, *Forbes* reported that President Liu's shares were worth $14 million, and that twenty-eight of Legend's earliest employees had a stake worth over $800 million, though values have retreated since. I now feel obligated to purchase shares.

sponsible for strategic acquisitions and investment planning. For someone so young, he has a remarkably critical job. Michael showed me around Legend's headquarters in Zhongguancun, the high tech section of Beijing, including its product exhibition hall.

KUHN: I'm fascinated by Chinese slogans. What does Legend's say?

MICHAEL: It's a play on words. In Chinese, our corporate name, "Legend," is similar to the word "imagination." So our slogan can be read two ways: "If the World Didn't Have Imagination, What Would the World Be Like?" and also "If the World Lost Legend, What Would the World Be Like?"

KUHN: Legend manufactures computer products under its own brand name, but it also represents foreign computer companies, like Toshiba. Aren't you competing against yourself?

MICHAEL: These products have different markets and different price points. Toshiba notebooks are high-end and very expensive; Legend notebooks are for the masses and are very cheap.

KUHN: From where does Legend recruit its employees? What's your background?

MICHAEL: We recruit from the best universities, such as Beijing and Qinghua. I graduated from Qinghua; my undergraduate degree was in electrical engineering and my master's was in economic management. You should know that Legend is concerned about our career development.

KUHN: Americans are used to seeing "Made in China" on clothing and toys. Will we start seeing it on computer motherboards?

MICHAEL: Our products are very good for the American market.

KUHN: What's your role in the company?

MICHAEL: I'm in charge of new business development. I analyze potential investments.

KUHN: Isn't it dangerous for a giant corporation to put so much trust in someone so young?

MICHAEL: I don't think so. The information industry is young and changes very rapidly. It needs new ideas and innovations. Being young is an advantage. The average age in our group is about thirty. We do have older people in the company, but we have a principle: we judge the work, not the age, of the worker.

KUHN: Tell me about Legend's investment opportunities on which you're advising.

MICHAEL: An opportunity may also be a trap. So first we have to do market research and collect industry information. That's very important. If we don't have enough information, we might fall into a pit instead of realizing an opportunity. In a recent transaction, we invested $4.5 million to acquire 30 percent of P-soft [an innovative Chinese software company]. Right now, I'm studying three or four potential investments.

KUHN: What are some of these potential investments?

MICHAEL: I mustn't tell you. If we want to merge with certain companies, it's top secret. We have to be responsible to our stockholders. We don't want to hurt their interests.

KUHN: When you make presentations to Legend's senior executives, are you sensitive because you're young?

MICHAEL: No, I'm confident. I know I'm competent in this position.

KUHN: Are your older colleagues jealous because you have such an important position?

MICHAEL: Ability is what's most important.

KUHN: Does Legend have problems, as IBM and Hewlett-Packard do, with counterfeiting?

MICHAEL: When you have a famous brand, others will try to pirate it. We have a brand protection organization in China, and Legend has won awards for our diligence.

KUHN: What's your career path at Legend?

MICHAEL: I'd like to lead a business unit at Legend. But my dream is to start my own company. Two years ago, very few young people had this dream, but today many do.

I conducted the following brief interviews while walking around Legend's headquarters unsupervised, speaking at random with employees working at their computers.

EMPLOYEE A: It's now common to jump from one company to another if you get a better opportunity.

KUHN: Did you jump to Legend because you got a better salary?

EMPLOYEE A: No. As a matter of fact, I get a little less here than I did at my previous company. I can accept that because I can learn a lot at Legend.

KUHN: Are there cultural differences between Legend and your previous company?

EMPLOYEE A: My previous company was a Korean company, which is like a Japanese company; they're very critical, and you cannot feel honor for your work. But at Legend you're appreciated for your achievements.

KUHN: How does Legend compare to traditional Chinese companies?

EMPLOYEE A: It's quite different. Although Legend is a state-owned company, the culture is modern. When I worked for a state-owned company in aerospace administration, I had a great deal of free time. Now I'm very busy.

KUHN: Are your friends envious of your job at Legend?

EMPLOYEE A: Yes, but their jobs are more stable. If I don't complete my plan, I may have to leave. At other companies, the risk is quite low.

— —

KUHN: Can employees access international websites?

EMPLOYEE B: We can access most websites that are relevant to our work.

KUHN: Are there restrictions?

EMPLOYEE B: Yes—no pornography, no violence, no politically sensitive topics. This is company policy, but it relies on individual self-control.

KUHN: As a computer expert, you do know how to find those sites.

EMPLOYEE B: The computer records the sites you visited.

KUHN: Is your creativity diminished because of such restrictions?

EMPLOYEE B: Somewhat, perhaps, but most stuff relevant to our work we can access.

KUHN: Is it helpful for other people to decide what sites you can and cannot visit?

EMPLOYEE B: If we aren't supposed to go to some websites, we don't go. It's a matter of self-control.

EMPLOYEE C: There's no mandatory policy. It all depends on your own discretion.

KUHN: Do you ever visit Western news sites, such as CNN, *The New York Times*, or the BBC?

EMPLOYEE C: I don't have time.

KUHN: Aren't you interested in different opinions or political ideas?

EMPLOYEE C: It's a sensitive subject. Perhaps we should move on to another subject.

—— ——

KUHN: *(looking at computer screen)* Is this your analysis of a potential acquisition?

EMPLOYEE D: Yes, here's the projected budget, sales plus profits. But I must shut it down; otherwise you'll see all our secrets. Sorry.

KUHN: I'm not an American spy, or a company spy. I'm just making a television documentary and writing a book.

EMPLOYEE D: I don't think a spy would say he was a spy.

KUHN: What percentage of your income is bonus?

EMPLOYEE D: For me, bonus and salary are about half and half. But if my performance is poor, I may not get any bonus at all.

KUHN: How much is your salary?

EMPLOYEE D: It's one of Legend's Four Rules that we must not disclose our salaries. If I tell you my salary, I have to leave the company.

KUHN: What are the other three rules?

EMPLOYEE D: We cannot take a second job. We cannot take bribery. We must not abuse our power.

KUHN: What happens if you break one of these rules?

EMPLOYEE D: You have to leave Legend.

KUHN: Do you have a girlfriend?

EMPLOYEE D: That's another secret.

In one of Legend's PC manufacturing plants, I interviewed a young female deputy general manager who, only three years after her college graduation (her major was communications management), is responsible for two hundred production workers, mostly male and mostly older.

KUHN: How many computers do you produce a day?

MANAGER: Between twenty-two and twenty-four hundred a day.

KUHN: Motherboards are a Legend specialty.

MANAGER: Yes, we make them ourselves, not only for our own computers but also for export.

KUHN: You're only twenty-five years old and have quite a responsible position. Is this unusual?

MANAGER: Most of the managerial personnel at Legend are young.

KUHN: Is it unusual for a woman to run a production department?

MANAGER: We have many women in managerial positions here. I think it's perfectly natural.

KUHN: What sort of work do your parents do?

MANAGER: They're governmental officials.

KUHN: How do your salaries compare?

MANAGER: My salary is much higher than theirs. In such an era, this salary difference between generations is a common phenomenon. But my work is more pressured than their work.

KUHN: Your husband also works at Legend.

MANAGER: Yes. We both came here directly from college.

KUHN: How does your salary compare with his salary?

MANAGER: Our positions are about the same, so our salaries are about the same. Salary has nothing to do with one's gender, only with one's capability and position.

--- --- --- --- --- --- --- --- --- --- --- --- --- --- --- --- --- --- --- ---

I was determined to interview a Communist official who worked for Legend. How would he or she justify communism's ideology with the needs of a world-class computer corporation?

KUHN: Mr. Li, you're the leader of the Communist Party branch in this Legend factory. Why does a modern computer corporation need the Party?

LI: We're here to make sure that Party policy is carried out in the corporation.

KUHN: What are some of the policies that you make sure are carried out?

LI: The Party branch can unite the workers to complete tasks so that the corporation can make more profit.

KUHN: So the Communist Party is interested in increasing corporate profits?

LI: Certainly. The workers, the Party, and the corporation's interests are the same.

KUHN: If the Communist Party helps to increase profits, won't the shareholders—the capitalists—get richer?

LI: Socialism wants to make profits, too.

KUHN: Why aren't all the workers Party members?

LI: Only the progressive proletariats are eligible to be Party members. It's not for everyone. Some aren't interested in politics; some are more interested in improving themselves by learning technology and enhancing their careers. Just as in America—where not everyone wants to run for senator.

KUHN: How do workers become Party members?

LI: They have to follow the Party constitution. First they apply and receive education from the Party. Then a Party committee decides whether they will be accepted. There's a one year period of probation before they become formal Party members.

KUHN: What happens when the interests of the corporation differ from the interests of the Party?

LI: There won't be conflict. The Party branch doesn't interfere with the daily operation of the corporation. The Party branch only ensures that, politically, the corporation takes the socialist direction.

KUHN: What kinds of policies do you make?

LI: We don't make policies; we only execute policies—for example, labor laws and workers' rights. We may have different points of view, and we can reach agreement through negotiations. For example, in the matter of dealing with laid-off workers, other political parties, which we have here, have put forward good proposals, and the Communist Party has adopted them. The Communist Party is the ruling party, but the other parties aren't puppets.

KUHN: I see all these slogans exhorting workers to increase sales and serve their customers. Thirty years ago, the slogans praised proletariat peasants and castigated capitalist corporations.

LI: Our thoughts have been liberated since the reform. Now we're more concerned with the development of the corporation, because the corporation's success affects the interests of the workers.

Outlook and Prospects

The Future of Communism

The Haier Group[26]—market-savvy, technically astute, and financially strong—exemplifies the new, successful Chinese enterprise, which is why its relationship to the Communist Party is especially instructive. With over $3 billion in annual revenues, Haier is China's largest appliance manufacturer—refrigerators, washing machines, air conditioners, electronic products—and, as we've seen (page 140) its brand name is known increasingly in world markets, including the United States. With an almost fanatical dedication to the market and attention to its customers, Haier plans to become one of the world's five hundred largest corporations, a goal I thought rather unrealistic,

With our CCTV camera crews, I visited Haier's campus-like facilities in Qingdao, a beautiful city on the Yellow Sea that was leased to Germans in 1898 for the establishment of the famous brewery of the same name ("Tsingtao," in the older spelling). It is a short flight from Beijing but Qingdao's clean ocean breezes, after being enveloped by the capital's dense pollution, make you remember that it's okay to breathe deeply.

I toured Haier's modern factories and slogan-draped headquarters and learned how Haier's corporate culture influences all their people and processes. My guide and host was Haier's president and chief executive of-

---

[26] The name "Haier" is German in origin, the product of an early joint venture with a German company to acquire world-class technology. The Chinese bought out the Germans but the name stuck.

ficer, Zhang Ruimin, one of China's most successful and distinguished business leaders. Mr. Zhang, who has become something of a celebrity for resurrecting the nearly bankrupt Qingdao General Refrigerator Factory that he took over in 1984 and turning it into a world competitor, has developed an intense management style that combines Western methods of quality control, Chinese cultural sensitivities, and his own unique perspectives.

He created a "Demerit Board" that lists publicly—right outside the company cafeteria—the names of employees, including senior executives, who are responsible for various kinds of failures, with serious consequences for repeat offenders; he famously ordered workers to smash defective products with sledgehammers; and he is absolutely obsessive about inculcating Haier's culture into all acquisitions. (*Business Week* selected Mr. Zhang as one of its "Stars of Asia" in June 2000.)

President Zhang's resume would not have suggested such success. Deprived of college because of the Cultural Revolution, he was a mid-level bureaucrat in the Qingdao municipal government, an unlikely incubator for a free-market visionary. But Zhang was reading Western management books by night and he harbored this peculiar belief that Chinese companies could produce goods of world-class quality.

As we toured his facilities, Mr. Zhang was explaining why he was serious that Haier would become one of the world's five hundred largest corporations, when deep within their modern, multistory headquarters and quite by accident I came upon a room that just looked oddly out of place, and when I asked, it turned out to be the "Activity Room of the Communist Party."

My attention now thoroughly diverted from mercantile matters, I asked Mr. Zhang if we could enter. He was most gracious and invited me into what seemed an anachronism—a room out of the 1950s, as if preserved for a museum. Here, nestled within Haier's striking edifice, whose walls were strewn with banners proclaiming the overwhelming importance of the market, was an unpopulated tranquil haven, a rectangular room roughly sixty by thirty feet with a huge table in the center and formal red flags dominating one's view. Along the walls were pamphlets and magazines preaching the primacy of proletarian doctrines, and on the walls were large photographs of fellows I knew—Marx, Engels, Lenin, Stalin, and Mao.

I discovered that the Communist Party operates a parallel organization within Haier, just as it does within all large enterprises in China, and just as it does within the government itself. (This is apparent on Haier's website, where alongside a column listing its operating departments is a parallel column listing the departments of its "Party and Masses.") I asked President Zhang if we could conduct our interview in the Activity Room. He agreed, and after opening with all the expected questions about Haier's strategy, structure, culture, market focus, managerial issues, executive compensation, and the like, I got down to what I really wanted to talk about.

ROBERT KUHN: What percent of Haier employees are members of the Communist Party?

PRESIDENT ZHANG RUIMIN: About 10 percent.

KUHN: What percent of Haier's management are members of the Communist Party?

ZHANG: About 90 percent.

KUHN: Doesn't that send a powerful message to all Haier employees that they had better join the Party in order to advance into management?

ZHANG: It's not necessarily so. The young people have their own ideas. Some of them want to join democratic parties. Some of them do not want to join any party; they just want to build their careers. And some of them want to go abroad. Since Party members constitute only 10 percent of Haier, this tells us that most of our employees do not want to join the Communist Party.

KUHN: Will Haier continue to have 90 percent of its management Party members?

ZHANG: That will change. Already some of our executives are not Party members, especially those who are young. [I was amazed to learn that three of Haier's four divisional presidents were in their early thirties.]

KUHN: What does the Party actually do for Haier?

ZHANG: The Party activities now are very different from what they were in the past. Now they only happen after work; in the past they happened during work. Party members are required to set a good example for other workers. Especially when conditions are tough, we require Party members to contribute more. We are working to become one of the five hundred strongest companies in the world. In accomplishing this, there will be difficult and urgent work; we expect Party members to do more. For example, when we acquire other companies, Party members volunteer to do extra work, such as integrating our corporate culture.

KUHN: How do you see the future of communism in China?

ZHANG: Our economy is a socialist market economy. We creatively make use of Marxism. It was impossible for Marx and Engels to predict what would be happening today, so we need to develop their thought. The theory that guides our work is more of a combination of Marxism and Deng Xiaoping's theory. So we carry on Marxism while developing it.

It seemed surreal, there in the Activity Room of the Communist Party, to be discussing executive compensation, stock options, the preeminence of the market, mergers, and acquisitions. I felt a delicious irony in forcing those fellows strung up on the wall to watch—Marx, Engels, Lenin, Stalin. Even in Russia, I thought, you can't find Stalin around anymore. Yet here they all were, enshrined in the heart of one of the most successful, market-driven companies in China.

Mao, I didn't mind so much, and this is why there is less contradiction here than first appears. Chinese communism, at its heart, was always more nationalistic than economic. Foreign domination was the gut issue, not exploitation of the working class. Chinese honor and pride was the real goal, not nationalized ownership of production. And so perhaps communism had its place in China's development, a place now being overrun by the competitive fury of the global market and China's determination to become one of the leaders.

With its nearly 62 million members nationwide, the Communist Party of China is the largest political party in the world. But what many of these Party members and officials are thinking about these days is how to make China stronger and richer—and, not infrequently, how to make themselves and their families richer at the same time.

If you take a close look at the Communist Party today, you find that it differs greatly from the one that Mao called his own. Communism, as we have seen, is embedded in the Chinese psyche, where it stands for far more than just a system of collective ownership and production. Communism provided the energy to restore China's national pride, and even today it is the vehicle for maintaining China's national stability. Communism, for China, must have a future. What to do?

There is a new notion making the rounds among communist theorists (perhaps as a trial balloon) that takes this justification of China's twenty-first century capitalism to a whole new level of theoretical creativity. Here's how it goes. It begins by reaffirming that communism is the best system for social equality, human economy and political governance, but then adds the temporal condition "ultimately." Ah, "ultimately"! The task is how to get from here to there: from today's reality of thousands of antiquated, ill-structured, ill-equipped, overstaffed, bureaucracy-laden, market-insensitive, money-losing, state-owned enterprises to tomorrow's wonderland of modern, efficient, market-savvy, profitable companies— and thence to the "ultimate" goal of an ideal (and so far conveniently undefined) "communism."

The key idea, these theorists claim, is that China's economy must pass through a stage that "looks a lot like capitalism." In fact, some clever theoretician must have asserted, with what seems like brazen overconfidence, the clever catch phrase that "capitalism is the first stage of communism." (A cheeky reply making the rounds: "Therefore capitalism is the period of high productivity between communism and communism.")

Let's consider this radical justification—that capitalism is the first stage of communism. How long does this first stage last, one might ask? How long will it take for transitory capitalism to bring about ultimate communism? The answer floating around seems to be "about a hundred years," a period long enough to be comfortably and conveniently beyond the lifetime of anyone in power in China today. This means that even a good communist society, professing all the communist ideals of equality and classlessness, can wholly embrace the free market economics of capitalism, a full-blown private sector, and a growing gap between rich and poor with a clear conscience—because in the end it will lead to the purest form of communism.

When I first heard this rationale, it sounded beyond rationalization, more comic than clever—a wry caricature of hack communist theorists leaked by intellectual cynics. But the hundred-year horizon is the serious opinion of at least some Chinese political theorists, and I have come to wonder whether there may be more vision here than is immediately apparent.

Capitalism, in its current form, has been a working economic model for several hundred years—since, say, the industrial revolution—and has passed through various incarnations, some of which were not so pleasant. If we project forward, as many have done in this year of millennial transition, to the twenty-second century, or surely to the third millennium, it is not unreasonable to expect a new working model of the global economy.

Although capitalism and liberal democracy seem to be the most effi-cient system at present,[27] it may not be so even a hundred years from now, given the extraordinary technological forces of change—in com-munications, computer science, biotechnology, nanotechnology, com-plexity theory—now sweeping the planet and rapidly turning it into one world. In a future that will undoubtedly differ from today's world more than today's world differs from that of the first millennium, it is un-likely that global economic systems will have remained static. The trans-formation of human life and society will be so astonishing that it is not at all clear what the prevailing economic systems and market mecha-nisms will have become.

Who knows what will happen to corporations, capital markets, cash flows, and governments at all levels, when we are all online all the time, when all the work of production is conducted by artificial intelligences, when the global network eliminates poverty and brings about worldwide equality among all peoples, when humans spend their time in creative ac-tivities and personal entertainment?[28] It would not at all surprise me if what will then exist—whether in a hundred years or a thousand years—might look a lot closer to classic communism than to classic capitalism.[29]

In any event, Chinese entrepreneurs and business leaders have plenty of time to become good capitalists; to pursue their dreams, make their mark, and build their wealth; to pioneer hot new marketable technolo-gies; to leverage China's huge domestic markets; to grow their companies into strong competitors in world markets—all the while allowing political theorists to proclaim that they are paving the way for the ultimate tri-umph of communism. Capitalism as the first stage of communism? Sounds silly at first, but if you think about it the idea becomes less far-fetched. When, as we've seen, the most populous country on earth is un-dergoing one of history's most profound transformations, such long-term political strategy may actually make sense.

---

[27] As the political and social scientist Francis Fukuyama argues in his seminal, though controversial, work, *The End of History*.

[28] Remarkable advances in science and technology will radically alter all aspects of the human condition. See *Closer To Truth*, by Robert Lawrence Kuhn (New York: Mc-Graw-Hill Trade Science, 2000), and www.closertotruth.com.

[29] According to Karl Marx, human societies would develop from primitive to slave to feudal to capitalist to socialist, and ultimately, to communist. Give the old guy his due; his day may yet come.

Personal Development

As our friend Yang Millionaire (page 148) told us, "I didn't become a millionaire overnight. I'm an opportunist, nothing wrong with that."

In the days of Mao, there were many different voices and personalities among the Chinese people, but they were hidden, says Professor Wang Lihua. It seemed there was only one voice then, Mao, who said: "Everyone must walk at the same pace." After the economic reform, all these different voices and personalities emerged.

Maintaining personal values, expressing personal opinions, and pursuing personal goals are new ideas in China—all the result of the market economy in which individual initiative is essential. The old communist models were selfless peasants who wholly devoted themselves to the communist cause, who sacrificed their individual desires for the national interest. The idolization of Lei Feng, a soldier who died in his early twenties protecting his fellow communists and countrymen, personified Mao's era. Young students were drilled to follow such examples and virtually all people held these same ideals.

The new social models are diametrically different. Chinese society is far more pluralistic and diverse, with people, especially young people, maintaining greatly varied values, opinions and goals. Money is a driving force for many people, and entrepreneurs are their heroes. As ordinary Chinese people say, "money is not omnipotent, but money does make things happen."

But even today, money is not the only motivation in China. People feel the excitement. They know what they are doing is important for China and they sense the historic mission. Chinese people have a good sense of history and they are thrilled to take part in China's profound transformation. A young Internet entrepreneur, one of Fanso's founders (page 219), said: "In the past, American entrepreneurs did better than us: look at Bill Gates. But we're different. We'll show the world what Chinese entrepreneurs can do."

It's as if there are no boundaries, that everything is possible. People are embracing the market economy with the same unvarnished enthusiasm that their parents did socialism. But socialism was not all bad, just as capitalism is not all good. The previous generation suffered through the punishing radicalism of the Great Leap Forward, the Cultural Revolution, the economic failures of collectivism, and they became utterly disillusioned. Now, some people, especially writers and artists, sense contradictions and problems in the market economy. There is no doubt that the market economy is good for China, but nothing social is simple, idealism fades quickly, and a realistic view is always the healthiest.

Policies and Politics

Westerners in general, and Americans in particular, can be naïve when dealing with China. It's often ironic (and occasionally embarrassing) how some policies seem to elicit responses quite at odds with their original intent. It makes no sense for China and the United States to be on opposite sides of great issues, since the well-being of both countries, especially on matters economic, relates directly to a cooperative, not competitive relationship. Yet opposite sides is where Chinese and American leaders often find themselves, sometimes intractably so, when real cultural differences are inflated by trumped-up political posturing. Nothing other than religion provokes the passions of people more than nationalism.

When American politicians talk China policy, "containment" and "appeasement" seem to define the domestic debate. Both betray scant understanding of China and neither are in any way helpful. Since human nature skews to the xenophobic, nationalism is always the easy card to play in internal politics, so that those countries whose interests seem to thwart your own are always convenient targets.

In policy analysis, simplistic solutions to complex problems are almost certainly wrong. The little devils of conflict resolution almost always reside in the little details of the particular issue. Facts are in constant flux and subtle differences in one place, applying chaos theory to geopolitics, can generate substantial differences in another, so that optimum solutions can differ in kind, not just degree.

Thus, although geopolitical policies must always be governed by the "what," some attention should be paid to the "who." The most important aspect of a specific policy might be whether it strengthens or weakens a key foreign leader. This does not mean compromising a nation's principles, but it does mean that policies should be thoughtfully constructed to satisfy those principles in reality, not just in theory.

If policy is what to do, and politics is how to do it, in China, as in the United States, policy and politics often collide. If President Jiang and Premier Zhu can be successful, and by extension and succession Vice President Hu Jintao, China will be America's positive, pragmatic partner in world affairs. Danger lies in their failure, and in the resulting recrudescence of reactionary forces, held in retreat since the early 1990s. So let's consider President Jiang Zemin, Premier Zhu Rongji, and Vice President Hu Jintao.

Jiang Zemin

Jiang sees himself in the historic tradition of Deng Xiaoping, a benevolent, reformist leader who brings about economic, social, scientific, and personal progress to his country and people. Jiang became general secretary of the Communist Party of China, the highest position in the country, under extremely difficult circumstances.

Paramount leader Deng Xiaoping had previously selected Zhao Ziyang, a popular figure, as his chosen successor. But Zhao, who as secretary general had guided the early economic reforms but whose advocacy for political reforms was threatening and already under severe criticism within the Party, sympathized with the change-seeking students who filled Tiananmen Square in the late spring of 1989, and was then ousted for not supporting the harsh military crackdown on June 4 in which hundreds were killed.

In what appears in retrospect to be one of his wisest, most prescient decisions, Deng selected Jiang Zemin, then Party chief of Shanghai and not the most obvious of choices, and elevated him (above other, higher-ranking members of his generation) to become the new general secretary of the Party. At the time, Deng's selection was not given much of a chance of long surviving the Byzantine politics of Beijing. Jiang did not have a deep power base (such as the army), nor was his personality particularly charismatic.

But Jiang provided some much-needed balance: he was not terribly liberal (he had fired a liberal newspaper editor in Shanghai) and he was not tainted by the fiasco in Tiananmen. In fact Jiang was credited with coolly diffusing the pro-democracy demonstrators in Shanghai in stark contrast to the carnage in Beijing. So Jiang was widely appreciated as a compromise candidate, and that was exactly what was needed at this tense time of mounting instability.

Widely minimalized in the West as hardly more than an interim leader, Jiang surprised most observers by putting his firm stamp on one of the most crucial ten-year periods in Chinese history. Beset with seemingly intractable economic problems and social contradictions, and having to tra-

verse the endless corridors of inner-sanctum Chinese politics, Jiang skill-
fully accelerated the economy and relaxed social controls while maintaining stability. Future historians may assess that it was during President
Jiang's term of office that China made its most critical and long-lasting
decisions, setting into motion what would become fundamental, irre-
versible, and robust transformation.

Jiang Zemin was born into an intellectual family in Jiangsu Province, in
eastern China. In an extraordinary gift of fate, Jiang became the legal son
of a Communist hero and martyr, a status that benefited his later career
in the Party. (His uncle had died fighting for the Communists in the Anti-
Japanese War, and since Chinese custom considered dying without leaving a male heir to be a tragedy, Jiang's father allowed him to be adopted
by his uncle's family.)

In 1946, at age twenty, Jiang joined the Communist Party to oppose Chiang Kai-shek. (He speaks with pride of his role in keeping a bombed-out factory operating after it had been attacked by the anticommunist nationalist
forces.) In 1947, he graduated from Chaio-t'ung University in Shanghai
with a degree in electrical engineering. After working in various factories, he
went to the Soviet Union in the mid-1950s to receive further technical
training. Jiang spent many years working in China's heavy industry sector, directing technological research institutes in various parts of China.

Jiang's career shifted from technical administration to government and
politics in 1980 when he became vice minister of the national commissions
on foreign investment and on imports and exports. He is given credit for
being a key planner behind the success of China's first Special Economic
Zone, Shenzhen (adjacent to Hong Kong), which was established in 1980 to
stimulate foreign investment and is considered a crucial breakthrough in
catalyzing economic reform. Jiang joined the Ministry of Electronics Industry as a vice minister in 1982 and became minister a year later. A member
of the Communist Party Central Committee since 1982, he was elected to
the Politburo in 1987. Jiang served in Shanghai as Party secretary from 1985
until 1989 and mayor from 1985 until 1988. He was an early and ardent foe
of corruption, a campaign that he continues to wage today.

Jiang enjoys culture and intellectual pursuits, including classical Chinese.
He speaks English and Russian, and reads French, Japanese, and Romanian.
He can quote Lincoln's Gettysburg Address; he is fond of literature and is
a great supporter of Western classical music. It is said that when asked by
large foreign companies what they can do to help China, President Jiang occasionally recommends donations to Chinese symphony orchestras.

A former U.S. under secretary of state for political affairs, Arnold Kanter, stated early on, "One shouldn't be fooled. Jiang is enormously smart and capable, but his persona is unpretentious and folksy, almost intentionally disarming." During a visit with Philippine President Fidel Ramos, President Jiang entertained—and shocked—everyone by dancing the cha-cha and singing a duet of "Love Me Tender."

But let no one underestimate Jiang's seriousness and conviction, which is underlined by his commitment to science and technology. With a successful pre-political career as an engineer (civil and power), he is proud of his science and technology background (which he contrasts, without value judgment, with President Clinton's legal background). In an extended interview with *Science* magazine (June 16, 2000), President Jiang reflected on China's "long history with splendid achievements in science and technology" and wondered why, starting from the last years of the Ming Dynasty (1368–1644), China began to lag behind: "The feudal rulers forbade traveling abroad and later imposed restrictions on entry into and exit from China via sea. That closed the door to external exchanges between China and the outside world."

Jiang credits China's many achievements to "reform" and "opening up" and to the casting aside of "bad legacies." Jiang is proud that China has established scientific links with more than 150 countries and regions, that "Chinese scientists have participated in 800 scientific collaboration projects launched by international organizations," and that "between 1978 and 1999, nearly 340,000 Chinese students and scholars went abroad to study."

In a guest editorial in the same publication, Jiang dealt with the importance of basic science and the personal freedoms required to do it well: "...we are encouraging scientists to conduct basic research in the fields where the needs of the state intersect the frontiers of science, and we applaud those who are driven by curiosity to pursue pure research. We recognize and respect the unique sensitivities and sensibilities of scientists; we understand that scientific creativity is the very source and lifeline of a knowledge-based economy" (*Science*, June 30, 2000).

Jiang concludes his *Science* editorial with a sweeping vision of China as a proud member of the world community: "By seeking common ground and common interests, I firmly believe that international scientific exchange and cooperation can transcend any differences in social systems, economic models, cultural traditions, and levels of development. The advancement of science in China is essential not only for China's welfare but also for that of the whole world. Chinese scientists look forward to joining with their counterparts in other countries in contributing to humankind's common cause. It is our solemn commitment that China's scientific development shall benefit all peoples."

Zhu Rongji

Premier Zhu Rongji, as the master strategist of China's economic, financial, and trade affairs, sees himself as a tough-minded administrator, who through sheer intelligence (protected by a mighty thick skin) seeks to change the course of China's economic and governmental structure. As mayor of Shanghai in the late 1980s he was nicknamed "one-chop Zhu," a complimentary appellation, for his well-known propensity to smash through the red tape of conflicting and bickering bureaucracies in order to establish worthy joint ventures. As premier he has streamlined the government by eliminating ministries and shrinking bureaucracies, thus earning the enmity of officials whose jobs were abolished. (Since Zhu, along with President Jiang and other senior leaders, comes from Shanghai, there is extra sensitivity when Beijingers lose their positions. The perennial competition between Beijing and Shanghai, not always with the grace of good spirit, can boil up quickly when power shifts.)

Zhu brooks no nonsense. He has not hesitated to humiliate incompetent officials in public or sack corrupt ones on the spot. (He once summarily fired a senior administrator who displayed a cigarette lighter that he could not possibly have afforded on his salary.) Zhu is not known to float a soft voice in the face of the ineffectual or display calm emotion when berating a bungler, and he has threatened to "chop off the heads" of bank officials who defy his edicts.

Zhu's career had been long locked in obscurity. A student activist who joined the Communist Party in 1949, an electrical engineer by training, and a rising star in the State Planning Commission, Zhu was labeled a "rightist" in 1958 and spent the next twenty years in low-level positions in the economic planning bureaucracy. During the Cultural Revolution, he was sent down to the countryside for punishment from 1970 to 1979. Although many of China's senior leaders suffered during the Cultural Revolution, few had also been double-punched and condemned earlier as a counterrevolutionary rightist.

It had been in response to Mao Zedong's "Hundred Flowers" campaign in 1957, when the Great Helmsman briefly encouraged open political and intellectual debate only to ruthlessly purge the debaters, that Zhu criticized Mao's policies of rapid economic growth as "irrational." Only after Mao's "Great Leap Forward" had turned into the greatest famine in human history and his disastrous policies had been finally halted was Zhu brought back in 1962.

When the Cultural Revolution ended, Zhu had his second rehabilitation and was appointed to the State Economic Commission where he served as vice minister from 1983 until 1988, when he was named mayor of Shanghai. Interestingly, Zhu has not reflected publicly on his own deprivations and humiliations, but the contrast between the way he handled student protests in Shanghai in 1989 and the way they were dealt with in Beijing is striking. While hundreds were shot in Beijing, Zhu made a televised plea in Shanghai that helped to persuade many protesters to leave peacefully. Four days after the Beijing massacre Zhu published a speech in the local papers, in which he eschewed the then-politically correct terms "turmoil" and "counterrevolution" used by Deng Xiaoping and Li Peng. He wrote: "The event that occurred recently in Beijing is a historical fact and historical facts cannot be covered up by anybody. The truth will always come out." On a visit to the United States in 1990 Zhu was called "China's Gorbachev," a designation he immediately rejected and said he preferred to be known as "China's Zhu Rongji."

Zhu has long held a concurrent position as dean of Qinghua University's School of Economics and Management, a title of which he is most proud. A former governor of the People's Bank of China (where he initiated sweeping reforms), he was appointed premier in 1998. When Zhu came to the United States in early 1999, he put his political credibility on the line to strike a deal on China's entrance into the World Trade Organization. When American politics put pressure on the American president to reject what he knew to be the right decision, our largest loss was that Zhu was diminished in his own country, and thus we undercut someone whose intrinsic interests were reasonably resonant with our own.

Hu Jintao

A fascinating expression of President Jiang's leadership—again, underreported in the West—is his expected, deliberate transference of national leadership. Jiang has reportedly informed senior Party leaders that he intends to relinquish his preeminent position of power as general secretary of China's Communist Party, at the Party Congress in 2002. (He must also step down as China's state president in early 2003, since China's constitution only permits two terms in this office.) Such changes in power—not through crisis, not by infirmity or death, and not conveyed to relatives—is hardly the mark of authoritarian regimes.

Jiang has mused with refreshing candor that he feels uncomfortable when meeting with younger world leaders such as U.S. President Clinton and U.K. Prime Minister Tony Blair. Not because of any intellectual inferiority or physical incapacity, but just because he feels that China needs to be represented on the world stage by vibrant, energetic leaders of the same age group. In fact, President Jiang has gone further by calling for the wholesale retirement of all older leaders of the Politburo Standing Committee, the Party's most powerful body, leaving only the two youngest members, Hu Jintao, state vice president, and Li Ruihuan, chairman of the Chinese People's Political Consultative Conference.

The appointment of Hu Jintao as vice president of the People's Republic of China in March 1998 symbolized the progressive maturation of China's collective leadership as President Jiang prepared for the future with an orderly plan of political succession. (Hu's ascension, though the more significant event, was overshadowed at the time by the appointment of Li Peng, enduringly stained by Tiananmen blood, as chairman of the National People's Congress. The 200 "no" votes against Li, along with the face-losing 126 abstentions—a protest by more than 10 percent of the 2,616 delegates—made the points that Li was not universally wanted and that the National People's Congress was no longer a rubber stamp.)

Catapulted to national prominence five years earlier by then Paramount Leader Deng Xiaoping who brought him into the Politburo Standing Committee, Hu's impeccable Party credentials and political savvy mark him as heir apparent to President Jiang and the odds-on favorite to become the next president. I can think of no better way of assessing China's future than by tracing Hu's background, which without doubt reinforces stability as the primary theme governing China.

Born in east China's Anhui Province, Hu studied hydroelectric engineering at Qinghua University, the country's most prestigious polytechnic university. An outstanding student, Hu once said that it was not his original intention to go into politics. After graduating in 1965, Hu remained at Qinghua as a researcher and political instructor until the start of the Cultural Revolution in 1966. In 1968, he was assigned to work in Gansu, one of China's least-developed provinces in the northwest.

After doing manual labor for one year on a housing construction team, he served successively as technician, office secretary, and deputy Party secretary in an engineering bureau under the Ministry of Water Resources and Electric Power, thus beginning his career in Party affairs work. In 1974, he was transferred to the Gansu Provincial Construction Committee and later became secretary of the Gansu Chinese Communist Youth League (CCYL). In 1984, he became the first secretary of the Central Committee of the Chinese Communist Youth League, the top leader of China's largest youth organization.

When he was elected into the Communist Party Central Committee, Hu was only thirty-nine, the youngest member at that time. In 1985, when he was forty-two, Hu became secretary of the Guizhou Communist Party, again the youngest of his rank in the country. He is proud to recall that in his two subsequent years in Guizhou, a poor province in south-central China, he visited eighty-six counties, cities, and prefectures. Hu said that economic development in poverty-stricken areas requires the effort of one full generation of dedicated people.

In 1988, Hu became Party secretary of the Tibet Autonomous Regional Committee, where he garnered general acclaim in a difficult environment. In 1992, Hu was elected to the Standing Committee of the Politburo, serving concurrently as president of the Party School since 1993. According to his former colleagues (speaking, seemingly, on the record), Hu is a very persuasive person and is "very good at coping with complex situations with firm principles and flexible tactics." ("Firm principles and flexible tactics"—what a wonderfully crafted phrase! How nicely it melds stability and reform, giving a nod to each side of the political spectrum.)

Hu said that "a good leader must have firm belief and lofty pursuit, do solid work, seek no fame or gain, do away with air of bureaucracy, and share the feeling of the masses of people." He added that, "a good leader should carry forward democracy and also be capable of taking resolute actions at critical moments, and must love life."

Hu is recognized in China as an intelligent, decent man of high integrity who is fundamentally committed to maintaining stability and continuing Jiang's policies of reform. Hu and his wife, who works in the Beijing Municipal Construction Committee, were schoolmates at Qinghua University. Hu, we are told, loves literature and art, and, most important in my book, he is said to play table tennis well.

At a high profile national conference for chiefs of Communist Party "publicity" (i.e., propaganda) departments, Hu noted that the next ten years will be a critical period for China, and the Party will face challenges brought about by the times. Therefore, according to Hu, an arduous effort must be made to consolidate the ideological foundation that will enable the nation to maintain stability and solidarity, so that all would "advocate patriotism, collectivism, socialism, and hard work." Hu pointed out that the Chinese media must uphold the Party and mobilize the people to safeguard stability and solidarity, and create favorable public opinion for continuing reform, opening up, and modernization. Hu said that the core of ideological work is to help the people cultivate lofty ideals and correct convictions. He stressed that cultural and "publicity" work should be strengthened, adding that artists should carry forth the nation's fine traditions and learn from foreign achievements. (Hu once noted that Chinese youth should be educated to appreciate reform's arduous and complex nature. "Do not place high expectations while your psychological capacity for endurance is low," he said.)

Although Chinese politics can change, occasionally without overt warning, it is surely true that Hu Jintao represents a cautious combination of continuity and progressiveness—stability and pride—and in the process of preparing for his coming leadership, he has elevated the position of China's vice presidency, itself a contribution to broad-based leadership. It is a master plan that maintains the policies of President Jiang, whose historical assessment will be tied to the ultimate success of his strategy for succession.

Americans and Misunderstandings

At our media conference in Beijing (see page 192), I was chairing an interactive session when a leading Chinese media executive asked my permission to tell a joke. Of course I assented. Jokes are not common in formal Chinese settings, particularly with foreigners, and especially not when sensitive subjects are being discussed. So as all American presenters paid close attention, I enjoyed a moment of private satisfaction since I knew that the simple request to tell the joke meant that the conference was going well and that the Chinese side felt confident in our friendship (though many of our comments were critical and pointed).

The Chinese media executive said he was quoting a former Rumanian dissent who, we were pre-comforted, usually directs most of his barbs at Russians:

"Why has every country in the world had a revolution except America?" the media executive asked rhetorically with a nervous smile, then paused only briefly.

"Because America is the only country in the world without an American embassy," he answered quickly, anxiously uncertain of our reaction.

The audience of more than forty Chinese media leaders laughed heartily as we Americans waited for the translation; then we laughed too, a bit muted perhaps.

After the session, the Chinese joke teller came up to me and rather sheepishly asked: "Did I offend our American guests?" I assured him that we were not only not offended, but pleased that our desire for openness and honesty was taken seriously and that he could have confidence in telling such a joke.

In the post–Cold War era, westerners (particularly Americans) remain fearful and suspicious of China. Many Chinese believe that it is not so much that westerners are unable to understand China as that they do not want to. I would put it differently: I think that in general westerners view China through polarized lenses that admit only certain images—images that conform to media-conditioned preconceptions.

I know of no Americans who have not come back from a first trip to China with impressions substantially different from those they held prior to the trip. One common misimpression is that Chinese people are all conformists—that all of them act in pretty much the same way. In fact, Chinese do not differ much from Americans in their degree of personal expression; the era of reform has heightened this individualism, not initiated it. Sun Yat-sen, the founder of modern China, described China as "sand in the wind"—a nation in which everyone is divided and free to do what he or she wants to do.

In general, the Chinese have a genuine affection for Americans, which makes it all the more perplexing to them that the United States is (as they imagine) intent on thwarting China's national interests. I have tried to discern the origin of this special affection. Part of it is undoubtedly the absence of a negative: other countries have at one time or another attempted, with varying degrees of success, to dominate or subjugate China. The United States, though it opposed China in the Korean War, never established a colonial or occupying presence on the Chinese mainland (see "Who Could Have Thought It?", page 204). Other countries, particularly England, took advantage of China in times of its weakness. And certainly the atrocities that the Japanese carried out will not be forgotten for many generations.

I think the fundamental compatibility between Chinese and Americans goes deeper, though. There are natural, personal similarities—a way of thinking that is practical, flexible, entrepreneurial, unencumbered by affectation. It may surprise Americans to know that many mainland Chinese—particularly those in Beijing, with whom I am most familiar—often feel more comfortable working with Americans than they do with overseas Chinese, say, from Hong Kong. The latter, though they speak the same language, often have an air of superiority toward their mainland cousins—the condescending attitude of supposed expert to apparent acolyte.

Some American geopolitical thinkers suspect that China has expansionist ambitions, to dominate other countries in Asia and perhaps the world. Their threats to Taiwan, their domination of Tibet, their claims of oil rights in the South China Sea, combined with their intent to build offensive missile capabilities, are used in the West to support a strategic position of Chinese containment.

Arguments about Tibet, in particular, are far more complex to Chinese than to Americans. Americans simply consider Tibet to be an occupied country, much like Hungary or Poland under the Soviets, unable to determine its own destiny. Chinese use historical analysis, however abstruse to the uninitiated, to justify their current policy, bolstered by a "higher good" claim of freeing the Tibetans from impoverishment and superstition. The bottom line, irrespective of the strength of their arguments or legitimacy of their positions, is that most Chinese feel that the sympathy the West has for Tibet, and the outrage expressed by Western activists, is just another example of Western efforts to contain and restrain the legitimate aspirations of China to become a great nation. To many Chinese, these foreign policy initiatives are manifestations of China's independence and their hard-won capacity to determine their own destiny and never again to be the object of coerced and humiliating treaties.

"Why does the United States not want us to build our own society in our own way?" is the question that diverse Chinese have asked me. And they ask further why Chinese should not have the same rights that Americans have to self-determine the best social system for their people. "China is different from America in terms of population and historical tradition," they say. "We must build our society in our way." The more astute will add that the Chinese way is really not all that different from the American way, and that the diverse paths to similar goals differ more than do the goals themselves.

A fascinating example of American misunderstanding is the bizarre report in the American media (and the hypersensitive reaction in the Chinese media) of a Chinese "plan" to take over the Panama Canal after its recent return to the government of Panama. Anyone familiar with Chinese foreign policy considers the notion preposterous, but such a report indeed made the rounds in American media—the story may have started when a Chinese company won a maintenance contract in Panama—and then this U.S.-concocted story became front page, big headline news in some Chinese tabloids, which used it to prove an American bias against China. Ironically, this kind of overheated Chinese reaction plays into the hands of China-bashing Americans, and the furor only escalates (see "Communication In and With China," page 198).

A story illustrating the complex relationship between China and America is set shortly after the tragic NATO bombing of the Chinese Embassy in Belgrade in which three Chinese journalists, including a young married couple, were killed. Chinese people, by a large margin (90 percent versus 10 percent), assume the attack to have been deliberate, while Americans, by a large margin (though probably less than 90–10), assume the attack to have been accidental. (I certainly count myself in the accidental camp.) Though the outcry from ordinary Chinese citizens seemed genuine, many Americans, myself included, blamed the Chinese government for stirring up xenophobia. But that analysis, I later discovered, was wrong: in fact most Chinese citizens (including my sophisticated and worldly friends in Beijing) did believe, with no goading from their government, that the bombing was no accident. In fact, Chinese students around the world launched protests and organized rallies. Chinese pride had been wounded and America, they believed, had inflicted it with malice aforethought. And the reason is fascinating.

Their thinking goes something like this: Since America is so powerful, so competent, and so technologically advanced, it is impossible for America to have made such a dumb mistake. Americans, on the other hand (myself included), are painfully aware that our government makes a lot of dumb mistakes and, more important, that the American media is so scandal-seeking and scoop-hungry that if there were a glimmer of a possibility of such a conspiracy, some news source would have ferreted it out. Of course, I cannot completely eliminate the remote possibility that some lower-level intelligence officer was up to some premeditated mischief in giving those ill-fated coordinates (as some non-U.S. newspapers have hinted), but the fact that no credible American news source even suggested that the bombing was deliberate is, to me, powerful proof that it was not.

The Chinese saw the American bombing as a reminder of the historical subjugation and wanton occupation of their land by foreigners. Americans saw the Chinese government as looking for any excuse to take
advantage of unfortunate situations to stir up anti-American resentment
for their own propaganda purposes. Such is the way that different perceptions of random events can lead to discord.

But there was one report of the air strike and its consequences that
combined irony with good sense. When angry Chinese students surrounded the United States Embassy in Beijing to protest the attack, one
of the students who was being interviewed expressed great indignation at
America's patronizing attitude—at America's smug sense that its system
is not only the best in the world but should be imposed on every other
country. His screed gained momentum and toward the end he was emot-
ing and hurling invectives. When the wearied interviewer asked him how
long his ranting would continue, he said matter-of-factly, returning to his
natural studious self, that he soon had to return home to study for his up-
coming GREs—which, of course, is the entrance exam for American graduate schools. Is there hypocrisy here? Not really; I think what it does
represent is the bifurcation in Chinese thinking about America: on the one
hand, haughty, arrogant, and domineering; on the other, leading the world
in education, freedom, and the good life.

There are many such opportunities for misunderstanding between diverse cultures. Another illustration is a story of far smaller import than
the dreadful American bombing. The story is personal and slightly embarrassing. First, the background. Chinese is a tonal language; in Mandarin
Chinese there are four tones—high (first tone), rising (second tone),
falling-then-rising (third tone), falling (fourth tone)—such that the same
sound pronounced differently takes on completely different meanings.
For example, the sound "ma" (first tone) means "mother," "ma" (second
tone) means hemp, "ma" (third tone) means horse, "ma" (fourth tone)
means curse, and "ma" (no tone and at the end of a sentence) indicates a
question. (If this tonality sounds strange to English ears, consider how
similar the following words sound, though their meanings have no relationship to one another—bow, hoe, mow, row, sow, toe, woe.)

So here's what happened. In one of my fledging efforts to learn Chinese, I was being tutored by a young Chinese woman, who was cute,
tough and many years my junior. I tell the truth, I had intended to say,
"I want to ask you a question," but instead of voicing "ask" with the
fourth (falling) tone, I hit the third (falling-rising) tone, so that my sen-

tence meant, "I want to kiss you." I do speak truth; like those American pilots, I was innocent.

Zhao Qizheng: "Tremendous Changes"

The following speech by Zhao Qizheng, minister of the Information Office of the State Council, discusses cultural, ideological, and lifestyle changes in China. It was delivered in Paris, during the China Culture Week in September 1999, co-organized by the Information Office, the French Ministry of Culture, and UNESCO.

Marco Polo, the Italian traveler, first informed Europeans about the existence of China. His travelogues, depicting the rich, powerful, and beautiful oriental country with a long-standing history, inspired curiosity and yearning. Theophile Gautier, a famous French writer of the nineteenth century, wrote a poem entitled "China Craze." It says, "My favorite girl is in China. She lives in a fine porcelain tower on the bank of the Yellow River, home to fish hawks. Her small feet can be played with in one's hands, and her skin is brighter than a bronze lamp. Every evening, like a poet, she chants verses about weeping willows and peach blossoms." The poem paints a romantic picture of China, but the poet might not have realized that the small feet were bound feet, a practice that brought great suffering to Chinese women.

I'd like to depict how China looks to the twenty-first century by reviewing the tremendous changes that have occurred over the past century, more [changes] than China has seen in its thirty-five hundred years of recorded history.... The Chinese experienced two revolutions in the twentieth century that dramatically changed their social status, lifestyles, and ways of thinking. The first was the 1911 revolution led by Dr. Sun Yat-sen, which overthrew the Qing court, which had ruled China for nearly three hundred years, and ended China's feudal society. After that, the wars between Chinese warlords and foreign aggression—particularly the Japanese aggression between 1931 and 1945—degraded China into a semifeudal and semicolonial country. The second revolution was the new democratic revolution led by Mao Zedong. The founding of the People's Republic of China in 1949 turned China into a new democratic and socialist country.

In 1978, China launched reform under the leadership of Deng Xiao-ping, who said that the reform was in the nature of a revolution centering on economic development. But reform and the opening of China do not contradict the practice of self-reliance and hard struggle, which history has determined that the Chinese must adhere to.

China entered the current century with a backward outlook and a humiliated spirit. A Dutch dictionary of the early twentieth century described the Chinese as "stupid people with mental problems." An American cartoon depicted the Chinese as pigs. Prior to 1950, China was called "the sick man of the East" by some people abroad.

The Chinese then could be likened to a woman with feet severely bound, moving slowly into the twentieth century with a serious deformity. The vile practice of foot binding became popular in the late years of the Qing dynasty, equally among rich and poor women.

Today, the Chinese are marching into the new century with healthy feet and steady steps. The performance of the Chinese women's football team at the last World Cup amazed the world. It would have been inconceivable fifty years ago for the Chinese to capture championships in the arena of global sports. It is said that the progress of Chinese women has surpassed that of Chinese men. The Chinese women have surged ahead in volleyball, football, gymnastics, and swimming.

In fact, it is appropriate to start our discussion of the Chinese people's conceptual changes by describing the changes in Chinese families and the role of women. In an old-style Chinese family, all the brothers lived together, even after they were married, while the girls had to leave the family for marriage. The richer the family, the larger its size. It was believed that the greater the number of children, the happier the life of a family. So it was common to see families with twenty or thirty people. The Chinese Confucian school stressed the control of "egoism" and encouraged "collectivism." A family was considered a kind of "collective." The Confucian school emphasized the importance of families, the loyalty to family, and the ruling position of the patriarch. Such a family lacked democracy, resulting in various kinds of tragedies. *Family*, *Spring*, and *Autumn*, novels written by the famous Chinese writer Ba Jin, profoundly depict the decline of such a feudal family.

After 1950, this kind of family was rarely seen, and now there are none. At present, the average Chinese family size is 3.63. But the Chinese have not changed their deep respect for family, nor has the sense of responsibility for one's family weakened. The decline in the average family size is related to family planning encouraged by the Chinese government. China's current annual population growth rate is only 9.5 per thousand, and some large cities have registered negative population growth.

The Chinese have also changed their concept of love and marriage. In the past, the marriage of young people was largely arranged by parents, a system that led to numerous romantic tragedies. Now people determine marriage on their own. Matchmaking via TV, ads, special agencies, and other forms has become popular. Some twenty years ago, mixed marriage was inconceivable. In 1977, when a Chinese student wanted to marry a French girl studying in China, the local civil affairs bureau did not dare to grant permission; later, with the consent of Mr. Deng Xiaoping, the two lovers were eventually married. Today, China has special provisions on transnational marriage to protect the people.

In addition, the quality of marriage has become important in China. For a long time, traditional concepts—for example, that a wife should be faithful to her husband until death—were strongly maintained by millions of Chinese families. Since reform, however, people's lifestyles have diversified and a consciousness of independence has developed. Now, when serious differences occur between the husband and wife, they will unhesitatingly divorce.

During the so-called Cultural Revolution [1966–1976], China's educational systems were disrupted in an unprecedented way. For six years, Chinese universities were closed. Chinese families, however, never ceased to attach great importance to education. Parents who had no chance to go to a university during the Cultural Revolution are nonetheless determined to send their children to a university.

One defect in China's education is its overemphasis on standardized examinations. Each summer vacation is the crucial moment for students to take the national university entrance examination. To enable more students to enter famous universities and middle schools, the principals of many secondary and primary schools do not hesitate to add classes during the students' spare time. China's current teaching system can be traced back to the imperial examination system. Emphasizing mechanical memorizing, it cannot instill in the students the thinking skills so necessary in modern society. The Chinese government is endeavoring to transform this examination-oriented educational system into one focusing more on general improvement of intellectual quality, with special emphasis on fostering the students' creative capacities.

In 1900, China had only ten universities. Now there are 1,022. Given the increasing pressure on higher education, the government called on universities to increase their enrollment in 1999, with the total enrollment reaching 1.53 million, an increase of 47 percent over 1998. At present, most Chinese universities are state-owned. Privately funded universities are expected to develop rapidly in the near future.

Before reform, most Chinese students favored the natural sciences, and there were only a small number of students majoring in economics, law, and management. Currently, the number of students choosing these specialties has increased significantly. Young people have also changed their concept of employment, a result of the development of a market economy. The classics of the Confucian school stress that "a gentlemen values friendship while a low brute stresses profit." In the past, China's social strata were ranked according to the order of official (first), peasant, worker, and merchant (last). Businessmen were of the lowest class. This culturally ingrained despising of commerce was one reason that China suffered an underdeveloped market for so long. At present, with the growth of a market economy, the Chinese no longer look down upon commerce and businesspeople. Many outstandingly talented people are now engaged in business.

Over the past fifty years, China's gross domestic product (GDP) has grown thirty-one-fold [8,319 billion *yuan*, or about $1,000 billion, in 1999], with the per capita GNP increasing elevenfold. At present, just twelve days of GNP is equivalent to the entire year of 1952. The per capita annual income of rural residents rose from 133.6 *yuan* in 1978 to 2,162 *yuan* in 1998 [2,205 in 1999], while the per capita disposable income of urban residents jumped from 343.3 *yuan* to 5,425 *yuan* [5,859 in 1999]. At the end of 1998, the balance of urban and rural residents' savings deposits approached 6,000 billion *yuan*, with that amount nearly equaling China's GDP of the year. The increased income has dramatically improved lifestyle and quality of life.

Restrained by the level of economic development in the past, the Chinese people had to spend a large proportion of their incomes on food. This situation has changed noticeably. The Engel's coefficient [proportion of income going to food] for rural residents dropped from 67.7 percent in 1978 to 55.1 percent in 1997, while for urban residents it declined from 57.7 percent to 46.6 percent. Urban residents are now beginning to stress nutrition and diversified tastes in food consumption. Though Chinese people are traditionally conservative about food, they are acquiring international tastes; indeed, French wine is gaining popularity in our country.

Twenty years ago, the Chinese were clad in blue "uniforms." It was limited income and ideological barriers, not personal choice, that turned China into "a fashion desert." In particular, the remnant influence of feudal ideology obstructed the development of women's clothes. In 1896, when Rodin made his *Kiss*, few Chinese could appreciate it. In 1914, when an artist in Shanghai for the first time taught his students figure painting by using a naked model, it was a major scandal, bringing him much trouble. Today, however, the Chinese market offers a great variety of clothes, including Western suits, T-shirts, dresses, miniskirts, and jeans. Innovative Chinese fashion draws worldwide attention, and Chinese fashion models have captured a number of world prizes. The fashion style of "a single look for many seasons" has been replaced by "many looks for a single season." Cosmetics were regarded as luxury goods before reform. Today, imported cosmetics are available in almost all cities.

After 1949, the responsibility to provide urban residents housing was taken over by the government, and rent was equivalent to 5 percent of a tenant's salary. China began to carry out the reform of its housing system on a trial basis ten years ago, encouraging individuals to purchase residences on their own.

Diversified sources of capital for housing construction has helped increase the per capita living space several times. While the living space for urban residents soared by 2.58-fold, from 3.6 square meters in 1978 to 9.3 square meters in 1998, for rural residents it grew by 2.92-fold, from 8.1 square meters to 23.7 square meters. Private dwellings have become a new consumer pursuit and a new sector of the economy. Interior decoration has also come into vogue and the furnishings of residences have become increasingly complete and more comfortable, beautiful, and harmonious. At present, 10 percent of urban households possess computers, and the number of Internet users has increased into the many millions.

Reform in China has been drastic, with entirely new concepts emerging. Environmental protection, for example, has entered Chinese consciousness, and this awareness has led to related lawsuits, with factories and even local governments as the accused.

Balzac, the renowned French writer of the nineteenth century, was also a "China fan." He frequently revealed his favor and appreciation of Chinese culture in his works. In one of them, he described the raw materials for matting paper and the techniques for printing in China—enumerating their advantages compared with French counterparts. He also wrote a long essay entitled "China and the Chinese," showing his appreciation of

Chinese culture. Similarly, the Chinese people like Balzac's works very much. Their circulation in China has far exceeded that in France.

Globalization has become one of the catchphrases in the world today. Jumbo jets, telecommunications, and the Internet have made the earth smaller. The rapid growth of worldwide trade and transnational investment has accelerated the process, which many people feel is deeply changing their lives. Some ask whether the cultural differences among nations will promote or obstruct globalization. And, more personally, what influences will globalization bring to the different cultures of mankind?

Undoubtedly, globalization will reinforce the mutual reliance of people from different cultures and societies, a trend that I believe to be highly beneficial. As they enter the twenty-first century, the Chinese people have gained the ideological and material foundation to join hands with all peoples to advance the progress of humanity.

Looking Forward I: Personal Predictions

Conventional wisdom likens predicting the future of China to reading the leaves of tea. Pundits relish giving austere alternatives for China, from an expansionist world power bullying Asian neighbors to internal fragmentation catalyzed by unemployment, social decay, and ambitious provincial chieftains or military warlords. These pundits do occasionally include a more benign image—progressively democratic, economically vibrant, internationally responsible—among their alternatives. The latter scenario isn't as sensational, of course, but it is what I feel will actually happen to China. In fact, I am quite confident of this.

I will make my prediction using only this one alternative; there will be no wiggle room in my assessment. Twenty years from now, in my opinion, China will be more democratic as well as more prosperous than it is now, and it will be taking its place among the leading families of great nations. China will be participating with America, as partners in peace and engines of prosperity, in maintaining geopolitical security and enhancing economic affluence. China's corporations will be competitive in world markets, its science and technology will be contributing to human knowledge, its society will be more diverse, its laws will protect its citizens far better, and its political leaders will be responsive to the will of its people. China as a nation will be a bulwark of stability in world affairs, and the pride of its people will be the highest in its long history. The key energizers for all this optimism will be the Chinese sense of civilization, entrepreneurial spirit, and an indomitable will to persevere and to change.

I'd like to give a personal example of these changes. It concerns "intellectual property rights"—"IP" as it's called in China—whose significance is far greater than it sounds. Everyone knows that China has had a terrible reputation for stealing content-rich things, from the mass pirating of CDs, movies, and designer clothes to the rampant, illegal copying of software. What most do not know is how seriously China is attacking this problem. New national laws have been instituted and are being enforced, and new nongovernmental associations and pressure groups have arisen. There is a determined national commitment to protect brands, technology and content.

When I submitted my first book *(Investment Banking Study)* for Chinese translation in 1994, rights and permissions were hardly discussed. When I submitted my second book *(Dealmaker)* in 1997, I was asked about my rights and then unquestioningly believed when I said that they had reverted to me. When I submitted my last book *(Closer To Truth)* in 1999, I had to *prove* that I had retained the Chinese rights in the original contract with my American publisher—my affirmative statement was not good enough—and, even though they knew me well, the Chinese publisher would not begin work until I had provided a complete copy of that original contract.

There are two reasons why China is now taking intellectual property rights very seriously. The first is obvious—external pressure: the insistence of world markets and China's imminent entry into the WTO. Second is not-so-obvious—internal pressure: the commercial reality that without protecting IP, there would be no incentive for Chinese knowledge-based companies to innovate and expand. Let's explore this second reason more deeply, because it closes a large loop.

Chinese Pride and Stability, to circle back to our primary themes, are inextricably bound to the capacity of Chinese technology and information companies to compete effectively in world markets: Stability, because the success of these innovative and growing companies is a primary uptake pump for reemploying workers laid off from moribund state-owned enterprises and for absorbing the legions of new workers continuously entering the labor force; Pride, because the Chinese believe that in order to regain their rightful position as a leading civilization and world power, they can, must, and will compete with anyone in science, technology, and information.

So, once again, we see the explanatory power of Pride and Stability. Only by appreciating their importance can one understand why the Chinese must be serious about protecting intellectual property; and conversely, China's obsession with protecting intellectual property reaffirms the paramount importance of Pride and Stability.

Will China, in the foreseeable future, have an elected, democratic government, precisely as we have it in the United States? I hope not, and I doubt it, too, because Chinese society has its own characteristics, which will remain distinct for at least several more generations. *Guanxi* will still count, but less so than it does today. I'm not sure that it ought to be a source of universal pleasure to see all nations amalgamated into a homogenized global culture, though that trend is probably inevitable.

I am often asked in China, after completing a grueling twelve to fourteen hour day of meetings, when do I take vacations, since my Chinese friends know that I have an extremely intense business and media life in the U.S. My answer sounds funny, but it is the truth. After finishing a meeting in Beijing at say, 11:00 at night, after a week of nonstop activities, I once said, "This is my vacation!"

I'm not kidding. Working in China, to me, is energizing and exhilarating, even when frustrating and challenging to one's patience. There is an infectious enthusiasm among the Chinese that is refreshing for us jaded Western types. Some may call my zest naïve, but I am invigorated by the new Chinese spirit. I find the fact that personal relationships, not just business competitiveness, still play a role in commerce satisfying—and I hope that these Chinese ways will not fall fast victim to the market economy. Perhaps those mysterious "Chinese characteristics" can continue to embed respect for traditional values such as honoring "old friends" *(lao pengyou)*.

At the end I come back to voices, for the Chinese people themselves, not any foreign observer, must give word to their spirit. When a society speaks with one voice, that voice by force is overbearing and repressive, such as in North Korea today and China during the Cultural Revolution. But the medicine of multiple voices is the best antidote to the poison of authoritarianism. Multiple voices express the multipart tonality of a multifaceted society, thus signifying growth, confidence, resilience, and robustness.

There is a new openness in today's China, a freewheeling sense that anything may now be possible, though the Chinese know full well the internal tensions and glacial slowness of their bureaucratic system. They are weary of the wait, yet they find ingenious ways to build and grow. The Chinese are natural entrepreneurs, and with the resoluteness to maintain national stability and the confidence to enhance national pride, it will be fascinating to watch as they bring their country to the fore so that China takes its long-awaited place at the high table of great nations.

Looking Forward II: Chinese Voices

We conclude with observations from several of our diverse Chinese friends. Here, from our PBS documentary, is how they envision the future.

DR. ZHENG SHIPING: No one has any idea what reform in China will end up looking like. Nobody can tell you that. But China has completely walked out of the era of Mao Zedong, and there is one thing ordinary Chinese people are sure of—they are determined to move forward even though it is into an unpredictable future. They have no choice.

YANG MILLIONAIRE: I remember when I was poor, how I dreamt to be rich. Now I'm a millionaire, the dream has come true, but I've begun to think it's not always good to be rich. I've become lazy. I no longer have the will to struggle. You know, there's an old saying: "After three generations have been rich, the fourth generation will be poor." That's just how money works. When you get rich, you don't have to struggle anymore and you'll eventually go down.

OLD XIAO: What did you learn today?

GRANDDAUGHTER: Nothing.

OLD XIAO: You learned nothing today?

GRANDDAUGHTER: Only some vocabulary words

OLD XIAO: Vocabulary words? Tell me, read them to me. Read them slowly, pronounce them correctly.

OLD XIAO: Overall my life may still look poor, but it's much better than before. I used to think about having lots of things but not anymore. How long can a man live? How much better can his house be? Desire is endless. As long as I am happy emotionally, that'll do it.

WANG HAI: Our government held a meeting on planning the economic direction for the twenty-first century. They invited all these entrepreneurs, including me. But now they don't invite me any more. They were disturbed by what I said. In the marketplace, the goals have been achieved. However, the obstacle to future reform, I believe, is still the political system. Without political reform, we will continue to be held back.

What better way to see the future than through the eyes of children? We interviewed several at an elementary school in Beijing.

GIRL #1: In the future everyone will live together in harmony and help each other out.

BOY #1: I think people should get better educated so they won't be so proud of being rich.

GIRL #2: I think we shouldn't value money too much. The meaning of life is to contribute to your country.

BOY #2: Because Beijing is our capital, it should become the first pollution-free city in China.

BOY #3: We'll invent a robot to be our servant; it will go shopping, cook, wash clothes, and all that.

BOY #4: In the future beds will be soft and comfortable so people will no longer have nightmares.

Finally, back to Old Xiao, as he continues teaching his granddaughter English. It is his mission and it is the closing image of our documentary (see photo).

GRANDDAUGHTER: "Shi de" means YES.... "Shi de" is YES...

Dr. Song Jian (center), vice chairman of the Chinese People's Political Consultative Conference and president of the Chinese Academy of Engineering, with Wang Yusheng (Mrs. Song, right) and Prof. Bi Dachuan (left).

Prof. Song Jian, with Lee Kuhn and Karen Troyan (Robert's mother and sister), at the Second Sino-U.S. Venture Fair in Beijing.

Tsinghua University: "China's MIT."

Fanso founded here in Tsinghua University dorm.

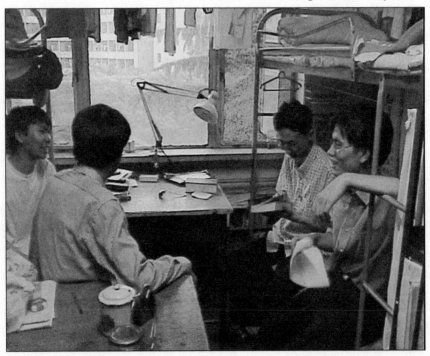

Fanso: Internet portal start-up founded by Tsinghua University students.

Fanso CEO Lu Jun speaking with potential investors at Tsinghua University Venture Fair.

Cui Xinshui at
launch site.

Rocket on side.

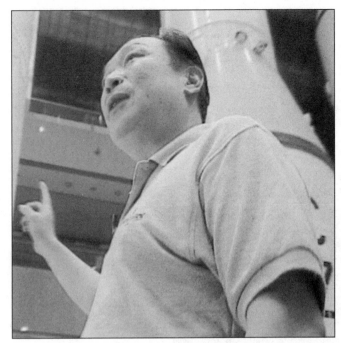

Cui Xinshui explaining the historical development of the Chinese aerospace industry.

Models of Chinese rockets.

Liu Chuanzhi, Legend Group chairman and CEO.

"Michael," Legend vice president of new business and development.

Deputy general manager supervising workers in Legend factory.

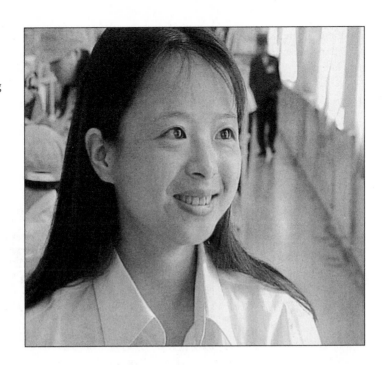

Communist Party secretary in Legend factory.

President Zhang Ruimin describing his grand vision for Haier.

Haier president Zhang Ruimin in the Activity Room of the Communist Party.

Old Man Xiao teaching granddaughter English.

"Little emperors" breakfasting in kindergarten.

"The best babysitters."

Old men
playing chess.

Cats and dogs waiting to be adopted.

Traditional hard-working Hui'an women.

Young girls at Beijing elementary school.

Fan dancing on the Bund in Shanghai.

Appendix: China Today

I selected the following articles, abridged from *China Today* magazine, to show slices of Chinese culture, life and society at the beginning of the new century. These small portraits of change evince a country no longer monolithic and a people desirous of further freedoms.

"China's Little Emperors"
By Lu Hui

It is time to reckon with the social consequences of family planning. Since the end of the 1970s, China has carried out a national policy of "one couple, one child," in order to hold population growth in check. The number of single children has grown to more than 70 million nationwide, and their emergence has brought about changes in relationships among family members, as well as in society. How China adapts to these changes is one of the questions for the new century.

To understand single children in China, one has to consider the traditional culture of the country. The parents of the first generation of single children, as with so many other parents in China, suffered much, both physically and mentally, during the Cultural Revolution (1966–76). Their experiences made them impart extra protection and love to their descendants and many "little emperors" and "little empresses" [which are China's special names for only children] were pampered and indulged.

Although this first generation of single children grew up sheltered, they have had other advantages. Since many of their parents were forced to work in the countryside when they should have been learning in school,

271

they wanted their offspring to receive the best possible education and become members of the intellectual community. Admission to a university was the only way to fulfill this hope, and parents believed that only through top scores on school exams could their children ensure good jobs and decent incomes. They therefore stressed the cultivation of intelligence rather than morality. They increased their investment in education with the result that the younger generation is much better educated. Many single children are well versed in literature but fail to make a living. Others know only how to ask, not give. Care and love, always forthcoming from their parents, were soon taken for granted.

Some parents limited social interactions for their single children, trying to protect them from the ugly side of Chinese society, but leaving many youngsters unable to communicate effectively. How will these only children compete in a rough-and-tumble world, with all its complicated human relationships? And how will they cope when starting a family of their own?

One only child who went to college met with constant criticism. The roommate who slept under his bed complained because he never changed his socks. Another complained because he never shut the room door when he went to the restroom during the night, letting in drafts. Finally, everyone told him that if he did not change his habits, he would have to find somewhere else to live. Later, the student said, "I had to learn what others were thinking rather than think of only myself. I had to learn the principles of how to get along with others, which is difficult for an only child."

Another college student who was the center of his family said, "When I was in elementary school, I never washed myself. My mother was a kindergarten teacher and treated me as another one of her charges. After I started living on campus, my mother came to my dorm every day before going to work to make my bed and bring me breakfast. My major is tourism. When I had my internship, I went to work in a hotel, and the lobby manager told us that if one could not do the least desirable jobs then he or she would never get promoted. My job was to open the door for guests and to bow to every one of them. I knew I had to do it, so I bowed a full 90 degrees to every visitor. The manager gave me a good job review. I guess I finally grew up when I had to become independent."

An only child of twenty said, "I have a special responsibility to my parents. Some say that single children do not know how to take care of others. Why are single children being blamed for the loss of morals in modern society? I don't have an inferiority or a superiority complex. I only know I am the only child in my family. For every gray hair on my parents' heads, I feel more responsible to them."

Chinese psychologists think that single children, though pampered by their families, eventually overcome these shortcomings upon reaching adulthood, or they take a turn for the worse. Su Songxing, director of the Juvenile Problems Institute with the Shanghai Academy of Social Sciences, has conducted comparative research between single children and those with siblings. Professor Su and his fellow researchers investigated seven thousand subjects over three years, and concluded that "an only child is not a problem child." Su found that single children lay greater emphasis on self-esteem, getting things done on their own, compared to other children with brothers and sisters. All children want to grow up and find a career that best fulfills their childhood dreams, earns them decent money, and promises stability. Su found, however, that single children tend to choose more challenging and ultimately more prestigious jobs, which is probably the result of their central position at home. They have a strong ego, which is often contrary to traditional Chinese values, but which tends to foster a strong sense of individuality more suited to the market economy.

In the traditional Chinese family, all life revolved around the patriarch. Today he must compete for attention with an increasingly assertive and liberated wife and an only child invested with substantial family resources. What will happen to the next generation of the nuclear family, and what will be the consequences for Chinese society?

Some experts say that when the "only child" generation takes over they will raise an incessant stream of demands, based on their more materialistic outlook and their already apathetic approach to interpersonal relationships. This alarmist view notwithstanding, other sociologists have noted new problems arising: many single children cannot stand the pressures of the workplace and tend to look for "easy jobs."

Another traditional Chinese concept of having one's children and grandchildren provide support in old age will also have to change. In the future there will be considerable dislocation as the only child, despite closer than normal bonds to his or her parents, seeks to move away from home and comes to expect social and government programs to care for his or her elderly parents.

Children pick up a lot from people around them. How Chinese parents behave in front of single children is a topic frequently discussed among parents, schools, and society. Zhu Min with the Beijing Academy of Social Sciences argues that parents should adjust their moods and expectations rather than place too much hope in their child's discretion. A more practical atti-tude is needed, but not a dilution of parental responsibilities. Parents have come to see that an education within the family can impart invaluable cul-tural, moral, social, and sexual mores to their son or daughter. As more sin-gle children become the norm, many parents invite children of neighbors and relatives to their homes in order to create a relaxed environment in which to foster communication skills and the ancient Chinese sense of col-lectiveness. Other schools have students participate in military training, so as to toughen them up and let them experience a little hardship.

It is a new century and a new generation of single children will soon be in charge. The implementation of the one-child policy has provided them with an environment where they received better education and better health care than their parents, and perhaps better than any Chinese gen-eration in history. Economic development has offered more opportunity, and everyone under the age of thirty has great hope for the future. Single children will have substantial impact on Chinese society and future his-torians will judge the result.

"China Faces an Aging Society"

By Li Jianguo

China has not only a huge population, but also the largest number of senior citizens—over 120 million. At present, senior citizens make up over 10 percent of the population, and the percentage is even larger in some big cities. In the twenty-first century, China will become an "aging coun-try"—by the year 2025, it is estimated that 20 percent of China will be elderly. An aging population is a reflection of social progress. However, it brings with it a series of social problems. Experts warn that the aging pop-ulation problem should not be neglected, because it will have great impact on the politics, economy, and culture of the whole society.

In the future, most Chinese families will have a "four-two-one" struc-ture—four elderly, a middle-aged or young couple, and one child. Leaving economic difficulties aside, taking care of the elderly will become a formi-dable task, since middle-aged couples all have their own jobs and old peo-ple often suffer from hypertension, arteriosclerosis, diabetes, apoplexy, paralysis, and senile dementia.

The Chinese people take kindness to be a foundation of society and taking care of the elderly is a strong tradition of Chinese culture. But as Chinese society continues to age and the size of Chinese families continues to shrink, a large number of parents who have only one child will enter old age facing an "empty nest." The chances for them to live together with their offspring will decrease greatly, and the ideal of "four generations living under the same roof" will become a memory of the past.

Following the modernization of the cities and urbanization of the countryside, many high-rise buildings have sprung up. Life in these monster edifices differs substantially from life in one-story house neighborhoods in which residents have a close relationship with their neighbors. Senior citizens living in high-rises can no longer enjoy socializing with neighbors in the alleys. Instead, they feel that life is dull and depressing. People are no longer satisfied with merely having enough food and clothing. With a lack of entertainment and diversion, they feel lonely and bored all day.

In modern society, people of different age groups differ greatly in lifestyle, such as choice of hobbies and habits, so that the generation gap can cause conflict. After their offspring grow up, some old people must leave home because of crowded housing; others are willing to continue to labor as servants or babysitters for their children—many are sad that their offspring do not care for them according to Chinese tradition.

Problems such as medical care and support for the elderly have arisen. Since most Chinese senior citizens who live in the countryside don't have pensions, 95 percent of these elderly must rely on their own old age work or on help from family or relatives. It is reported that among the senior citizens living in the countryside, 3 percent are maltreated by their offspring. The living conditions of the old people in towns and cities are much better than that in the countryside, but they have their own difficulties—their biggest complaint is "the fixed pension and price fluctuation." Some retirees are worse off still, with no guarantee of pension since the enterprises they had worked for are likely in debt.

China is in transition from a planned economy to a market economy. In the process there are many urgent problems that demand immediate attention so that the problems of senior citizens are often neglected. For school dropouts, there is Project Hope, for disabled people, there is a federation of the disabled, but for 120 million senior citizens, society is not as generous.

China does not have enough old folks' apartments designed specifically for senior citizens, and it is hard for them to find places for entertainment, leisure, and shopping that suit their needs. The special needs of old folks are seldom considered in city planning. A nongovernmental hospital that takes care of the dying elderly met with numerous difficulties. The lack of forceful measures to guarantee old people's safety causes frequent traffic accidents involving senior citizens.

China is known for its tradition of respecting and protecting the old. Recently, a new branch of science has taken shape—sociogerontology. Obviously, there is still much work to be done to meet the coming of an aging society. Old age welfare, unemployment, and medical insurance reforms need to be accelerated and a social insurance system must be formed, combining social insurance, relief, welfare, and special care. Only in this way can China prepare for the coming of the aging society in the twenty-first century.

"Life Begins at Sixty"

By Li Jianguo

"I am old and I have a poor memory. So I always keep a slip of paper in my pocket, and I look at it whenever I must," said Zou Shumei, a grandmother. On the slip was written two English sentences: "How are you?" and "Sit down." To learn to pronounce them, Chinese characters are used as phonetic notations. Several women in their sixties laughed heartily. They all had similar paper slips in their pockets.

These old people live in Dalian City, Liaoning Province in northeast China, and learning English is a hobby for them. They say it doesn't matter how much they learn. "We are just interested in it. When we meet a foreigner, we speak to them in English. In the past, people of our age had nothing to do but cook in the kitchen. Now we feel we are energetic, and want to do something."

In the eyes of young people, their grandpas and grandmas are incredible. They learn to speak English, use computers, wear bright-colored garments, and dance; those who have lost their spouses seek to remarry, known as "sunset love" by the Chinese people. Not long ago two old people in their seventies got married in an old folks' home in Shenyang, the capital of Liaoning Province. The old couple, just like young couples, quarrel occasionally but reconcile quickly. Nowadays more and more old people remarry.

Compared with old people in Western countries, most old people in China put more energy into their offspring, and family is always their spiritual pillar. Ms. Hua, who is retired, goes to work every morning like every other wage-earner, but she goes to take care of her one-year-old granddaughter in her daughter's home. She performs her duty with heart and soul. Both her daughter and son-in-law are busy with their work. Being with the baby is a great pleasure for her, and she feels much younger for it.

From Harbin in northeast China to Guangzhou in southern China one can see old people dancing in parks, in the squares and open air dancing grounds. A simple tape recorder is all the oldsters need to have a good time. In the smoky jungle of karaoke bars, microphones are often occupied by grandpas or grandmas. Though their voices are not very good, they are willing to show off, and are happy to hear praises from the audience.

"I never permed my hair when I was young," said an elderly woman. "But in my old age I have my hair done fashionably. All the people are changing so I must too." Not long ago, each of four women in Dalian, all in their sixties, bought purplish-red overcoats. Many old people complain that garment designers too seldom take them into consideration. As a result, they cannot find suitable fashions.

Many old people say, "The longer I live, the more energetic I am. Don't think I am too old physically, I am young at heart." As members of the society, they are unwilling to be forgotten, and want to participate in society. Many older professionals are busy working on the streets, in workshops, on construction sites, or in designing offices. They have formed a gray-haired work force.

Mr. Sun, senior editor for a newspaper before retirement, is famous in press circles for his writings. After he retired, he accepted the task of cooking and taking care of his grandchild. Though he worked hard, he was not familiar with household chores. The other family members were not satisfied with his work, and he himself felt helpless. He decided to change his life and found employment with another newspaper. He is responsible for three pages, which he edits wonderfully; they are very popular with readers. Mr. Sun commented, "My aim in returning to the post of editor is simple. I must say goodbye to the days of cooking around the stove and running after my grandson. Those days are unbearable to recall."

There are many similar cases. When the Zhejiang Provincial Museum announced that it was going to hire twelve workers for its exhibition hall, twenty-two hundred old people responded. Many of them said that getting a job is more difficult than college entrance examinations.

A sociologist holds that the reform and opening of China has influenced the Chinese people's modes of thinking, behavior and lifestyle in a comprehensive way. These changes have also greatly affected the senior citizens, who are no longer the conservative group they used to be. On the contrary, since they were subject to so many restrictions when they were young, now that they have the chance, they are even more eager than young people to express themselves and try their hands at new things. In a way, their "return to youth" epitomizes the new era.

"Chinese Democracy: Progress Finally"
By Li Fugen

In 1997, a delegation of seven American and Canadian advisors from the Carter Center in the United States monitored grassroots elections in Fujian and Hebei provinces. Robert Pastor, the delegation leader, noted that "almost all the villagers came out to vote, a ratio much higher than in American elections. The concern of Chinese rural voters was greater than I expected."

As an example of this new democracy in action, the village committee in Tuntou, Henan Province, planned to build a new office building, but their plans were thwarted at a village meeting where villagers proposed using the money for education, and instead voted to use the funds for two new school buildings.

After publicizing its financial affairs and accepting public supervision, Baodi County in Tianjin has cut "nonproductive expenditures." Public bids on land, orchard, and fishpond contracting have risen, on average, three thousand *yuan* per hectare.

These instances illustrate that elections, policy decisions, administration, and supervision now being promoted in China's rural areas are gradually taking root among the nation's 800 million peasants.

How can China, a despotic nation for so long, suddenly embrace democracy? There have been problems. At the second popular election in Liaoning Province in 1992, Huang Xinran, the former director of the village of Fangshen near Benxi, did not vote for himself nor buy other villagers' votes. He was honest, but his opponent wasn't, and Huang was voted out of office. His case caused concern at the start of democratic reforms—many village cadres as well as town, county, and city leaders opposed elections, saying peasants could not understand democracy, and that "elections manifested resentment against cadres and were too troublesome" and would cause disorder.

It is true that in some places villagers have not properly exercised their democratic rights. Many were indifferent or voted at random, which invalidated their ballots; some harbored grudges or favoritism, while still others sold their votes to the highest bidder. Village elections still leave much to be desired as some candidates try to rig elections, some town leaders refuse to hold elections saying they are "unsuitable to China's actual conditions," and some villages become subject to nepotism or other factional interests. But progress is being made.

Citizens in Fashi, Fujian Province gathered at the village headquarters, a building festooned with red banners and posters promoting candidates for village director, deputy director, and other posts. Villagers eighteen years and older cast specially marked red, brown, and yellow ballots in secret. The voting lasted from 6 A.M. to 12 noon. At 2 P.M., specially picked supervisors monitored the four ballot boxes as they were opened and the ballots counted. Tallying showed only three people out of an electorate of 2,435 failed to vote, a turnout of 99.88 percent.

Elections have finally become common in rural areas. Peasants across the country participate in elections, usually with a turnout exceeding 90 percent. The media also has helped by publicizing election irregularities and disputes, thereby making it easier for villagers to plead their case.

Village elections originated with the Law on the Organization of the Village Committees of the People's Republic of China (Trial Implementation), passed by the National People's Congress Standing Committee on November 24, 1987. [Little known in the West,] the law stipulates that directors, deputy directors, and village committee members will be elected directly by villagers for three-year terms.

Earlier elections date back to the people's communes when production brigades used the electoral system for selecting commune member representatives. After village committees were set up in rural areas in the early 1980s, the Simplified Regulations on Village Committee Organization, which state that village committees should be directly elected, were formulated in Beijing, Hebei, Tibet, Xinjiang, and Inner Mongolia. Elections were held in some places, but before 1987 these often were done more in name than in reality: most village committee directors and deputy directors were appointed by town governments.

Economic changes in the countryside, new affluence, and the emergence of joint-ventures and foreign investment have necessitated a greater distribution of power. Local issues such as building roads and schools and distributing money and manpower can't be decided in some county seat a hundred miles away.

The election in Fashi followed the newly-revised village Committee Election Procedures of Fujian Province. For the past ten years, village elections across China have gradually improved, expanding from just the right to vote to the right to nominate. In early 1995, Lishu County in Jilin Province took the lead by selecting candidates through preliminary elections.

The establishment of secret voting booths signified more progress. In contrast to traditional public voting, secret ballots allow Chinese peasants to express their wishes. Speeches and electioneering help voters understand the issues better and compel candidates to make and keep campaign promises. There are also question and answer sessions.

Village leaders have several incentives, such as salaries linked to performance, but the restraint mechanisms are perhaps more compelling. Unlike appointed village cadres, elected cadres must be responsible to higher authorities while satisfying their constituents. When handling village affairs, appointed cadres seldom consider villagers' interests and tend to rule by caprice. Many are corrupt and flaunt the law. But elected cadres must get along with villagers and maintain popular support.

In the village of Xiaoqingbao in Hebei Province, new roads were promised several years ago, but the project was delayed for a lack of funding because villagers would not give money to the appointed cadres. After village affairs became more democratic, the village collected two hundred thousand *yuan* in three days for its road construction fund.

The town of Shuangwang in Hebei also illustrates the relationship between democracy and honesty. Indulgence in food and drink was common among local village cadres, but in the three months following the implementation of public discussion of village and financial affairs, entertainment expenses dropped substantially [thus confirming the growing significance of public accountability, one of the hallmarks of democracy].

"We Will Have More Freedom in the New Century"
By Li Yinhe

As a sociologist at Beijing University, I believe that Chinese people will enjoy a more pluralistic and mutable society in the twenty-first century. People are already taking hold of their own lives. To illustrate, only twenty years ago, all Chinese were expected to marry and have children. In the early 1980s, unmarried people over thirty accounted for only 3.8 percent of the total population. But in recent years, more and more young people are opting either for the single life or for "live together" situations. No longer do all married couples want children, and no longer do single parents fear public ridicule. In the future, everyone in China will be able to choose whether they want to marry, have children, or to be heterosexual. We may not be able to reach this state of freedom in the twenty-first century, but China will definitely be closer to it.

In any society, two things limit people's freedoms: laws and social norms. Such restrictions are necessary, of course, for the functioning of society, since restrictions prevent one's liberties from harming others. The quality of a people's social life may be determined based on the following: in a poorly run society, people have little freedom and few opportunities—the benefits do not justify the restrictions. In a well-run society, restrictions are imperceptible, and the benefits outweigh any sacrifices.

It is my firm belief that Chinese society will one day be a very positive one. Some may say I am over-optimistic in my predictions. Although social progress lags behind economic development, all Chinese can feel the subtle changes taking place in our ways of thinking and living.

"Literature Should Not Preach"

By Hong Zicheng

Popular novels that appeared in the late nineteenth century are considered by some historians to be contemporary rather than classical literature, although the orthodox concept is that China's contemporary literature started from the May 4th Movement of 1919, when revolutionary literature was initiated. Popular literature is created for all Chinese, not just intellectuals and elites. After the founding of the People's Republic in 1949, popular literature almost completely disappeared. But since China began opening up in the early eighties, the genre has been experiencing a rebirth.

More and more writers today are writing popular literature—pieces that are not literary masterpieces, but rather stories that may be enjoyed by anyone, educated or not. Because the Chinese were denied such fiction for so long, the popular literature market has become extraordinarily lucrative. Really, this trend makes me rather sad. But I understand that China does not need so many refined literature writers. We just need a few who can concentrate on spiritual and artistic pursuits so that our nation can continue to produce excellent writers. In my opinion, human emotions and fears can only be truly expressed through more serious writings. There is no substitute for refined literature.

But, unfortunately, for decades, China's best literary geniuses have been using their talents to serve political means, thereby turning people away from more challenging reads. These writers claim that it is their responsibility to instill moral and political values into their readers. Really, literature should influence its readers through its examination of the human condition—literature should never preach.

As dean of the Chinese Department of Beijing University, I believe that in this new century, Chinese literature will cater more to common people, not to intellectuals. Writings will reflect changes in thinking brought on by economic reforms and will speak with more self-conscious and independent tones. Writers, hopefully, will learn to balance their artful craft with their responsibility to reflect changes in our society and act as our society's voice.

"Lawyers: Stepping into the Lives of Ordinary People"
By Xia Er

Lawyers are becoming increasingly popular in China, and this signals that big changes are coming to Chinese society. There are about 900,000 legal consultants currently employed by Chinese enterprises, and some high-income people are now retaining private lawyers.[30] Lawyers have entered into the life of ordinary Chinese people.

In 1995 the Jinhua Law Office in Tianjin opened a family legal consulting service, causing a sensation. Within a month, more that 100 families signed contracts with the office. The first one to sign up was an ordinary worker named Qi Heying. The Jinhua Law Office had helped his sister win a lawsuit in the countryside and he decided to retain a lawyer for his family. He said, "Nobody wants to get into any trouble, but sometimes accidents just happen. For example, quarrels between neighbors,

---

[30] Only a small number of these 900,000 people working on legal matters in China have been trained at the graduate level and have formal, bar-like certifications— as is required for the appellation "lawyer" in most developed countries. However, the number of fully professional lawyers, with graduate educations and professional certifications, is now growing rapidly in China, another product of the market economy.

traffic accidents, or work injuries. With a family lawyer, we will know how to handle the situation."

An entrepreneur of a private enterprise owed one hundred thousand *yuan* to another enterprise because of some payment problems. One morning, the creditor demanded immediate payment of the debt, declaring that if he didn't pay, they would take his son away. Frightened, his wife telephoned their family lawyer. The lawyer arrived immediately, persuaded representatives from the enterprise to solve the problem reasonably, suggested a solution, and the tumult subsided.

As the legal system is improving in China, laws are growing more relevant to daily life. Actually, much of our normal behavior is related to the law—for example, marriage, neighborhood relationships, and economic activities. Without the help of laws, many people would get into trouble.

As the economy is developing rapidly, opportunities and risks are growing together. In order to protect their own rights and avoid trouble, many people use the law as their weapon and shield. There are about a hundred family lawyers in Shenzhen, Guangdong Province, and in Shanghai, the number is over a thousand. Most people who employ family lawyers are self-employed businessmen. As one of them said, "We know very little about law, but in our daily life and economic activities, we encounter many legal problems. With our family lawyers, we can consult them whenever we are in difficulty." Similarly, as more intellectual property rights cases are being brought to court, some writers have hired lawyers so that they can relax and concentrate on their writing.

At present, lawyers are found not only in big cities, but also in the vast rural areas. In Qingzhou City, Shandong Province, more than twelve hundred peasant families have their own legal consultants, and the trend is spreading to Hubei, Hunan, Jiangsu, and Fujian provinces.

All this reveals the rapid development of a legal system, and of democracy, in China. And as the Chinese people become more legally conscious, Chinese society will quickly catch up with developed countries in all respects.

"Insurance: Making Its Way Into Everyday Life"
By Luo Xi

China is finally waking up to the idea that guarding against the unexpected makes good sense. Consider Fangfang, a worker at the Beijing Milk factory, who had managed to purchase some property worth a few thousand *yuan*. Nobody could have known that one day in 1994 her home would burn to the ground. Fortunately, before this tragedy occurred, the factory had invested five thousand *yuan* for every worker in home and property insurance, rescuing Fangfang from further misfortune.

"If I had purchased the insurance myself, things would have been easier after the fire," Fangfang said later with the benefit of hindsight. The fire taught her a hard lesson about what being insured means, and how it helps protect one's family against the possibility of unexpected loss.

If anyone had discussed insurance ten or more years ago, Chinese would have thought the idea strange, and would have even laughed at the idea of going to an insurance company to buy a policy. Yet today insurance has made its way into every level of society; there are close to one million enterprises and 100 million Chinese residents who have signed up for property and life insurance. China, whose annual growth in insurance surpasses ten percent, will one day be Asia's brightest insurance market, whose value may exceed 200 billion *yuan*. Life insurance is especially popular here and activity could set new records for the world insurance industry.

However, the current situation is not so simple. For many Chinese, it will take time to appreciate life insurance. Most Chinese still consider insurance as an extravagance, not a necessity. For two generations, the state has taken care of people from cradle to grave, in sickness and in death, providing homes and care for one's children. Moreover, influenced by tradition, people don't like to discuss accidents or death. Ordinary people still have no concept of insurance, and think that if one has money they need only put it in the bank, and that will be "insurance" enough. But as the state is taking less responsibility for social services, insurance will surely become a necessity in China.

"Reflections on Divorce"
By Chen Xinxin

Do rising divorce rates bode ill for China's traditional society? Twenty years ago, Chinese people prided themselves on their low divorce rate in contrast to developed countries. But since 1978, when China began shifting from a planned to a market economy, the country has changed socially, politically, and culturally. During this transitional period the divorce rate has increased steadily and has become a topic of concern.[31]

Many people believe that the increasing divorce rate results from more liberal attitudes. Economic growth has affected Chinese views of marriage and family, causing some people to take a reckless, laissez-faire attitude toward family and morality.

As to whether a high divorce rate leads to social instability, researchers note that countries with high divorce rates may remain socially stable (e.g., northern Europe) while those with low divorce rates may be unstable (e.g., Africa). Employment status and education play more important roles in social order, and the dissolution of a bad marriage may contribute more to order and harmony than to instability. Perhaps divorce's so-called adverse influence on social stability is based on an imaginary cause-and-effect relationship.

Is divorce good or bad? One answer can be found in the old Chinese saying: "It is better to dismantle ten temples than to dissolve one marriage." This deeply rooted opinion that divorce is bad has made it difficult, historically, for unhappy couples to split up. In China before the 1980s, divorce was dishonorable as well as difficult.

Although most people today try to view divorce objectively, some scholars and policymakers want to increase the effort couples must make in getting divorced, in order to limit the negative impact that so many rapid changes have had on modern relationships. Other scholars oppose this argument. Divorce frees people to whom marriage means nothing but suffering, they say. As for children, a bad marriage is not better than divorce. Sociologically, a divorced couple serves society more efficiently than those who are always depressed from an unfulfilled marriage. Therefore, it is meaningless to make moral judgments about divorce. What should be done is to ease the suffering that accompanies divorce rather than increase the difficulty in getting divorced.

Li Hong lived with her daughter after she divorced her husband for infidelity. The court ruled that the father must provide the daughter with eighty *yuan* per month, according to the payroll he provided to the court. But Li Hong knew that besides his salary, her ex-husband earned extra pay for works he publishes, bringing his monthly income to an average of two thousand *yuan*. But her knowledge could not be used in court.

---

[31] There are about one million divorces a year in China, compared with about 10 million new marriages a year and 250 million registered families in total.

Whether a wrongdoer should be punished in a divorce has also become a focus of discussion. A survey conducted in China's coastal areas, where culture, morality, and ways of living have inevitably changed as a result of reform, reports increased bigamy, concubines, extramarital affairs, and cohabitation before marriage.

As early as the 1980s, women in these areas who had been deserted by their *nouveau riche* husbands organized the Qin Xianglian Mission and petitioned then-leader Hu Yaobang for government support. Qin Xianglian was a virtuous woman in ancient Chinese legend who endured many hardships to support the education of her husband. The husband, however, married the daughter of the emperor, concealing his first marriage. The story ends with justice for Qin Xianglian, who has become a symbol in China for the wronged woman, when the emperor orders her husband beheaded. Owing to this popular legend and the common consensus that immorality in men accompanies wealth, many people support punishing a guilty party in a divorce case.

The counterargument is equally strong, because if legal punishment is to be meted out in civil litigation, close attention must be paid to specific details. First, the prosecutor must produce evidence to justify judgment against the wrongdoer. Second, if punishment and asset distribution are based on the degree of offense, it is necessary to clarify the economic situation of the wrongdoer, which inevitably increases the work of the court and prolongs and complicates the divorce process. Mentally and emotionally, divorce already is painful, so punishing one party based on evidence given by the other party only inflames passions. These delays make everyone—wrongdoer, wronged, and society—suffer more. And, frankly, women are usually hurt more that men.

Some unhealthy traditions die hard and in some places divorced women are discriminated against. If they live with their children, they have less chance of being accepted by men. Some had married, not for love, but to alleviate the burdens of life, leading to crises. Generally speaking it is difficult for single mothers to remarry and it has become a social problem in China today. Gao Xian, thirty-five, is a bright woman with a university education. She divorced her husband because the two could not get along. With her personality she didn't expect to have much of a problem in finding a good man, but although she has tried many channels of introduction for over two years, she has had no success.

So what is the state of marriage in China? Having surveyed six thousand couples from four provinces, Xu Anqi, a fellow with the Shanghai

Academy of Social Sciences, says marriage in China is quite stable. More than 80 percent of those surveyed are satisfied or quite satisfied with their marriage; only 11 percent think frequently or occasionally of divorce. Xu opposes the view that 60 percent of Chinese families are just "making do," and believes that divorce may not see a rapid increase in the near future, even though married life can be monotonous and very few marriages are based on real love.

"In Love of Abandoned Pets"
By Sun Lina

Wang Entong and her dog Huzi were the center of attention at a reception sponsored by the China Small Animal Protection Association (CSAPA). Wang related Huzi's life story and many in the audience were moved to tears. Three years ago Huzi had been abandoned in a village where he lived with a herd of sheep. When Wang heard of this from friends, the dog had already been there for a year and another northern winter was about to begin. Wang traveled to the countryside and found that Huzi's emaciated body was riddled with ruts and his long hair was filthy and matted into cement-hard bundles. Wang and her husband took him home, giving him a second chance in life.

Huzi's is but one of a host of stories told by members of the association. Established in September 1992, CSAPA now has more than a thosand members and has done much to promote the welfare of small animals. Among other activities, it introduced World Animal Day, popular around the world for more than twenty years, to China.

CSAPA has saved hundreds of dogs and cats. At first the association was short of money, but that never stymied the members. Septuagenarian Lu Di was ridiculed when she announced the establishment of CSAPA, but she persevered and helped make the association what it is today. Many lent their support. A Buddhist leader wrote a letter to Lu Di saying, "I wholeheartedly support your aims in establishing such an organization" and enclosed a donation.

According to Lu Di, the CSAPA has now passed the most difficult period. Its Sijiqing Animal Health Center often receives help from volunteers like Jackson, an American who works in a zoo. He and seven of his colleagues often go to lend a hand. In addition, young students regularly pitch in.

CSAPA actively seeks new members and aims to become truly national. New chapters in Guangdong, Shanghai, Tianjin, Chengdu, and Anhui will be established, and the association receives sympathy and support from animal lovers everywhere. Receptions and other events are always popular, with the animals often at center stage, such as cat and dog races and awards for beauty. At the same time, orphaned animals are introduced to people who may be willing to adopt a new pet.

The CSAPA animal hospital, complete with an operating room, was opened in 1998. An American vet is currently providing care. "Our work is difficult," Lu said. "I appreciate the help of all these good people and thank them for all they have done for our animals. We hope that more people will come to understand what we are doing and support our cause.

"China's National Minorities"

China claims to be a "multinational unified state," with a total of fifty-six ethnic groups, the largest being the Han.[32] According to the 1990 census, there were just over one billion Han, accounting for 91.96 percent of China's population. The total of the other fifty-five ethnic groups, referred to as minorities, numbered just over 90 million, making up 8.04 percent of China's total.

Among China's national minorities, the Zhuang's population is the largest, with more than 15 million. The ethnic group with the smallest population is the Lhoba, with only 2,300 people. There are 17 minorities having a population of above 1 million, including the Zhuang, Hui, Uygur, Kazak, Dai, Yi, Miao, Manchu, Tibetan, Mongol, Tujia, Bouyei, Korean, Dong, Yao, Bui, and Hani.

The distribution of China's national minorities has the following characteristics: first, wide distribution over large areas. The minority population is less than one-tenth of China's total, but it is dispersed and occupies

---

[32] The Constitution of the People's Republic of China states that China "is a unitary multinational state created jointly by the people of all its nationalities. Socialist relations of equality, unity, and mutual assistance have been established among the nationalities and will continue to be strengthened. In the struggle to safeguard the unity of the nationalities, it is necessary to combat big-nation chauvinism, mainly Han chauvinism, and to combat local national chauvinism. The state will do its utmost to promote the common prosperity of all the nationalities."

over half of the country's total area. Yunnan is the province with the most minority ethnic groups, thirty-five in all.

Second, various ethnic groups live together in compact communities. Over 90 percent of China's population is Han; even in autonomous regions, Han people are the most numerous. For example, of the 4.5 million Tibetans, only 2 million live in Tibet; the others live in Gansu, Qinghai, Sichuan, and Yunnan provinces. This distribution shows close relations between the Han majority and various minorities. This is the foundation of China [in the Chinese language] as a united and multinational state.

Third, minority areas possess rich resources and products. Minorities almost all live on plateaus, mountains, greenlands, or in forest areas that have rich mineral deposits, developed animal husbandry, and various crops. Forest coverage in minority regions makes up 37 percent of the country's total.

Fourth, many minority regions are located on China's frontiers, which are important for national defense and developing friendly relations with neighboring countries. But these border areas have backward economies, because of their wide area, out-of-the-way locations, sparse population, and poor transportation facilities. Since the establishment of New China in 1949, great changes have taken place in these regions, but compared with the places that the Han live, the minority regions still have a long way to go.

Almost all of China's fifty-five national minorities have their own spoken languages, but only twenty-one of them have their own writing systems. Languages of China's minorities belong to different language families. Those belonging to the Han-Tibetan language family are the most numerous. Other languages belong to the Altai, South Asian, the Indo-European and Nandao language groups.

China's minorities generally all believe in some kind of religion, and Islam, Buddhism, and Christianity have had deep influence on China's national minorities. In addition, some minorities also maintain their original belief systems, such as ancestor worship, witchcraft, and shamanism.

After the founding of New China, the Chinese government formulated a series of policies toward ethnic groups and practiced regional national autonomy. Now China has five autonomous regions (Guangxi Zhuang, Inner Mongolia, Xinijian Ugyur, Ningxia Hui and Tibet) and 124 autonomous counties. The Chinese government also helps national minorities to develop their economies and culture. It set up a national committee in the state's supreme organ of power—the National People's Congress—and the State Nationalities Affairs Commission in the central government, both of which are specially responsible for formulating, implementing, and examining the laws and policies regarding national minorities. To support and help minority areas' development, the central government gives aid in finance, goods and materials, science and technology, culture, and personnel. The purpose is to narrow the gap between the Han and minority areas.

"The Kingdom of Women"

By Ri Nong

Hui'an County on China's southeastern coast is described as a "world of stones and the kingdom of women." It is famous for its stone carvings. Stone houses, bridges, benches, tables, dragons, lions, and slabstone paths can be seen everywhere in Hui'an. However, Hui'an is best associated with women. For many centuries Hui'an women have played a key role in both housework and farming and are known as women of virtue and resolve. Today they still wear traditional dress—cone-shaped yellow hats, floral-patterned scarves, waist-length blouses, silver belts and baggy black pants. But underneath the traditional dress, life has changed.

Of Hui'an's 900,000 residents, women make up 50 percent, including 240,000 female farmers, or 85 percent of the total rural labor force. The majority of Hui'an men are engaged in fishing or leave home to work as laborers in other areas. In old times, Hui'an women had to do heavy labor that was usually considered men's work in other communities, but they suffered no less discrimination than Hui'an men. Today, Hui'an women have become independent individuals and have won themselves equal status with men both at home and in society as a whole. We spoke with two Hui'an women.

The vice chairwoman of the standing committee of the county congress, Xu Ruchen, age fifty-seven, is a doctor who has worked as a gynecologist for three decades. Her father was a doctor of traditional Chinese medicine. He always urged her to work for her own people in Hui'an because they had few doctors. When Xu was little, she recalls, she heard people say that Hui'an women were very unfortunate because they were required to perform the roles of both women and men and had to do the heaviest labor. She felt sorry for them.

The county hospital was very small. The gynecological department had only two doctors. Xu became the third. During the first few years she often went around villages offering physical checkups and treatment for women. Most men were away either fishing or making money, and women were left behind to assume all the duties at home and on the farm. They married early and gave birth early. Some became grandmothers in their thirties. Pregnant women had no health care and didn't get proper rest. In a fishing village, Xu says, "I saw a housewife, heavy with child, carrying two buckets of water. When I saw her going to the field two days later, her stomach was flat. I knew she had just given birth. I asked her to stay at home and get some rest. She told me that her husband was out and she had to take care of the fields."

Many Hui'an women suffered from postpartum diseases, such as prolapse of the uterus. Xu dedicated herself to treat these kinds of ailments and spent over ten years going around the country studying these diseases and looking for both traditional Chinese and Western cures. Meanwhile, the state earmarked funds and the provincial government sent medical teams to help local doctors like her. As a result, health care for Hui'an women steadily improved.

Hui'an is a leading producer of stone sculptures in China. In the past, this trade was monopolized by men, while women only helped with some odd jobs, such as carrying stones. Since the 1980s the trade has developed greatly, giving rise to a group of outstanding women sculptors and female entrepreneurs. Li Yuwei, age sixty-one, was an ordinary farmer. She owes her luck to the county's reform and, in 1984, she opened the county's first family carving factory.

Li had helped her mother in the field when she was small and received no schooling. When she was eighteen, she was elected head of her village because she was "warmhearted." When she was twenty-two, she married into the fishing village where she lives now. Soon after the wedding, her husband left home to find work. He returned only on holidays. Li did all the hard work at home—farming, fishing, cutting firewood, not to mention housework. She also served as head of her new village for some years.

The village had not enough land to support its population, and Li discussed with other village leaders how to find a way to improve their lives. In the 1960s they set up a stone carving workshop. Li says, "I was its director for some years, but there were too many obstacles and restrictions at the time, and the workshop was taken over by others."

In the years of reform and opening, the government encouraged farmers to improve their lives through hard work, and they allowed private enterprises. Li seized the moment. "I was still in good health; I saw an opportunity to set an example for my fellow villagers. My husband and son supported my idea, so we rented a small storehouse, hired a few stone artisans and set up a factory for 4,000 *yuan*. I myself worked very hard, going about looking for raw materials, sculpture patterns, and markets. The first year, our output amounted to 10,000 *yuan* and by the third year had shot up to 130,000 *yuan*. With a growing building industry, demand for stone sculptures increased and my factory expanded rapidly. I now employ over 200 workers and we have an annual output of 8 million *yuan*. Three years ago I went to Southeast Asia to study the market there and acquired a loan for the import of some advanced equipment, mainly for increased production. We now produce over a hundred varieties of sculpture and receive many orders from foreign countries. We are going to expand again this year to enlarge production.

"I mainly hire workers from my village, giving preference to those from poor families and the handicapped. I also train female technicians and managers. Now the typical woman worker in my factory can earn 2,000 *yuan* a month. The best can make 4,000 *yuan*. I also help other villagers set up stone carving factories, and have brought the number of such factories to twenty-three in my village. The village per capita income has increased from 200 *yuan* in the mid-1980s to 2,000 *yuan* at present."

"What's So Special About Dragons?"

By Pang Jin

Dragons appear throughout China. They are carved upon buildings, painted on vases, mimed in dances, featured in Chinese movies and operas, and even used as metaphors in daily conversation. But how is it these exotic creatures have become so closely intertwined with Chinese culture? Experts are still not certain, and theories abound about their origin.

Dragons possess the best features of all the zodiac animals—the deer's beautiful antlers that symbolize health and longevity, fish tails that symbolize agility and zeal, powerful tigers' eyes, lions' noses that symbolize wealth, horses' teeth that represent hard work, oxen's ears, donkey's mouths, snakes' bodies, and eagles' claws. Some say dragons are either descendants of a wild gulf crocodile named Jiao or of snakes because of their snakelike bodies. Others argue that dragons were either formed out of rising and twisting clouds, unpredictable lightning, fish, or sea tides. Most believe, though, that the dragon sprang from the curiosity and fear ancients felt towards reptiles such as crocodiles and snakes and natural weather phenomena such as lightning and thunder showers. The earliest dragon records date back to the late Paleolithic Period and the early Neolithic Age. Back then, people believed that all creatures had souls, and most tribes had their own totems.

The dragon is said to have separated earth from heaven, made all the creatures on the earth, and to have helped mankind reproduce. According to one Chinese fairy tale, the first dragon's name was Fuxi. Fuxi had a dragon's body and man's head. He wanted to become the forefather of mankind but could not find a woman who was able to bear him a son. So he married his sister, Nuwa, who then gave birth to the first group of men and women on earth. In the stone carvings of the Han Dynasty, there are pictures of Fuxi and Nuwa embracing each other, either with mascots in their hands or with their two tails twisting together.

According to legend, fighting occurred after the birth of mankind. When the fighting became fierce, the land splintered into pieces. The well-known Yellow Emperor was the first to bring order out of the chaos. The Yellow Emperor also had a dragon's body and a man's head, and so some storytellers call him the Yellow Dragon. The Yellow Emperor's brother, Emperor Yan, had the same mother but a different father. He also had the body of a dragon. Some say the Chinese people are descendants of the Yellow Emperor and Emperor Yan and are thus descendants of dragons.

There are both good and bad dragons and the symbolism of each is strong. It is said that on the Central Plain, Nuwa killed a black dragon who always brought disasters to the local people, and in the Wuxia Gorge, Yu the Great slew a stupid dragon who had created a water channel in the wrong area. Conversely, some dragons in Chinese folktales are imagined to help kind and poor people, drive away evil, and appear when one is in trouble—sort of like Superman in America.

Dragons are considered water gods because many of their zodiac animal features need water to survive. Dragons are responsible for administrating water affairs and are said to exist in seas, lakes, rivers, and springs. Whenever floods or droughts occurred, people used to pray to dragons and offer sacrifices of pigs and goats. Many dragon king temples still exist in China today.

Dragons also symbolize imperial power. Admiring their ancestors, later Chinese emperors would compare themselves with the powerful creatures and sometimes dress up like them. Since dragons are in charge of water both in heaven and on earth, they would report the conditions of the earth to the celestial god, and then pass on orders to civilians. The emperor is said to be the imperial dragon, the son of the celestial god. His duty is to receive orders from heaven and to administer the earth.

Many Chinese emperors associated themselves with dragons. Emperor Qinshihuang of the Qin Dynasty (221–206 B.C.E.) was called the ancestral dragon. Emperor Gaozu of the Han Dynasty is said to be the son of his mother Liu Ao and the flood dragon. Emperor Jingdi of the Han Dynasty once dreamed of a red pig turning into a red dragon; afterwards, his son Emperor Wudi was born. When Emperor Taizong of the Tang Dynasty was born, two dragons were said to have been seen playing in a pool in Wugong County.

Since the emperors were considered dragons, special terms were created to describe their activities. Regime conflicts were called "dragon fighting," the beginning of a new imperial regime was called "dragon's rising," and a crown prince was called "a dragon in concealment." Once a prince succeeded to the throne, he was called "a dragon in flight."

As the symbol of imperial power, the dragon often bears a ferocious expression with bare fangs and brandished claws. Living under the tyranny of imperial rule for so long, some people became very passive—they obeyed rules, avoided conflict, and kept away from imperial power. Thus, when we see dragons carved or painted in imperial palaces, although they are beautifully decorated in bright colors, they always seem to keep their distance from people.

During important holidays and festivals, there are always dragon dances. The dragons are made of different materials including bamboo, wood, straw, rattan, cloth, and paper. Sometimes, patterns of lotus flowers and butterflies are put together to make the "Hundred Leaves Dragon." People run, jump, and sing with the dragons as a prayer for good harvest and luck as well as an amusement activity. Working in the fields, Chinese farmers seldom had an opportunity to relax and let themselves go. During the dragon dances, they were free to perform all kinds of movements. Also the dances posed a good opportunity for young fellows to show off their abilities to girls.

Through the dragon dance people show their disrespect for imperial power by pushing down its head, twisting its body, and grasping its tail. The dance climaxes when onlookers either throw firecrackers at the dragon or stuff its body with gunpowder and light it. Fire spews from its mouth and tail, and the creature crumbles. But today, the dragon has lost a bit of its mystique and has walked into the lives of ordinary people, making us feel closer to it.

"Stories of Jade"
By Huo Jianying

During the Neolithic Age, people discovered that some stones were more beautiful, finer in texture, and more solid than others, and they used them to make tools, arrowheads, and ornaments. These were the prototypes of jade ware. The materials used by the ancients included not only hornblende jade but also other gemstones, such as serpentine, turquoise, malachite, and agate. Ancient Chinese called these beautiful stones *yu*, or jade. The first Chinese dictionary, *Explanation of Words and Phrases*, published in C.E.100 during the Eastern Han Dynasty, defines the meaning of "yu" as "the most beautiful stone."

Jade has been blessed by nature with many fine attributes—jade is solid in texture, beautiful in color, comfortable to the touch, and produces a pleasant sound when tapped. These qualities matched the ethical standards and codes of conduct of the ancient people and were hence personified. Confucius (552–479 B.C.E.) concluded that jade had eleven virtues, such as benevolence (being smooth and lustrous), fidelity (the feel never irritates the skin), polite etiquette (there was an order of wearing), and sincerity (a flaw in jade never hides itself). The Confucian culture advocated that a gentleman should define his manners and conduct in accordance with the virtues of jade.

For a long time, wearing jade ornaments was in vogue. They were either a single piece of jade or comprised of as many as nine pieces strung together. People used the ornaments, which were carved with auspicious designs and words that wished good luck and happy lives, to show their social status. Wearing jade was most popular during the Qing Dynasty (1644–1911). Those who did not wear them were considered improperly dressed, and houses without jade decorations were not considered homes.

For women, jade bracelets took up most space in their jewelry boxes. Bracelets received as engagement and wedding gifts were as precious as today's diamond wedding rings. The Chinese describe a good marriage as a "gold and jade marriage."

Jade has not only been idealized and personified, but also mythologized, particularly in ancient times when jade vessels were dedicated to rituals and divination purposes. The ancients believed that jade was formed where phoenixes had landed and where there were accumulations of the essence of *yang*.[33] Proper panning was conducted during moonlit nights by naked women. It was believed that only by using *yin* [women were philosophized as *yin*] to absorb *yang* could pure jade, the core substrate of earth and sky, be obtained. This belief influenced the Chinese for many centuries. *Exploitation of the Works of Nature*, a description of ancient production techniques published in 1637 during the late Ming Dynasty, recorded that naked local young women dredged up jade from rivers during moonlit nights. The book explained that by "attracting the vital energy of *yang*, jade would easily be obtained."

The ancient Chinese also believed that jade staved off corrosion and evil spirits. Many jade burial objects have been found in tombs that date as far back as the Zhou Dynasty (eleventh century B.C.E.). The Zhou people began using flat pieces of jade to cover corpses. In the Han Dynasty (206 B.C.E.–C.E. 220) this custom developed even further. Flat and square jade pieces were sewn by gold thread into burial suits for rulers so that their physical beings would never vanish. In 1971, the tombs of Prince Jing of the Western Han Dynasty and his wife were excavated, yielding two jade suits. However, the bodies inside had decomposed long ago.

Myths about jade faded with the passage of time. However, many people today still believe that wearing jade is good for one's health. Face massagers made of jade have been used since the Qing Dynasty. There are also jade pillows and seat mats. Some claim that jade contains trace elements needed by the human body.

During the times of Yellow Emperor in about 4600 B.C.E., the use of jade was regulated. Articles of state power, such as rulers' seals and tokens, and vessels for important rituals and ceremonies had to be made of jade. Jade was a symbol of social status, and nobles liked to wear jade ornaments.

An old Chinese saying, "Gold has a price, but jade does not," is not technically true. In traditional Chinese literature, gold and jade are often mentioned together and are seen as symbols of wealth. Even today the price of high quality jade is no less than a piece of gold of the same weight.

---

33 *Yang* represents the masculine principal in nature—bright, forceful, expansive, and
   movement out and up. *Yin* represents the feminine principal in nature—dark,
   withdrawn, receptive, passive, and movement down and in.

The earliest jade artifacts thus far unearthed in China are eight thousand years old. This indicates that jade has played a continuous role in the course of human development, though today it has stepped down from its ancient sacred altar and has come into the lives of ordinary people.

"Experimental Art in Shanghai"
By Cui Li

Shanghai was China's first open port and an important city in Chinese history of contemporary art. As the gateway through which Western art was introduced, Shanghai has evolved into a cosmopolitan city with a energetic, humanistic atmosphere. The splendor of "Shanghai school" Chinese painting and the rise of modern art education demonstrate Shanghai's ability to respect tradition while ushering in the future. In the 1980s, Shanghai's modern art scene became very active, and Shanghai youth drove artistic innovation.

After 1992, Shanghai's young and middle-aged artists began to participate in art shows abroad. Starting in 1996, the Shanghai Fine Arts Biennial and Shanghai Arts Exposition have been held, and Shanghai's young artists continue to add vitality to the prosperity and development of Shanghai's art world.

During the Shanghai Arts Exposition held in late 1999, there was an exhibition called "Shanghai New Vision." Of the twenty young artists presenting their works, although each had his or her unique style and temperament, they all shared a common aim—to pursue new visual emotions and create unique visual spaces. Li Lei, exhibition planner and one of the participants, says that a characteristic of Shanghai artists is that they don't seek to be like each other. Their styles are diversified. Li Lei goes on to say, "Shanghai artists are a bit egoistic; they like innovation and seeking something different. So Shanghai's abstractionist school and avant-garde arts are more advanced than those in other places. Shanghai artists think more about culture, and they demonstrate a deeper concern for society."

Shanghai's economic and cultural development has provided many opportunities for artists, as well as a great deal of pressure for them to develop their arts. Li says, "Shanghai's young artists have not poured as much energy into traditional arts as artists from other areas have. Shanghai's artists are clever and intelligent, but their work lacks depth."

Visual arts can depict themes of literature, history, philosophy, and religion, but no matter what their theme, they must still strike a balance between perception and rationality. The artists at the "Shanghai New Vision" exhibition included teachers, students, and professional artists, some of whom had given up their jobs for their art. Most of them create abstract art in different styles and use their rich imaginations to challenge viewers' visions. Some are experimenting with realistic representations to examine an industrialized society and their environment. A few like Liu Yanchi create dreamlike images with a method that is both surreal and symbolic. Others explore traditional Chinese paintings with their works of *gongbi* (fine brushwork) or *xieyi* (freehand brushwork).

Zhang Yong's works are unique and avant-garde. His use of transparent paper gives viewers a feeling of obscure beauty, and his subtle brushwork forms complete and indispensable parts, challenging people's imaginations. He describes his own works saying, "My paintings have a kind of fresh, sparkling theme with personal wildness. The uncertainty of things excites me. In the present life, not much is interesting. So, I am always painting. Other people's comments to me are illusive. Actually I have been in a state of illusion, a high-class state of illusion. I am heavy-hearted. I don't know for what a man lives. In my opinion, the life of living things is fascinating and shining. It attracts me. I think sincerity and passion are the most precious traits. I think I will be famous in the future."

The artists who participated in the "Shanghai New Vision" exhibition express their different understandings of life and society though independent thinking, showing artistic diversity and unlimited possibilities. "They are very young and have bright futures," Li Lei says. "Young Chinese artists see the world; they are inspired by Western culture, and at the same time, they look to Chinese tradition. They know what they should do is not to imitate."

The exhibition called "The Popular Scenes of the 1990s" held during the Shanghai Arts Exposition demonstrated Chinese artists' thinking about life and art and modern society's influence on them. The popular scenes reflect problems existing in modern society as well as people's expectations and hopes. The works force people to look inward, to think about their own lives. Many of these scenes are not pretty, and some even make people feel unpleasant. However, the scenes are familiar—they portray what happened in the past or what is happening now. According to Ma Qinzhong, planner of the exhibition, "Popular scenes are a 'dictionary' that concentrate various commercial aims. Here, people can see sociological problems involving people's subsistence and desires. The exhibition provides an angle from which to observe humanitarian ecology in the 1990s."

The "popular scenes" refer to scenes that are predominant in mass media and are closely linked with people's daily lives. These scenes are related to the development of a commercial society and urbanization. The changes of popular scenes in the mass media and people's daily lives serve as a barometer for modern people's ideals.

Due to differences in location, artists' interpretations of popular scenes are also different, forming distinctive contrasts. In general, Beijing artists seek to criticize popular trends, but because Shanghai artists' concern for popular culture is still in its initial stages, they choose to engage in abstract art creation. Artists from Guangzhou are the most active in representing popular scenes.

Jiang Hong's latest series, entitled "Beauty and Fish," features beautiful women in different postures and swimming fish. The colors of these motifs are the same; the only changes are in the color of the women's fingernails. In his opinion, beautiful women are a special symbol of a commercial society that takes the era as its carrier medium. Through these beautiful images, people can derive aesthetic enjoyment. He tries to find connections between beauty and commerce.

Ma Yun from the Yunnan Art Institute depicts the theme of love, and the facial expressions of all the characters in his paintings show nostalgic sadness and the pursuit of beautiful things.

Popular social trends penetrate into every facet of people's lives. Popular scenes may soon become a primary form of visual art, reflecting people's different cultural pursuits and varied attitudes toward life.

Afterword

Jiang Zemin, the President and the Man

On September 3, 2000, as this book was going to press, an interview with Jiang Zemin, president of the People's Republic of China, was broadcast on the top-rated CBS newsmagazine 60 Minutes. I believe that what was said, and what happened, cries out for commentary.

President Jiang's historic role in transforming China into a modern nation, apparent to insiders for years, could be appreciated in his remarkably candid and confident interview on *60 Minutes* that was at once insightful, revelatory, intimate, and courageous. Americans saw, probably for the first time, the real human being who is the leader of the most populous country on earth. Questioned toughly and cleverly by legendary correspondent Mike Wallace, Jiang came across as poised and personable, a good-spirited fellow with a ready smile and disarmingly game to address any query. He had some daunting positions to defend.

In a first for Western television, the interview was conducted at the seaside resort of Beidaihe, where China's senior leaders go each August to plan the nation's business. President Jiang said he wanted to convey through *60 Minutes* his best wishes to the American people and to express his feelings of friendship and desire for mutual cooperation. Wallace introduced the piece by stating that he would only do the interview, which the president had requested just prior to his trip to the United

States, if Jiang would be "willing to level with us," then adding with a lilt-
ing voice evocative of surprise, "and he was."

It was a risk going head-to-head with the notoriously contentious Wallace, who would ask all the questions, choose all the footage, and have final
cut on the edit. No doubt Jiang and his staff anticipated the relentless prob-
ing of sensitive subjects. But the gamble paid off: Americans got to see Jiang
Zemin the man, and I think many were surprised by what they saw.

Forget all the peppering about China's anti-American propaganda, their
xenophobic reaction to the bombing of the Chinese Embassy in Belgrade,
human rights, trade imbalances, the Falun Gong cult, and Internet blocking,
it was clear that Mike Wallace liked Jiang Zemin. Though Wallace hinted that
we should not be lulled—he referred to the president as a "silk-rapped nee-
dle," putting us momentarily on edge—watching Jiang indeed made it easy to
believe Jiang. Avuncular and plainspoken with oversized black glasses framing
expressive eyes, Jiang seemed to be enjoying the give and take. He sang a
protest song from his youth ("Arise Fellow Students to Defend the Motherland")—the president carries quite a good tune—when brave young Chinese
were demonstrating against the hated Japanese occupation forces. He recited
multiple lines from Abraham Lincoln's Gettysburg Address with obvious an-
imation (which is more than most Americans can do). His displayed calm understanding that while China can be a convenient target in American election
campaigns, American presidents, once in office, recognize the importance of
mutual respect and good relations (". . . someone told me not to pay attention
to the unfriendly remarks candidates might make about China during the
campaigns, because once elected they will be friendly—I only hope that's
true"). And his occasional English, clear though accented and suggesting sincerity, seemed to bridge a long-standing barrier between China's remotely
austere leaders and America's internationally unsophisticated citizens.

Wallace was the determined aggressor, showboating at times, pressing
points over the top, as if he had to prove that he was neither awed nor
cowed. President Jiang, on the other hand, was largely self-assured without being cocky, and he just looked like an elderly chap in a tough situation. In fact, no matter what your political orientation, by the end of the
interview, you found yourself rooting, at least a little bit, for the president.
Jiang was like Rocky, the good guy, and Wallace, well, he was like that in-
vincible Russian fighting machine in Rocky IV. It was as if , to use an older
metaphor, David and Goliath had reversed roles. So we cheered when,
after Wallace complained that Jiang's answers were too long, Jiang came
right back and said that his answers were the same length as Wallace's

questions, so that if Wallace wanted shorter answers he should ask shorter questions! (To Mike's credit, he too enjoyed the repartee.)

One gets the impression that President Jiang doesn't take himself so seriously, though he takes his responsibilities very seriously. Americans admire such traits, especially in their leaders. Pomposity looses and down-to-earth wins—it's just that simple—and this is why when Jiang comes across genuinely he comes across well. Few will remember his precise explanation why China has outlawed the "evil cult" Falun Gong (i.e., its founder considers himself a reincarnation of the Great Buddha and Jesus Christ, predicts doomsday, and breaks up families) or why Chinese newspapers claim that the United States is a threat to world peace (i.e., U.S. economic power and leading-edge science and technology cause America to overestimate itself). And few will recall his defense of religious freedom (i.e., "...under China's constitution people have the freedom of religious belief, but Falun Gong is a cult—it is totally different from Christianity") or his noticeable discomfort justifying why China blocks certain Internet sites (i.e., pornography and disruptive political views harm society) or his strained continuing contention that the American bombing of the Chinese embassy was not an accident (i.e., American state-of-the-art military technology combined with clear identification marks on the Chinese embassy) or his definition of a free press in China (i.e., "...We do have freedom of the press, but such freedoms should be subordinate to and serve the interests of the nation—how can you allow such freedom to damage the nation's interests?"). But everyone will remember that President Jiang is a thoughtful, engaging man who sincerely wants America and China to be real friends and work together for the common good.

Here is a man who is not so self-possessed with his own importance that he cannot sing and dance in public. Here is a man who is not afraid to try some halting English to connect with his audience. Here is a man who radiates a pleasant even boyish pride when he recites the Gettysburg Address. Here is a charming man with little pretense. So when viewers see President Jiang joking with Wallace, giving as good as he was getting, they see a man that they can like—and "like" is the first step in making friendship work.

Wallace used humor to score points. When the president said, "I have a lot of friends among the leaders of both parties, Republican and Democrat," Wallace retorted with mock seriousness, "So you give money to both their campaigns?" The president then showed his serious side: "Are you just joking? We have never done such things. I have read the campaign platforms of both parties and whoever becomes president will be friendly [to China] because this is in the strategic interests of the whole world." When Wallace thrust with "That's spoken as a true politician; there's no candor in it," Jiang parried with, "I do think that 'politician' is a very nice word."

An interesting political theory was embedded in what seemed to be a simple thought. Since President Jiang had studied Lincoln's Gettysburg Address as a student ("this had a great influence on students when I was young") and had such admiration of its ideas, why, Wallace asked, doesn't Lincoln's ideal government "of the people, by the people, for the people" apply to China? Why doesn't China allow free elections of its national leaders? Doesn't China trust its own people?

President Jiang responded by stating that he believed that what Lincoln described "still remains the goal of American leaders today." He then patiently explained, "I am also an elected leader, though we have a different electoral system. Each country should have its own system because our two countries have different cultures and historic traditions, and different levels of education and economic development."

There are many layers here. What Jiang is saying, in a sense, is that political admiration is neither the equivalent nor the precursor of political application, and that context is critical for ascertaining the practicality of systems. This means that while he can admire the American system of government as applicable in the United States, it would be inappropriate if not arrogant for Americans to assume that the same system would apply in all societies, especially when different countries have different conditions. Appreciation and respect for diversity without robotic insistence on ubiquitous applications, Jiang asserts, would be a powerful and refreshing mechanism for promoting mutual understanding among nations and peoples.

Perhaps the most spirited exchange took place when Wallace badgered the president about Wen Ho Lee, the Chinese-American, Los Alamos-based nuclear scientist accused of spying for China. After the usual barbed questions and simple denials ("If you are out to condemn someone, you can always trump up a charge"—Jiang quoted this Chinese proverb), the president turned the tables on the wily reporter and asked, with a twinkle in his eye, whether he, Mike Wallace, thought Lee was guilty. Wallace was suddenly seized in his own trap. What could he say, since no one really knows whether Lee is guilty in this muddled and controversial case? Off balance and unaccustomed to being flustered—Wallace is always the "flusteror" not the "flusteree"—he hemmed and hawed, offered the safety-net excuse that he was not the one being interviewed, and lamely changed the subject. But give the old correspondent his due—Mike had the good spirit not to edit out his awkward moment.

WALLACE: "You seem defensive for the first time in this interview. I sense this [Wen Ho Lee] is a difficult subject for you."

JIANG: *(in English)* "No, not difficult for me. This is your feeling. Maybe under the lights? What do you think?"

WALLACE: "I'm not supposed to think."

JIANG: *(starting to smile)* "Chinese spy or not?"

WALLACE: "I think?"

JIANG: *(broader smile)* "That's right."

WALLACE: [silence]

JIANG: "You will consider carefully."

WALLACE: "I am considering carefully; you stopped me."

JIANG: *(still in English)* "This is the first time I discover your face [having] difficulty to answer the question."

WALLACE: "Yes that's true; I probably shouldn't answer it."

WALLACE: *(in voiceover narration)* "If there was any time to change the subject this was it."[34]

---

[34] Less than two weeks after the *60 Minutes* broadcast, Federal prosecutors suddenly dropped fifty-eight of the fifty-nine felony counts against Dr. Wen Ho Lee—who had been charged with helping "a foreign power" (i.e., China) steal the "crown jewels" of the nation's nuclear secrets—and in a plea agreement he was released after more than nine months in solitary confinement. (His only guilty plea was to "mishandling classified information," something even a former CIA director had admitted doing.) Racial profiling is suspected: though long a U.S. citizen, Lee was born in Taiwan and is an ethnic Chinese. *Time* magazine wrote, "Wen Ho Lee's most fervent pursuers had proclaimed his case the biggest thing since the Rosenbergs, but the historical parallel may in fact be closer to the Dreyfus case ... [in which] the turn-of-the-century Jewish Frenchman [was] falsely accused of treason in a blaze of anti-Semitism and finally vindicated after a spell in prison." Although Attorney General Janet Reno refused to apologize, the U.S. District Judge, James Parker, who presided at the trial, did: "I sincerely apologize to you, Dr. Lee, for the unfair manner in which you were held in custody by the executive branch." Former Deputy Assistant Attorney General Jeffrey Harris said the Lee case "appears to be one of the darkest episodes in the Department of Justice's handling of criminal prosecutions."

One of the more contentious moments of the interview was Wallace's simplistic and anachronistic labeling of the Chinese government as a dictatorship, as if China today were to be categorized with the likes of North Korea, Libya, Iraq, and Cuba, where one man exercises absolute power absolutely, where the omnipotent dictator's word is law and his persona is worshipped, and where all citizens are intimated and all society is repressed. Anyone who has been to China can put the lie to this mischaracterization. Anyone in China can just feel the flexibility and sense the opportunity that pervade economic, social and individual lives, even though public politics is still under tight control. And anyone who knows China can appreciate how much real freedom people now have in their private behaviors and personal beliefs. Ironically, it was Jiang's unruffled, matter-of-fact explanation of how the political process in China works that helped Wallace escape embarrassment here.

WALLACE: "You are, it seems to me, a dictator, an authoritarian..."

JIANG: *(in English)* "What means dictatorship?"

WALLACE: "A dictator is somebody who forcibly, whether it's a free press or free religion or free private enterprise—now you're beginning to come a little closer to that—[your system is like] 'father knows best,' and if you get in the way of 'father'—[and here Wallace made the sign of a throat being slit]—father will 'take care of you.'"

JIANG: "Your way of describing the way things are like in China is as absurd as the *Arabian Nights*."

Wallace then retreated into what he thought would be the safe harbor of Tiananmen Square: "When I see the picture of that one young man in front of the tank in Tiananmen Square, that means to me Chinese dictatorship. That's a wonderful symbol, that hits me in my heart about dictatorship in China."

Jiang, in English, cut off his translator: "I don't need translation; I know what you said—I am very willing to answer these questions."

What then came forth was momentous. The quiet simplicity of President Jiang's words almost belied their import. For it was President Jiang's considered remarks about Tiananmen Square, a touchstone of the Chinese body politic, that signaled his vision and confirmed his leadership. His softly worded statement shone with clarity, frankness, and freshness, and at the same time was anchored in his need to respect and strengthen the State. He seemed to suggest the impossible: bridging the gap [chasm!] between antagonists on polar opposite sides of Tiananmen. The president dealt with historical truths while defending the legitimacy of the Communist Party and incumbent government. His new framework for understanding the events of Tiananmen suggests, for the first time, what could mature into a reasonably acceptable account of the single most contentious matter about China, a symbol of oppression seared into Western minds with images of tanks and turmoil and hundreds of dead and injured students—events with which Jiang Zemin was not personally associated. Only discerning analysis and honest history can put to rest this virulent and tenacious issue. This in truth is how China can best maintain national stability, and this, it seems, is what President Jiang is determined to do. It would be a great day for China.

Here's what Jiang said in the interview: *"In the 1989 disturbances we truly understood the passion of students who were calling for greater democracy and freedom. In fact, we have always been working to improve our system of democracy."* Though he defended the crackdown by stating that "we could not possibly allow people with ulterior motives [whom he did not identify] to use the students to overthrow the government under the pretext of democracy and freedom," there was no doubt that President Jiang was heralding a bold new view.

The relatively cool code word "disturbances" was a clear relaxation from the previously prevailing hot terms "counterrevolution," "riot," and "turmoil," and his overt sympathy for the "passion of students" was genuinely startling. However, it was President Jiang's carefully constructed statement that *"we have always been working to improve our system of democracy"* which I believe is actually the most revealing and potent. Who is the *"we"* here? Clearly, his own tenure of office. *". . . always been working"* suggests that Jiang's long-term personal motivation, not appreciated in the West, has been to enhance Chinese people's freedoms in the broadest sense. *"Our system of democracy"* expresses the general consensus in China that people's rights, material and behavioral, can best be expanded in a still-developing society, not by multiple parties who contest one another through opposition and public election (which, Chinese leaders believe, can lead to political chaos and social turmoil when educational levels are still not uniformly high), but through the leadership of a single party exercising enlightened and farsighted rule, thus providing the greatest amount of benefits for the largest number of people. Most Americans will not agree with this analysis—we do not promote the stability of society above the rights of individuals—but we must admit that the great majority of Chinese in fact do.

"Why must we have opposition parties," Jiang asked rhetorically? "You are trying to apply the American values and the American political system to the whole world, but that is not very wise." He went on to say that while China and America differ in our values, "we want to learn from the West about science and technology and how to manage the economy. But this must be combined with specific conditions here. That's how we have made great progress in the past twenty years."

Asked in the trickiest question of the long interview whether he felt inspired by the courage of the lone protestor who faced down that long line of tanks during the Tiananmen assault—the indelible image is of one of the most memorable of the twentieth century—President Jiang made a remarkable statement: "I know what you are driving at, but what I want to emphasize is that we fully respect every citizen's right to fully express his wishes and desires. But I do not favor any flagrant opposition to government actions during an emergency. The tank stopped and did not run the young man down." He noted that the man was not arrested—an interesting piece of news—then made a fascinating observation loaded with subtleties: "I don't know where he is now. Looking at his picture I know he definitely had his own ideas."

Wallace then coolly switched subjects, while maintaining focus. He alluded to the Tiananmen students protesting against corruption and quoted from a speech that President Jiang had given about one month after the attack: "Corruption is growing in the soil. If all our party and our government organs use their power to seek material benefits, isn't this just like fleecing the people in broad daylight?" Wallace then asked Jiang whether the students had an effect "on you and your party?"

Confirming his straightforward, tough-minded attitude toward this most sensitive of subjects, the president agreed that in the area of corruption—against which he has staked his career—the students in Tiananmen were ahead of their time and were indeed resonating with current policy.

"I hate corruption," Jiang answered with a flash of anger—one could see the depth of his contempt for corruption in the sudden contortion of his face. "You are right that during the 1989 disturbances students were chanting slogans against corruption, so on this specific point, the party shares the same position as the students."

And when Wallace drew an allusion to Jiang's own days of a student protestor (in 1943 in Shanghai against the Japanese occupation), the president did not contradict the analogy.

The simple reality is that in his short statements about Tiananmen,

President Jiang gave notice that he will take leadership in bringing to closure the divisive events that occurred in the spring of 1989. There is no doubt that, in the West, the issue of Tiananmen will never go away until some plausible explanation is given and the decade-old "official version" of what happened is reversed (or at least greatly modified). The events prior to and on June 4 of that year will continue to impair and impede China's full entry into the family of civilized nations. Only a fair and forthright assessment of Tiananmen will free China for its manifest future. Opinions may differ but the president's overt willingness to address this gnawing issue begins the long process of healing the open wound that still tarnishes the image of China.

The president's reasoned comments about Tiananmen, delivered in a way that conveyed serious and long-time consideration, may enable the issue, ultimately, to enter the public forum in China. It will surely help damp the unproductive cycle of charge and countercharge in escalating rounds of accusations about Tiananmen. What President Jiang suggests is far more fundamental than compromise. It deals honestly with the motives and ideals of the students in Tiananmen while it strongly supports the legitimacy of the current government in maintaining national order. People on all sides will not agree with everything President Jiang said about Tiananmen, but all should admit that his views were thoughtful, helpful, perceptive, conciliatory, bridging, and designed to begin to put an end to this disruptive chapter in Chinese history.

One can only guess that President Jiang's new thinking about Tiananmen is not universally appreciated by China's old-guard leadership, particularly among those who were involved in those tragic events, though surely his historic assessments are shared by the vast majority of the Chinese people. By openly mentioning the unmentionable and seeking reconciliation, President Jiang shores up the moral authority of the government, maintains the stability of the state, and affirms his personal integrity and credibility.

It is difficult for non-Chinese to appreciate the courage and depth of conviction it took for President Jiang to make the statements he did, particularly about Tiananmen. This was the act of a great leader acting with greatness, displaying wisdom, exemplifying his vision, and solidifying his mark in history. It was, in its entirety, a startling exchange—President Jiang was responsive, bold, accurate, truthful—and I believe this interview will help catalyze positive developments in China, accelerating the reforms and achievements of the Chinese people in their ancient motherland. Speaking personally, as I watched President Jiang face down that long line of questions during the Mike Wallace assault, I felt inspired by *his* courage. It was a masterful performance.

Americans watching *60 Minutes* that evening came away with a fresh opinion of President Jiang Zemin, and by extension, the American impression of China became richer and more nuanced. The television camera is merciless in exposing insincerity and hypocrisy and it humiliates those who posture and puff. President Jiang succeeded because he is sincere and direct and because he does not posture or puff. The truth is that *60 Minutes* and the perceptive (and often relentless) Mike Wallace liked Jiang Zemin and so generally did the large audience viewing the interview.

President Jiang concluded, in English, by stating, "I'm convinced that this interview will further promote the friendship and mutual understanding between our peoples. I trust in that." If President Jiang's objectives were to challenge the stereotypical portrayal of China and to convey his admiration of America and his desire for good will between China and America, he succeeded beyond expectations.

Robert Lawrence Kuhn
September 4, 2000

Index

311

About the Author

Dr. Robert Lawrence Kuhn is an investment banker and corporate strategist, author and editor, and television producer and host, who has long-established relationships in the People's Republic of China. He is president of The Geneva Companies, one of the leading and largest financial advisory firms specializing in mergers and acquisitions of privately held middle market businesses. He is also Chairman of K^2 Media Group, a television and media production company.

Since 1989, Dr. Kuhn has advised ministries and enterprises in the People's Republic of China, including the Information Office of the State Council, the Science and Technology Ministry, the State Economic and Trade Commission, the State Property Bureau, the State Administration of Radio, Film and Television, and China Central Television (CCTV). Dr. Kuhn is the creator and executive producer of the first documentary series, co-produced with CCTV, on China's economic reform versioned for both Chinese and American audiences. The eight-part Chinese-language version, *Capital Wave*, was broadcast nationwide across China on CCTV in 1999. Receiving wide acclaim, it was CCTV's first series on mergers and acquisitions. The English-language version, *In Search of China*, is a ninety-minute PBS documentary that gives fresh understanding of the new China through intimate access and character-driven stories. It was broadcast nationally on PBS in the U.S. in September 2000 (concurrently with the publication of this book) and syndicated internationally thereafter. WETA (Washington, D.C.) is the presenting station for PBS, and *Made In China: Voices from the New Revolution* is the companion book.

Dr. Kuhn is Chairman of the Kuhn Foundation which operates educational, scientific, cultural, and humanitarian projects, including the pursuit and dissemination of new knowledge in science and scholarship, the sponsorship of classical music performances in various countries, and the conduct of various activities to promote cultural exchanges, media education and good relations between the United States of America and the People's Republic of China. In January 2000 in Beijing, the Kuhn Foundation sponsored, and Dr. Kuhn organized and co-chaired with Zhao Qizheng, minister of the State Council Information Office, a closed conference on "Media in the United States."

Dr. Kuhn is the author or editor of more than twenty-five books, including the seven-volume Dow Jones-Irwin *Library of Investment Banking*, McGraw-Hill's *Handbook for Creative and Innovative Managers*, and the first investment banking book published in Chinese (*Tou Zi Yin Hang Xue*, published by Beijing Normal University Press). His book *Dealmaker* (John Wiley & Sons) was recently translated into Chinese (*Jiao Yi Ren*, published by China Economic Science Press).

Dr. Kuhn is the creator and host of a new 28-part national public television series, *Closer To Truth*, which presents the world's foremost scientists, scholars and artists discussing the fundamental ideas and issues of our time. Broadcast on public television stations across the U.S., *Closer to Truth* has developed (at Caltech) an innovative, high-content website for deliberative discourse (www.closertotruth.com). The companion book, *Closer To Truth: Challenging Current Belief*, is published by McGraw-Hill (Trade Science); the Chinese version (*Zou Jin Zhen Shi*) is published by China Economic Science Press.

Dr. Kuhn has an A.B. in human biology (Johns Hopkins–Phi Beta Kappa), a Ph.D. in anatomy/brain research (UCLA Dept. of Anatomy and Brain Research Institute), and an M.S. in management (MIT Sloan School/Sloan Fellow). He has taught psychology at MIT, anatomy at UCLA, and business and financial strategy at NYU where he was adjunct professor. He is Senior Fellow at the IC^2 Institute of the University of Texas at Austin and has lectured at Beijing and Qinghua universities in China. Dr Kuhn has advised the governments of China, U.S., Germany and Israel on economics and technology.